Not

m

D1530237

Free Speech

Free Speech

Other books in the Current Controversies series:

The Abortion Controversy
Afghanistan
Alcoholism
America's Battle Against
    Terrorism
Assisted Suicide
Biodiversity
Capital Punishment
Censorship
Child Abuse
Civil Liberties
Civil Rights
Computers and Society
Conserving the Environment
Crime
Developing Nations
The Disabled
Drug Abuse
Drug Legalization
Drug Trafficking
Espionage and Intelligence
    Gathering
Ethics
Family Violence
Garbage and Waste
Gay Rights
Genetic Engineering
Guns and Violence
Hate Crimes
Homeland Security
Homosexuality
Illegal Drugs
Illegal Immigration
Immigration

The Information Age
Interventionism
Iraq
Marriage and Divorce
Medical Ethics
Mental Health
The Middle East
Minorities
Nationalism and Ethnic
    Conflict
Native American Rights
Police Brutality
Politicians and Ethics
Pollution
Poverty and the Homeless
Prisons
Racism
The Rights of Animals
Sexual Harassment
Sexually Transmitted Diseases
Smoking
Suicide
Teen Addiction
Teen Pregnancy and Parenting
Teens and Alcohol
The Terrorist Attack on
    America
Urban Terrorism
Violence Against Women
Violence in the Media
War
Women in the Military
Youth Violence

Free Speech

John Boaz, *Book Editor*

Bruce Glassman, *Vice President*
Bonnie Szumski, *Publisher*
Helen Cothran, *Managing Editor*

Current **CONTROVERSIES**

GREENHAVEN PRESS
An imprint of Thomson Gale, a part of The Thomson Corporation

THOMSON
™
GALE

Detroit • New York • San Francisco • San Diego • New Haven, Conn.
Waterville, Maine • London • Munich

THOMSON

™

GALE

© 2006 Thomson Gale, a part of The Thomson Corporation.

Thomson and Star Logo are trademarks and Gale and Greenhaven Press are registered trademarks used herein under license.

For more information, contact
Greenhaven Press
27500 Drake Rd.
Farmington Hills, MI 48331-3535
Or you can visit our Internet site at http://www.gale.com

Cover credit: © Wally McNamee/Corbis. People protest for tighter restrictions of Internet content.

LIBRARY OF CONGRESS CATALOGING-IN-PUBLICATION DATA

Free speech / John Boaz, book editor.
    p. cm. — (Current controversies)
Includes bibliographical references and index.
    ISBN 0-7377-2204-5 (lib. : alk. paper) — ISBN 0-7377-2205-3 (pbk. : alk. paper)
    1. Freedom of speech—United States. I. Boaz, John. II. Series.
KF4772.Z9F735 2006
342.7308'53—dc22
                                                                    2005046225

Printed in the United States of America

Contents

Foreword   12

Introduction   14

Chapter 1: Should Free Speech Be Limited?
Chapter Preface   17

Yes: Free Speech Should Be Limited

Flag Burning Should Not Be Protected Speech
  by the Citizens Flag Alliance   18
   Desecrating the American flag, a cherished symbol of national unity,
   demeans the United States. A constitutional amendment to ban flag burning is the only way to safeguard this most important emblem of America.

Hate Speech Should Be Limited *by Laura Leets*   23
   While a direct link between exposure to hate speech and perpetrating hate
   crimes is difficult to prove, evidence suggests that hate speech can influence a listener. Until the connection between hate speech and violence is
   better understood, hate speech should be limited.

Colleges May Restrict Some Types of Speech *by Derek P. Langhauser*   27
   Colleges and universities have a vested interest in maintaining an environment that is conducive to the free exchange of ideas. Thus, colleges
   may restrict speech that creates hostility.

Pornography Should Be Censored *by S. Michael Craven*   31
   Pornography encourages the separation of the sex act from intimacy and
   thus objectifies people. With channels for the dissemination of sexual
   content at an all-time high, pornography must be regulated.

No: Free Speech Should Not Be Limited

Flag Burning Is a Legitimate Expression of Dissent
  by Ralph G. Neas and Marge Baker   42
   Central to any free nation is the protection of speech, even when the
   means of expression, such as flag burning, is offensive. A flag protection
   amendment can only have adverse effects on First Amendment freedoms.

Speech Codes Threaten the Free Exchange of Ideas on College
  Campuses *by Eugene Volokh*   46
   Although classroom speech must be controlled to promote a free

exchange of ideas, instructor censure, not speech codes, should be the instrument of enforcement.

Limiting Hate Speech Threatens Legitimate Debate
  by Ira H. Mehlman   49
  Squelching any speech that is offensive to the listener creates an environment in which open debate is stifled. Social censure of offensive speech is
  superior to government restrictions.

The Government Should Not Define Obscenity for Its Citizens
  by Jeffrey Rosen   52
  Given the proliferation of obscene and pornographic material in America,
  the U.S. Supreme Court should not try to enforce a universal understanding of obscenity. Deciding what constitutes community standards regarding pornographic expression is now impossible.

The Government Should Not Censor Art
  by the American Civil Liberties Union   59
  Any attempt to censor artistic expression is dangerous to a free society
  because it leads to the suppression of other modes of speech.

Chapter 2: Is Free Speech Threatened?

Chapter Preface   66

Yes: Free Speech Is Threatened

Media Consolidation Threatens Free Speech *by Robert W. McChesney*   68
  The American media system, which increasingly allows for media conglomerates, is the product of regulation that favors broadcasters, not
  viewers. Media consolidation must be stopped in order to serve the public
  interest.

Library Internet Filters Block Access to Vital Information
  by the Kaiser Family Foundation   76
  The Child Internet Protection Act requires schools that receive federal
  tax dollars to use Internet filters in order to block access to pornographic
  Web sites. The filters, however, block access to vital health information
  along with pornography.

Campaign Finance Reform Limits Political Expression
  by John Samples   82
  Large sums of money are required in order for a candidate to get a campaign message across to the voting public. Campaign finance reform that
  limits a candidate's ability to raise funds restricts the public's access to
  political expression.

Freedom of the Press Is Threatened *by Charles Lewis*   88
  The Bush administration has implemented policies that have limited press
  coverage of the federal government's actions. Freedom of the press is a
  necessary check on governmental power.

No: Free Speech Is Not Threatened

Campaign Finance Reform Could Enhance Political Expression
by John Kerry   95
> The U.S. Supreme Court has held that campaign finance reform does not
> violate the First Amendment. Limiting the amount of money spent on
> campaigns might improve campaign discourse, issue discussions, and
> voter education.

Filters and Ratings Systems Are Protecting Free Speech *by Jeffrey Cole*   100
> Voluntarily using Internet filters and TV and movie rating systems can
> head off dangerous censorship of entertainment media.

Media Consolidation Does Not Threaten Free Speech *by Adam Thierer*   104
> Deregulation of the media has provided citizens with greater access to
> news, information, and entertainment. Government attempts to regulate
> the media amount to censorship.

Chapter 3: Does the War on Terror Threaten Free Speech?

Chapter Preface   109

Yes: The War on Terror Threatens Free Speech

Free Speech Is Often Restricted During Wartime *by David Hudson*   110
> From America's Revolutionary War to the Vietnam era, First Amend-
> ment rights have often been restricted during wartime. The global war on
> terror gives every indication that Americans once again face restrictions
> on free speech.

Criticisms of the War on Terror Are Being Suppressed *by Alisa Solomon* 116
> Playing on Americans' fears following the September 11, 2001, terrorist
> attacks, the Bush administration is fostering an environment hostile to
> political dissent. Criticisms of the 2003 war against Iraq are particularly
> discouraged.

Anti-Terrorism Policies Threaten First Amendment Protections
by Elizabeth Dahl and Joseph Onek   125
> Several anti-terrorism policies were established following the September
> 11, 2001, terrorist attacks. These policies pose significant threats to pro-
> tections guaranteed by the First Amendment.

The Patriot Act Discourages the Free Exchange of Ideas
by Eleanor J. Bader   133
> The Patriot Act allows the FBI to track library patron borrowing habits
> and the purchases of bookstore customers. Government investigation into
> what citizens read discourages people from seeking information on partic-
> ular topics for fear of being investigated.

No: The War on Terror Does Not Threaten Free Speech

The Right to Dissent Has Not Been Threatened in the War on Terrorism
by Bobby Eberle   136
Numerous leftist celebrities have complained that they have been punished for criticizing the war on terror. However, whatever repercussions
they experienced were the result of public opinion turning against them,
not governmental suppression of free speech.

The Patriot Act Does Not Threaten Free Speech by John Ashcroft   139
After the September 11, 2001, terrorist attacks, Congress passed the
Patriot Act to give law enforcement the tools it needs to fight terrorism.
Despite claims to the contrary, the act does not threaten First Amendment
rights.

Embedded Reporters During the Iraq War Improved War Coverage
by Jeffrey C. Bliss   145
During the 2003 Iraq war, reporters were embedded within military units,
enabling them to report on events as they occurred. The embedding process
fostered freedom of the press and led to more and better war coverage.

Chapter 4: How Should the Right to Free Speech Apply to Corporations?

Chapter Preface   154

Corporations Should Be Granted the Same Free Speech Rights as
Individuals by Kathy Cripps   155
The California Supreme Court has set a precedent forbidding corporations
from defending themselves against their critics. By denying corporations'
First Amendment rights, the decision undermines democracy in America.

Corporations Do Not Have the Right to Free Speech
by Carl J. Mayer and Brenda Wright   158
Corporations are not entitled to the First Amendment protections that
individuals enjoy. Company responses to critics constitute commercial
speech, made with the intent of protecting profits, and are not eligible for
free speech protections.

Broadcast Media Conglomerates Promote Free Speech
by Anthony J. Dukes   168
Media conglomerates have a vested interest in diverse programming since
a larger audience translates into expanded viewership and more advertising revenue.

Consolidation of Media Outlets Raises Concerns About Limits on Free
Speech by Gal Beckerman   172
Deregulation has allowed more media outlets to fall into the hands of
fewer owners. As a result, concerns have arisen that there is less media
accountability and diverse programming.

Telemarketers Should Be Able to Contact Potential Customers
by Solveig Singleton   182
Telemarketers are a nuisance, but they are not the type of irritant that
demands federal regulation. Limiting the free speech rights of telemarketers could lead to less freedom for everyone.

Telemarketing Is Not Protected Free Speech *by Bill Lockyear et al.*   187
Regulation of commercial speech has long been upheld by court decisions
in the United States. In the case of telemarketing, the right of private citizens to be left alone in their own homes trumps the rights of telemarketers
to make unsolicited calls.

Corporations Threaten Freedom of Speech *by Lawrence Soley*   197
Private citizens are protected from government censorship under the First
Amendment, but corporations can restrict expression on their property. In
an increasingly privatized, corporate culture, corporations represent a
tremendous threat to freedom of speech.

Organizations to Contact   207
Bibliography   211
Index   214

Foreword

By definition, controversies are "discussions of questions in which opposing opinions clash" (Webster's Twentieth Century Dictionary Unabridged). Few would deny that controversies are a pervasive part of the human condition and exist on virtually every level of human enterprise. Controversies transpire between individuals and among groups, within nations and between nations. Controversies supply the grist necessary for progress by providing challenges and challengers to the status quo. They also create atmospheres where strife and warfare can flourish. A world without controversies would be a peaceful world; but it also would be, by and large, static and prosaic.

The Series' Purpose

The purpose of the Current Controversies series is to explore many of the social, political, and economic controversies dominating the national and international scenes today. Titles selected for inclusion in the series are highly focused and specific. For example, from the larger category of criminal justice, Current Controversies deals with specific topics such as police brutality, gun control, white collar crime, and others. The debates in Current Controversies also are presented in a useful, timeless fashion. Articles and book excerpts included in each title are selected if they contribute valuable, long-range ideas to the overall debate. And wherever possible, current information is enhanced with historical documents and other relevant materials. Thus, while individual titles are current in focus, every effort is made to ensure that they will not become quickly outdated. Books in the Current Controversies series will remain important resources for librarians, teachers, and students for many years.

In addition to keeping the titles focused and specific, great care is taken in the editorial format of each book in the series. Book introductions and chapter prefaces are offered to provide background material for readers. Chapters are organized around several key questions that are answered with diverse opinions representing all points on the political spectrum. Materials in each chapter include opinions in which authors clearly disagree as well as alternative opinions in which authors may agree on a broader issue but disagree on the possible solutions. In this way, the content of each volume in Current Controversies mirrors the mosaic of opinions encountered in society. Readers will quickly realize that there are many viable answers to these complex issues. By questioning each author's conclusions, students and casual readers can begin to develop the critical thinking skills so important to evaluating opinionated material.

Current Controversies is also ideal for controlled research. Each anthology in the series is composed of primary sources taken from a wide gamut of informational categories including periodicals, newspapers, books, United States and foreign government documents, and the publications of private and public organizations. Readers will find factual support for reports, debates, and research papers covering all areas of important issues. In addition, an annotated table of contents, an index, a book and periodical bibliography, and a list of organizations to contact are included in each book to expedite further research.

Perhaps more than ever before in history, people are confronted with diverse and contradictory information. During the Persian Gulf War, for example, the public was not only treated to minute-to-minute coverage of the war, it was also inundated with critiques of the coverage and countless analyses of the factors motivating U.S. involvement. Being able to sort through the plethora of opinions accompanying today's major issues, and to draw one's own conclusions, can be a complicated and frustrating struggle. It is the editors' hope that Current Controversies will help readers with this struggle.

Greenhaven Press anthologies primarily consist of previously published material taken from a variety of sources, including periodicals, books, scholarly journals, newspapers, government documents, and position papers from private and public organizations. These original sources are often edited for length and to ensure their accessibility for a young adult audience. The anthology editors also change the original titles of these works in order to clearly present the main thesis of each viewpoint and to explicitly indicate the opinion presented in the viewpoint. These alterations are made in consideration of both the reading and comprehension levels of a young adult audience. Every effort is made to ensure that Greenhaven Press accurately reflects the original intent of the authors included in this anthology.

"The war on terror had begun, and with it, a battle over freedom of speech."

Introduction

Following the September 11, 2001, terrorist attacks on New York and Washington, D.C., President George W. Bush was quoted as saying, "Freedom itself was attacked this morning by a faceless coward, and freedom will be defended. . . . Make no mistake: The United States will hunt down and punish those responsible for these cowardly acts." The war on terror had begun, and with it, a battle over freedom of speech. Just a few days later, political comedian Bill Maher made the following comment on his late-night talk show, *Politically Incorrect:* "We [Americans] have been the cowards lobbing cruise missiles from 2000 miles away. That's cowardly. Staying in the airplane when it hits the building, say what you want about it, it's not cowardly." When Ari Fleischer, press secretary for the Bush administration, was asked about the White House's response to Maher's comment, he said that all Americans "need to watch what they say, watch what they do." While many saw Maher's comment as unpatriotic, some viewed it as an important, if ill-timed, exercise in free speech. Similarly, many thought Ari Fleischer's reaction was a legitimate call for discretion in wartime, while numerous civil libertarians saw it as an official crackdown on American free speech and civil liberties during the war on terror. The stage was set for the debate over what constitutes legitimate free speech in wartime, arguably the most important free speech issue today.

The right to freedom of speech has always been contentious despite the First Amendment's seemingly unequivocal affirmation that "Congress shall make no law . . . abridging the freedom of speech or of the press." It has been widely acknowledged that certain forms of speech, especially those that cause harm, are not protected by the First Amendment. Yelling, "Fire!" in a crowded theater is the classic, oft-cited example. Clearly, yelling "Fire!" could induce panic and put people at risk. But not all cases are so clear-cut. During wartime, especially, the cases become difficult. For example, is it appropriate in a time of national tragedy to characterize the perpetrators of terrorist acts as brave? Are certain forms of speech absolutely inappropriate in wartime? During past wars, laws were passed restricting freedom of speech in order to enhance national security. Many contend that the war on terror should be treated as any other war. According to judge Richard A. Posner, "The events of September 11 have revealed the United States to be in much greater jeopardy from international terrorism than had previously been believed. . . . It stands to reason that our civil liberties will be curtailed." However, as many experts point out, the war on terror is unlike other wars because it is ongoing. Thus laws regulating what people say could become permanent, rather than temporary, restrictions on free speech.

The USA Patriot Act, passed in October 2001, quickly became the focus of debates over wartime freedom of expression. The act granted unprecedented power to the Department of Justice to prosecute the domestic war on terror. One particular part of the Patriot Act, Section 215, has been widely criticized by groups such as the American Library Association (ALA) and the American Civil Liberties Union (ACLU) for infringing on the privacy rights of library patrons, book buyers, and charitable organizations. Section 215 allows federal law enforcement officers to seize records in secret if it is believed that they are related to terrorist activities. The ALA and ACLU contend that this section is in violation of the First Amendment because it could have a chilling effect on people borrowing or buying books on potentially sensitive subjects, such as international terrorism or Islam. The U.S. Justice Department, however, argues that it is a necessary tool for combating terrorism.

The right to political dissent is another area of controversy. In February 2003, just as the United States was preping for war in Iraq, a man was forced to leave a mall in upstate New York because he was wearing a shirt that said "Peace On Earth." In another example, the popular country band The Dixie Chicks was pulled from the playlists of many radio stations because the lead singer of the band said that she was ashamed of President Bush for his support for the war in Iraq. During 2004 presidential campaign stops, dissenters were often relegated to "free speech zones," located far away from the sites of presidential rallies and speeches. They were thus not seen by the news media, and their messages were not disseminated.

As the war on terror continues, Americans struggle between their desire for security and their wish to preserve their cherished right to free speech. An annual poll conducted by the Freedom Forum, known as the First Amendment survey, has consistently shown that since September 11 a majority of Americans believes that the First Amendment goes too far in the degree of freedom that it grants citizens.

People feel vulnerable to terrorists and are willing to endure some restrictions on what they can say if such limitations make the nation safer. With no end in sight, the war on terror will certainly continue to test the willingness of Americans to trade freedom for safety. Americans have often been sharply divided over pornography, flag burning, hate speech, speech codes, and the extent of corporate free speech, but they have become especially polarized over whether speech should be restricted so that anti-American or antiwar statements do not jeopardize the war effort and make Americans more vulnerable. Throughout *Current Controversies: Free Speech*, authors debate where the line should be drawn between appropriate and inappropriate expression, and explore the ramifications that a post–September 11 world has for free speech.

Chapter 1

Should Free Speech Be Limited?

Current **CONTROVERSIES**

Chapter Preface

Threats to free speech have become more numerous and varied as communications technologies have developed. To address these concerns lawmakers have passed numerous bills regulating these technologies. For example, on April 27, 2005, President George W. Bush, in a private ceremony and without comment, signed into law the Family Entertainment and Copyright Act. The law addresses a main concern of Hollywood film studios and the recording industry in general: bootlegging, the illegal copying and for-profit distribution of copyright-protected movies and music. The film industry has long maintained that the most widespread source of movie piracy is the recording of first-run films by theater patrons with camcorders. The Family Entertainment and Copyright Act makes it a federal crime, a felony, to record first-run films in movie theaters with camcorders. Doing so carries with it a penalty of up to three years in prison for a first offense.

Another part of the act addresses DVD content and how it may be altered legally: Section 202 authorizes "the making imperceptible, by or at the direction of a member of a private household, of limited portions of audio or video content of a motion picture, during a performance in or transmitted to that household for private home viewing, from an authorized copy of the motion picture." This means that anyone who purchases a legal copy of a film on DVD can view that film however he or she chooses. Certain video companies, such as Utah-based CleanPlay, have developed DVD filtering technologies that allow viewers to omit undesirable content—such as sex, violence, and profanity—from a film's playback.

Filmmakers, in general, are greatly opposed to this portion of the act because they believe it opens the door to unauthorized tampering with their artistic vision. But lawmakers and filtering companies contend that, since the DVD disc itself is not altered in any fundamental way, use of the filtering technology does not constitute censorship. Advocates of the technology maintain that, just as the viewer has a right to adjust the volume of DVD playback, or to look away during material that he or she may find objectionable, utilizing technology that allows a viewer to simply omit or alter parts of the film for viewing, without harming the director's original vision, is perfectly constitutional.

The communications technology revolution has challenged lawmakers to craft laws governing the use of electronic devices while respecting the right to free speech. Flag burning as political expression, freedom of the press, speech codes on college campuses, pornography, and hate speech are discussed in this chapter.

Flag Burning Should Not Be Protected Speech

by the Citizens Flag Alliance

About the author: *The Citizens Flag Alliance is a coalition of organizations that have come together to persuade Congress to propose a constitutional amendment to protect the American flag.*

Why amend the Constitution to authorize congress to prohibit physical desecration of the American flag?[1]

Amending the Constitution is the only available means to further the government's legitimate interest in protecting the flag.

Amending the Constitution is the only way. While it would be preferable to protect the flag by federal statute, the Supreme Court has, in two narrow 5–4 decisions, breaking from 200 years of precedent, overturned statutes prohibiting physical desecration of the flag. By these definitive rulings, the Court has sent the message that a Constitutional Amendment is the exclusive means for protecting the flag.

The Government Has a Legitimate Interest in Protecting the American Flag

- Protecting the flag affirms the most basic condition of our freedom: our bond to one another in our aspiration to national unity. Our system of democracy, the Constitution, and all of the freedoms, rights and laws which flow from each are based on this unity. The flag forms the basis and is a symbol of this unity. The flag remains a single unifying embodiment of our unceasing struggle for liberty, equality, and a basic commitment to others for all citizens, regardless of language, culture and heritage. To protect the laws and freedoms that are based on this unity, we must protect the flag upon which this unity is grounded.

1. To date, no flag protection amendment has been passed.

- The Flag is the "trademark" of our nation. The values that the flag embodies are the "intellectual property" of our nation that the government has an interest in protecting through the "trademark" of the flag. Just as the government has a legitimate interest in protecting ownership rights for inventors, writers and artists, so it also is charged with promoting respect, understanding and adherence to the values which make self-government possible.
- We must protect the flag to protect its role as an incident of sovereignty.

Our Founding Fathers and those who led the nation thereafter did not permit the desecration of the American flag. They knew that America's adversaries would interpret this as a sign that our flag is a symbol that is meaningless, rather than an embodiment of our rights and freedoms. As a result, today, there is a unique respect for the flag of the United States abroad. (This respect for the American flag overseas was demonstrated during the Persian Gulf War, when foreign tankers in the Gulf flew the American flag. An act of aggression against the tankers in the Gulf would have been the equivalent of an attack against the United States and its sovereign interest in protecting allied vessels in wartime). Because our government has a strong interest in the physical protection of American citizens and property abroad, it has a corresponding interest in protecting the flag from physical desecration, on behalf of all Americans who benefit from the rights and freedoms the flag embodies.

> *"Our Founding Fathers and those who led the nation thereafter did not permit the desecration of the American flag."*

- The proposed amendment protects from further injury the fundamental value of aspiration to national unity.

Since the Supreme Court rules that the freedom to physically desecrate the flag is more important than the unity which underlies all freedoms, the flag has been decaying as an embodiment of this unity. This decay justifies the proposed amendment which will restore to the people the right to protect their common objective of democracy which underlies our freedoms. . . .

- If the values are worth fighting for, the symbol and embodiment of those values deserves protection

The freedom and ideals of liberty, equality and tolerance that the flag symbolizes and embodies have motivated our nation's leaders, soldiers and activists to pledge their lives, their liberty and their honor in defense of their country. Because our history has demonstrated that these values and ideals are worth fighting for, the flag which uniquely symbolizes their power is itself worthy of protection from physical desecration. . . .

Amending the Constitution to authorize Congress to prohibit physical desecration of the flag is entirely appropriate and consistent with the principles set out in the Constitution. The drafters of the Constitution realized changes would be necessary, and provided the Article V amendment process precisely for this purpose. The amendment process is intentionally rigorous and methodical so that only those proposals with overwhelming public support are enacted. Furthermore, the notion of "upholding" the Constitution, which all elected members of Congress swear to do, embodies the privilege of exercising all the rights within it, including the right of the people to amend the Constitutuion consistent with the Article V process.

The proposed amendment does not reduce our freedoms under the Bill of Rights, it merely restores the Constitution to the way it had been understood prior to 1989—to the notion that the people had the right to protect the flag from physical desecration. This is how the Constitution had been interpreted for 200 years. The Article V amendment process is the time-tested manner in which the people express their disagreement with Supreme Court construction of the Constitution, as was done in the case of the Eleventh, Thirteenth, Fourteenth and Sixteenth Amendments. Protecting the flag is just as important as the issues which resulted in these prior amendments. (Professor Steven B. Presser, Northwestern University School of Law, in a letter to Marty Justis, Executive Director of the Citizens Flag Alliance.)

First Amendment rights have never been absolute. There are existing laws against libel, slander, perjury, obscenity and indecent exposure in public. Just as the government has a legitimate interest in regulating these types of speech and conduct, it has a similar interest in limiting certain conduct which damages an incident of its sovereignty, or infringes on the rights

> *"If free speech is to truly flourish, we must protect the bond that unites us, including the substantive parameters of the right to free expression."*

and freedoms embodied in our national symbol, by prohibiting the physical desecration of the flag. *United States vs. Eichman*, 496 U.S. 310, 322 (1990) (Stevens, J., dissenting), *Texas vs. Johnson*, 491 U.S. 397, 430 (1969) (Rehnquist, C.J., dissenting).

The First Amendment right to free speech includes a substantive component. The right is not merely process-based and one-dimensional. Rather, it is multidimensional, and includes the correlative duty, when one is exercising his/her free speech right, to respect the rights of others. The proposed amendment validates this corresponding responsibility by restoring to the people the right to defend their collective rights. Specifically, this proposal would empower the people to apply their right to protect the flag from physical desecration.

If free speech is to truly flourish, we must protect the bond that unites us, including the substantive parameters of the right to free expression. We must strengthen the bonds that hold us together, and so make it possible to engage in robust disagreement with each other. Protecting the flag lays the foundation for this objective.

The proposed amendment would not "amend" the First Amendment. Rather, the proposed amendment and the First Amendment would both be interpreted in light of each other. Just as the Equal Protection Clause of the Fourteenth Amendment is interpreted in light of the First Amendment without any fear of diluting the latter, our courts are equally capable of harmonizing a provision to authorize protection for the flag with the First Amendment.

Consistent with Supreme Court Precedent

The proposed amendment is consistent with Supreme Court precedent. The Supreme Court determined that protecting a flag by statute amounted to the government "choosing sides" in favor of a specific point of view, in violation of the First Amendment. The proposed amendment poses no challenge to the notion that the government is prohibited from "choosing sides" for a specific view. Rather, it questions the assumption that protection of the flag is just another "point of view". The government does not create reverence for the flag when it acts to protect it, for the previous 200 years of history had already established this reverence. The proposed amendment merely recognizes this respect, and affirms that the flag forms the basis of our aspiration to unity. This aspiration nurtures, rather than undermines, freedom of speech. The Court thus retains the full power to harmonize the two amendments by interpreting the proposed amendment in light of the First Amendment. (*Texas vs. Johnson*, 491 U.S. 397, 429, 434)(1989)(Rehnquist, C.J. dissenting).

The proposed amendment would reinforce the Constitution. The flag symbolizes our aspiration to national unity and democracy, upon which the Constitution is grounded. Thus, amending the Constitution to authorize Congress to protect the flag would further strengthen the Constitution and the laws and freedoms which form from it.

The Flag Is a Cherished Symbol

The flag is an instrument of expressing honor as well as a symbol of honor. We honor and cherish members of the Armed Services and other individuals through the process of honoring and protecting the flag. Draping a flag over the coffin of a fallen soldier, placing a flag near a grave, or hanging a flag on one's house on Memorial Day are all ways we express our honor and appreciation for those who have fought and died to secure the freedoms we have as Americans. Allowing others to physically desecrate the flag diminishes the honor and recognition that we bestow upon such individuals. Thus, we must protect the flag to respect the substance of what the flag embodies, along with what it symbolizes. To appropriately honor the individual, we must honor the flag.

Displaying the flag is a medium for demonstrating that the freedoms the flag represents are recognized, protected and upheld. Courtrooms, schools, the halls of Congress, other government buildings—wherever the flag is displayed signifies that it is a place where the substance of our freedoms and rights is protected. Thus, we must protect the flag to preserve the significance and weight that displaying the flag in such forums conveys.

The proposed amendment does not regulate speech or discriminate against any specific messages. The proposal would merely regulate one mode of expression—physical desecration of the flag. Regardless of the specific "message" intended, laws enacted pursuant to the proposed amendment would impose a single narrow regulation on the mode of the message: It could not be expressed by physically dasecrating the flag. (*Texas vs. Johnson*, 491 U.S. 397, 432 (1989) (Rehnquist, C.J., dissenting).

The American people deserve the right to choose to protect the flag. The practice of democracy binds our nation. The flag symbolizes and embodies this bond, and thus in turn symbolizes our system of democracy. The American people should be authorized to require a minimal respect for this one symbol that binds us to one another, to protect the freedoms upon which it is based.

Hate Speech Should Be Limited

by Laura Leets

About the author: *Laura Leets is an assistant professor in the communication department at Stanford University.*

There's been a groundswell in the past several years to increase diversity in journalism, both in news coverage and in newsroom staffing. The goal of several diversity initiatives is to increase the number of voices that regularly appear in our newspapers, magazines, broadcasts and Web sites.

It's important to seek different perspectives and ideas, and the goal of such initiatives is an admirable and productive one. There are some voices, however, that have demonstrably adverse effects. So while the journalism community, judicial system and American public generally support tolerance of diverse viewpoints, some perspectives and types of speech still warrant concern.

One problematic voice is that of hate. Whether it is the dragging death of an African-American behind a pick-up truck in Texas, a gay student's murder in Wyoming, a racially motivated shooting spree at a Los Angeles Jewish community center or a bloody rampage by two high school students enamored of fascism, the rising incidence of hate crimes and the groups who appear to encourage them is attracting public interest. In particular, the World Wide Web has provided marginalized extremist groups a more notable and accessible public platform. The Internet has put the problem of incendiary hate into sharp relief.

Hate Speech Has a Slow-Acting Effect

In several research studies where I have focused on short-term message effects of hate speech, it is difficult to demonstrate with certainty the linkage between hate expression and violence or harm (deterministic causality). In a recent study, I asked 266 participants (both university and non-university students recruited online) to read and evaluate one of 11 white supremacist Web pages that I had randomly sampled from the Internet. Similar to previous studies, the data showed that the content of the hate Web pages was perceived to be in keeping with the Court bounds for First Amendment protection. Yet the participants acknowledged an indirect effect that, on the other hand, may suggest hate speech effects are more slow-acting—and thus imperceptible in the short term (probabilistic causality).

Specifically, participants in the cyberhate study rated the indirect threats from the World Church of the Creator (WCOTC) Web page as very high (Mean=6, on a seven-point scale where seven represented the highest score). Is it coincidental that a former WCOTC member recently shot 11 Asian Americans, African-Americans and Jews, killing two, before committing suicide? Or that two brothers associated with WCOTC were charged with murdering a gay couple and fire-bombing three Sacramento synagogues? While WCOTC leader Matthew Hale does not endorse this lawlessness, neither does he condemn it. Part of their ideology is that all nonwhites are "mud people," people without souls, like animals eligible for harm.

Current legal remedies may be missing the real harm of racist indoctrination, which may not be immediately apparent or verifiable. For instance, hate expressions tend to encourage a set of beliefs that develop gradually and that often can lie dormant until conditions are ripe for a climate of moral exclusion and subsequent crimes against humanity. Moral exclusion is defined by Susan Opotow, an independent scholar affiliated with Teachers College at Columbia University, as the psychosocial orientation toward individuals or groups for whom justice principles or considerations of fairness are not applicable. People who are morally excluded are perceived as nonentities, and harming them appears acceptable and just (e.g., slavery, holocaust).

It is not the abstract viewpoints that are problematic. Rather, it is the expressions intending to elicit persecution or oppression that often begin with dehumanizing rhetoric. In my research, I argue that communication is the primary means by which psychological distancing occurs. Arguably, it may be the long-term, not short-term, effects of hate expression that are potentially more far reaching.

The Internet May Require Special Regulation

Even though prevailing First Amendment dogma maintains that speech may not be penalized merely because its content is racist, sexist or basically abhorrent, Internet law is a dynamic area and as such is not completely integrated into our regulatory and legal system. Consequently, many questions remain about how traditional laws should apply to this new and unique medium.

The Internet can combine elements of print (newspapers and magazines), broadcast (television and radio) and face-to-face interaction. Moreover, unlike users of previous media, those on the Internet have the power to reach a mass audience, but in this case the audience must be more active in seeking information, as cyberspace is less intrusive than other mass media.

It is unclear whether content-based restrictions found in other technological media may be permissible for the Internet. For example, the FCC ruled that indecency was unsuitable for broadcast media because of ease of access, invasiveness and spectrum scarcity, yet cable and print media are not subjected to this form of content regulation.

In 1996, the United States Congress passed the Telecommunications Bill, which included the Communications Decency Act (CDA). The CDA regulated indecent or obscene material for adults on the Internet, applying First Amendment jurisprudence from broadcast and obscenity cases. Later that year, the Supreme Court declared two provisions unconstitutional in *Reno vs. ACLU*. Congress and the Court disagreed on the medium-specific constitutional speech standard suitable for the World Wide Web. Congress argued that the Internet should be regulated in the same manner as television or radio, but the Court decided not to apply that doctrinal framework. Instead, the Court viewed the Internet as face-to-face communication, deserving full protection.

> *"Arguably, it may be the long-term, not short-term, effects of hate expression that are potentially . . . far reaching."*

Issues of Internet regulation naturally lead to the question of whether such regulation is even possible. Cyberspace doesn't have geographical boundaries, so it is difficult to determine where violations of the law should be prosecuted. There are enforcement conflicts, not only between different countries' legal jurisdictions, but also among federal, state and local levels in the United States. Although Americans place a high premium on free expression, without much effort most people can find Internet material that they would want to censor.

Some argue that cyberhate oversteps this idea of "mere insult" and warrants liability. The Internet is a powerful forum of communication with its broad (world-wide) reach, interactivity and multi-media capability to disseminate information. These features inevitably result in concerns about impact, especially when viewed as empowering racists and other extremists. It is common for people to wonder whether white supremacist Web pages cause hate crime. This question is similar to people's concerns regarding whether TV violence causes aggression in viewers. The issue of causation (claim: x causes y) is an important one to address.

Hate Speech May Influence Actions

It is important to differentiate between language determining (or causing) an effect and language influencing the probability of an effect. In terms of a strict social science approach (deterministic causation) we can't say language has an effect unless three conditions are met: (a) there must be a relationship between the hypothesized cause the observed effect, (b) the cause must always precede the effect in time (x must come before y), and (c) all alternative explanations for the effect must be eliminated. The problem with making a strong case for a causal effect lies with the second and third conditions. For example, most media (television, Internet etc.) effects are probabilistic, not deterministic. It is almost impossible to make a dear case for television or cyberhate effects because the relationship is almost never a simple causal one. Instead, there are many factors in the influence process. Each factor increases the probability of an effect occurring. The effects process is complex.

The U.S. Supreme Court has traditionally viewed speech effects in terms of short-term, deterministic consequences, and has not considered more far-reaching effects.

While more research is needed on the long-term effects of hate speech, it may be worth considering some very limited restrictions on some hate expression. American jurisprudence has not fully realized the harmful nature and effects stemming from hate speech, which has the ability both to directly elicit immediate behavior (short term) and to cultivate an oppressive climate (long term).

Colleges May Restrict Some Types of Speech

by Derek P. Langhauser

About the author: *Derek P. Langhauser is general counsel of Maine's public two-year college system.*

One should never agree to write briefly about free speech in the college and university setting. With their essential purpose being to inspire the exchange of new and challenging thoughts, colleges and universities are precisely the marketplaces of ideas that the framers of our Constitution had in mind when they committed the nation to protect both the process and the product of free speech under the First Amendment.

Indeed, there is currently no shortage of issues involving free speech on our campuses: student protests, commercial solicitations, Web-based expression, and student fees, just to name a few.

In judging these shifting contexts and the diverse viewpoints they encompass, we are asked to apply a maze of legal nuances. Nonetheless, it bears recalling that, for those of us who search in good faith for where the lines of constitutionality fall from one matter to the next, there is meaningful stability in the framework of what is generally called the "forum analysis."

Defining the Nature of the Speaker

This analysis—which may be helpful to administrators and not just college attorneys—requires identifying the speaker, type of speech, location where the speech will be expressed, and the timing and effect of any restriction on the speech. While this analysis is required as a matter of law for public institutions, it can also serve as guidance for private schools that struggle with the same issues.

The first step is to identify the speaker and determine whether the speech is generally protected under the First Amendment. For example, members of the college community (that is, students and employees) typically have a more secure right to speak than persons from outside that community (like vendors and external interest groups).

There is also a difference between an individual speaking on her own behalf (such as through a leaflet) and an individual seeking to compel the institution to incorporate her speech into the institution's own speech (for example, through an essay in a college publication), the former having more established rights.

Finally, there is a threshold difference between simple expression and expression that furthers unlawful ends. The latter, which enjoys no First Amendment protection, is that which promotes the imminent prospect of illegal or violent conduct, or which otherwise constitutes defamation, obscenity, pornography, gross disobedience of legitimate rules, false advertising, promotion of religion in violation of the free exercise or establishment clauses of the First Amendment, or the use of public resources to promote partisan political activities in violation of state or federal law.

Determining the Type of Speech

The next step is to categorize the type of speech, distinguishing political speech from commercial speech. Political speech is comprised of ideas, whereas commercial speech relates to products. While the distinction between these is not always clear (consider, for example, the late Supreme Court Justice William Brennan's question whether the phrase "Be a Patriot; Buy American Cars" constitutes a political or commercial utterance), the distinction is important because, in a democracy, products are not as constitutionally significant as ideas. Accordingly, colleges have greater authority to regulate commercial speech than political speech.

The next step is to define the scope of the location, or "forum" as the courts call it, that the speaker intends to use, and determine whether that location is public or non-public. If a speaker seeks general access to a piece of property, such as a building, then that building is the relevant forum. If a speaker seeks more limited access, such as to a bulletin board inside of a building, then that bulletin board is the relevant forum.

> *"Speech that would disrupt, interfere, threaten, or otherwise be incompatible with the purpose of a forum is not protected."*

Regarding the public or private nature of a forum, there are two types of public forums. "Traditional" public forums are areas, like a sidewalk or a quadrangle, where colleges have typically permitted broad expression. "Designated" public forums are more limited areas, such as an auditorium or lobby, that a college has specifically designated for either open expression or expression limited to certain groups (either internal and/or external) on certain subjects (like commercial and/or political expression). By contrast, non-public forums are those areas, such as offices, where public speech has typically not been permitted because it is incompatible with the legitimate operations of that area.

Distinguishing a public from a non-public forum is not always easy, and it requires a close examination of the forum's purpose and nature. A forum may have one or several purposes (such as, educational, administrative, governmental, and/or commercial), and, if it has several, a college may give certain types of speech priority over others. Speech that would disrupt, interfere, threaten, or otherwise be incompatible with the purpose of a forum is not protected.

As regards the nature of a forum, one should examine the college's intent, policy, and practices in recognizing and using that forum. Specifically, courts examine the stated purpose of any written policy and the consistency with which it has been enforced. Courts are suspicious of post-hoc policy formulations and selective enforcement of an otherwise inoperative policy.

Consequently, courts examine whether access to the forum is objectively controlled—that is, who determines which speech, if any, is permitted; the standards used to determine which speech is permitted; and whether a fee for access is charged. Finally, courts ask whether there is, in addition to the restricted forum, an alternative public forum in which the speech can be effectively expressed. Such availability enhances a college's argument that a disputed forum is non-public and, therefore, subject to more limitations.

Timing and Effect

The last steps in analysis turn to the timing and effect of any restriction on speech. Regarding timing, restrictions can either restrain a speaker before he acts, or punish him afterward. Generally speaking, colleges have less authority to issue prior restraints (such as denying a permit) and more authority to issue post-speech penalties (for example, suspending a student).

Regarding the effect of a restriction, it is crucial to distinguish those restrictions that limit the content of the speech (that is, the idea itself) from those that simply limit the circumstances in which the speech is expressed (such as the time, manner, and place of the expression). Colleges retain in all forums—public and non-public—the authority to regulate the location, duration, and volume of the speech regardless of its content if the restrictions protect an important and legitimate administrative or pedagogical interest; if the restrictions minimize, where practicable, intrusion into the speaker's opportunity to express content; and if they are evenly applied to all speakers.

A college, however, must exercise great care in all forums when it restricts speech because of its content. In any public forum, a college may restrict speech because of its content only by proving that the restriction is necessary to serve a compelling interest, and that the restriction is narrowly drawn to achieve that interest.

This is a very difficult test to pass (because a threat of violence must indeed be imminent). Note, however, that in non-public forums, a college may restrict speech because of its content by proving that the restriction is reasonable. Reasonableness is assessed in light of the purpose and nature of the forum and all surrounding circumstances. This is often an easier test to pass (such as removing students who "sit in" at the president's office).

In many instances, the right of free expression is, as it should be, broadly protected. The right, however, is not absolute. Indeed, courts balance this right against the many legitimate and important administrative and pedagogical interests of a college. By designating reasonably, clearly, and consistently which speech is permitted in what locations, colleges and universities can comply with the Constitution, meet their diverse administrative needs, and honor their legacy of meaningful ideological exchange.

Pornography Should Be Censored

by S. Michael Craven

About the author: *S. Michael Craven is the vice president of religious and cultural affairs for the National Coalition for the Protection of Children and Families. He is a former director of the Center for Decency in Dallas, Texas, and has been a featured speaker on various college campuses and network news shows.*

Robert George, the Princeton Law Professor, pointed out in his book, *The Clash of Orthodoxies*, that, ". . . legal prohibition of anything works well only when supported by a widespread recognition of the evil of the thing prohibited." This it seems is our first challenge when addressing the issue of pornography and the proposed restriction thereof in a society that seems to no longer hold to the 'widespread recognition of the evil' that pornography represents.

As a result of the proliferation of pornography, there are many today that have removed pornography from any moral category altogether and simply regard this as a First Amendment issue. In fact, according to research by George Barna conducted in November 2003, 38 percent of American adults surveyed stated that pornography was morally acceptable. This is the first supposition that we must address: is pornography morally acceptable or is it in fact immoral? And if we suppose it is immoral, on what basis do we make this distinction?

Pornography Harms Public Morality

Regardless of one's religious beliefs, most rational people can agree that behavior that does harm could be categorized as immoral, evil or wrong. Therefore we can likely agree that we, as a society, have an interest in and responsibility to prohibit or restrain certain behavior in order to eliminate or minimize the harm to both individuals and society. This would be regarded as "public morality."

Robert George offers an excellent definition of public morality. "Public morality, like public health and safety, is a concern that goes beyond considerations of law and public policy. Public morals are affected, for good or ill, by the activities of private parties, and such parties have obligations with respect to them." Contrary to the assertion that the private exercise of behavior or in this case the private use of pornography is not the concern of anyone else—private behavior is of concern simply because it does in fact affect public morals and therefore does have public consequences. For example, even apart from laws prohibiting the creation of fire hazards, individuals have an obligation to avoid placing persons and property in jeopardy of fire. While this example addresses a health and safety issue it is nonetheless the same with respect to the moral obligations imposed by society upon private behaviors which produce public consequences.

It is with this in mind that we examine the issue of pornography in an effort to first understand how this "private" behavior affects public morality and our society as a justification for governmental restriction and/or prohibition of pornographic materials.

So, we begin with the simple question: Does pornography cause harm? To adequately answer this question we must first make an argument for a proper view of sex.

A view of sex that integrates the psychological, emotional, physical and life-giving or procreative potential is a comprehensive and proper view of sex. This perspective provides the only foundation for intimacy built upon mutual love and respect with a high view of humanity. Intimacy by its very nature is something deeply personal marked by the sharing of one's innermost self, an act of unrestrained exposure to our most vulnerable physical and emotional self. . . .

The other view of sexuality, and frankly the more pervasive view in today's culture, is by contrast a disintegrated view separating the physical from every other aspect. Sex is reduced to mere copulation and persons are instrumentalized or viewed as objects of sexual gratification. . . . This view is inherently dehumanizing, reducing persons to nothing more than instrumental value. Our perceptions of men and women are brought down to their most base form as "objects" whose sole purpose is to meet the "objectifier's" needs. This shift in thinking denies the intrinsic value of people made in the image of God and renders them less than human, fostering a low view of humanity. History has demonstrated that a society of people who have a view of others as less than human will necessarily become desensitized and indifferent leading to a culture in which the abuse of those so objectified increases. This might account for the unprecedented increase in violence against women and the epidemic rape rates in this country just in the period since the so-called sexual revolution began.

A Disintegrated View of Sexuality

In addition, this *dis*integrated view of sexuality is inherently selfish and narcissistic; sex is divorced from love and relationship and instead is viewed as sport producing a conquest mentality. Intimacy has no place in such a system.

Sex is no longer an act of sharing and vulnerability but simply self-centered gratification. The gratification of self above all else becomes the purpose and aim of all sexual encounters. Again, this is in sharp contrast to a proper view of human sexuality which advocates and achieves the highest satisfaction through an emphasis on the other instead of self. . . .

This is the view of sexuality and human relationships that pornography promotes and idealizes to the exclusion of all others. This would explain why, in large part, pornography has such strong appeal among men because the difficult and sometimes challenging aspects of relationships are completely removed, giving the viewer unabated access to sex without any prior or subsequent commitments. Couple this with the visual medium, a powerful sexual stimulant to men, and you have the makings of a potent platform for the perversion of male views pertaining to sex, relationships, and women in general.

> *"Public morals are affected, for good or ill, by the activities of private parties."*

As one researcher put it, "Pornography presents a graphic, degrading picture of human life and invites the viewer to wallow in it. It [pornography] plunges him into imaginative preoccupation with autoerotic fantasies wherein he entertains himself by violently or sexually feeding, vicariously, on the helplessness or willing vulnerability of a no-longer-human animal."

Possible Links to Mental Health

Dartmouth Medical School recently completed one of the most compelling research studies to date on the growing mental health crisis among U.S. children and adolescents titled, *Hardwired to Connect: The New Scientific Case for Authoritative Communities*. The results of this research are simply astonishing and should serve as a wake up call to the escalating danger in our nation. The report, undertaken by the Commission on Children at Risk, sought to address the rising rates of mental problems and emotional distress among U.S. children and adolescents.

The report stated that, "we are witnessing high and rising rates of depression, anxiety, attention deficit, conduct disorders, thoughts of suicide, and other serious mental, emotional and behavioral problems among U.S. children and adolescents." In answer to the question; what's causing the crisis? The report offered the following:

> In large measure, what's causing this crisis of American childhood is a lack of connectedness. We mean two kinds of connectedness—close connections to other people, and deep connections to moral and spiritual meaning.

Since the report goes on to say, "the scientific evidence shows that the human child is hard-wired to connect," I would argue that the pornographic culture with its disintegrating view of persons and relationships is at the very least exacerbating this condition and at most *central* to creating them.

According to the psychiatrically trained anthropologist, David Gutmann:

> Acquiring a moral identity is largely based on a profound redirection of the idealizing tendency, from being introversive and reflexive (that is, fixed on the self) to being focused on some worthy version of otherness. We can say that adulthood has been achieved when narcissism is transmuted, and thereby detoxified into strong, lasting idealizations and into healthy narcissism. . . . Instead of himself, the true adult venerates ideal versions of his community, his vocation and his family.

In other words, adults that remain self-centered and narcissistic, the central theme of the pornographic message, may actually experience a retardation of moral development. This *moral retardation* then inhibits healthy relationships, which in turn produces a sense of disconnectedness from other persons as well as any transcendent sense of meaning and purpose. This then affects society in two ways. First, if those using pornography are spouses and parents then this dysfunctional relationship is modeled between mother and father and experienced directly between parent and child. Secondly, the proliferation of pornography and its messages into mainstream media is promoting this same dysfunctional view of sex and relationships as the norm for an entire generation.

Pornography's Adverse Behavioral Effects

If pornography does indeed promote this disintegrated view of sexuality, which all of the social science seems to confirm, then we must ask, "Does such a view actually produce any tangible negative consequences?"

Victor B. Cline, Ph.D., professor of psychology at the University of Utah, identified as early as 1985 that exposure to pornography was in fact capable of producing profound psychological and behavioral changes. Cline conducted a clinical-case history study of approximately 225 male patients who had sexual pathology or family disruption resulting from their involvement with pornography. He reported that of those males who became immersed in pornography there appeared a near universal four-factor syndrome characterizing their experience with and the effect of pornography use.

> *"Sex is no longer an act of sharing and vulnerability but simply self-centered gratification."*

This four-factor syndrome identified by Cline is as follows:

The first thing that happened was an ADDICTION effect. There seemed to be a clear psychological addiction to this material. Once involved the men kept coming back for more and still more. The material provided a very powerful sexual stimulant or aphrodisiac effect followed by some kind of sexual release.

Secondly, there was an ESCALATION effect. With the passage of time these men required more explicit, rougher, more deviant kinds of sexual material to get their "highs" and "sexual turn-ons." In one sense it was reminiscent of individuals afflicted with drug addictions. In time there is an increasing need for more of the stimulant to get the same effects as initially. If their spouses or girlfriends were involved with them the same thing occurred. They pushed their partners over time into doing increasingly bizarre and deviant sexual activities. In many cases this resulted in a rupture of the relationship when the spouse or girlfriend refused to go further leading to conflict, separation or divorce.

> *"Adults that remain self-centered and narcissistic . . . may actually experience a retardation of moral development."*

The third thing that happened was DESENSITIZATION. Materials that were originally perceived as shocking, taboo breaking, repulsive or immoral (even though still sexually arousing) in time were seen as acceptable and commonplace. These behaviors, in a sense, became legitimized. There was also, increasingly, a sense that "everybody does this" or at least many people do, which gave a kind of permission to do likewise.

The fourth thing that occurred was an increasing tendency to ACT OUT the sexual activities witnessed in the pornography viewed. This involved a great variety of acts including the sexual seduction of children, sexual aggression against women, as well as an increasing repertoire of sexual activities in the bedroom with one's current partner. Group sex and partner switching were other outcomes. Voyeurism, exhibitionism, fetishism, and necrophilia were other examples of acting out behavior.

This is not to suggest that every person who views pornography will inevitably experience any or all of these four stages but it demonstrates the progressively degenerating potential of pornography consumption. There is something very powerful taking place within the psyche of a person with long term exposure to pornography. . . .

This demonstrates the unique aspect of sexual stimulation and its influence on a person. There are very few other influences capable of producing such strong chemical and physiological responses than that of sexual stimulation. This in and of itself is not necessarily bad; this is the natural design of human sexuality—it is most definitely a powerful human experience, and we ignore this fact to our own peril. This is precisely why sex should never be treated casually. A casual or recreational approach to sexuality is by necessity a disintegrated view of sex.

In pornography, sexual stimulation is achieved visually (excluding phone sex) and the chemical and physiological process begins. However, the object of arousal is not a person in an anthropological sense but an artificial image of a person existing outside of any relationship to the viewer. The viewer is focused on his own gratification to the exclusion of all others even if he is viewing the pornography with a sexual partner.

Furthermore, by integrating pornography into his sexual experience he is becoming dependent upon the stimulation of the image and not a "live" person. This provides the condition described by Cline above in which the person enters the ESCALATION stage. In addition, this person is becoming more and more disconnected from relationship as the context for sexual gratification.

Nowhere do you find *any* positive effects resulting from habitual exposure to pornography. There are no documented "improvements" in a person's attitude toward the opposite sex or relationships in general, for example. The tendency is NOT toward a higher view of sex, relationships and humanity but in every case, a perverted view of intimacy, a dysfunctional view of relationships, and a dehumanizing view of women.

Cline accurately stated, "If there is some suspicion that the drinking water, for example, is contaminated and people are getting ill after drinking it the burden of proof shifts to proving it is safe—rather than having final conclusive proof that it is indeed toxic. I think that this situation now pretty clearly applies to the pornography area."

Pornography Affects Society

What has been addressed thus far is the fact that pornography most certainly and in almost every way adversely affects the person using pornography and those in relationship to them but the question remains, "how does this affect society in general?"

If a commitment to the prohibition or restriction of pornography necessitates a broader impact than that upon the individuals that I have just described, then let us examine the collateral social effects of pornography to which all of us are exposed.

Let's begin by examining the unprecedented proliferation of pornography that has taken place in the last four decades and then attempt to correlate these facts with a number of related societal ills.

In 1973, Americans spent approximately $10 million on pornography. By 1999 the pornography industry took in more than $8 billion dollars. More recently that figure was placed at $10 billion. This is more than all revenues generated by Rock-n-Roll and Country music, more than Americans spent on Broadway productions, theater, ballet, jazz and classical music combined! In addition, it is estimated that online sex sites generate at the very least another $1 billion in annual revenues. These figures, of course, do not even begin to include the "free" pornographic material presently available in abundance on the Internet, not to mention the estimated 2.5 billion pornographic e-mails that are sent each day!

> *"There is something very powerful taking place within the psyche of a person with long term exposure to pornography."*

However, this raises the "supply and demand" question. In other words, did the increase in availability produce an increase in demand or were pornographers simply responding to existing market demands? To answer this we have to examine several converging factors that will demonstrate that it was the supply that preceded the so-called demand for pornography.

Lax Regulation Encourages Pornography

Since the founding of America there has always been some form of legal prohibition against obscene or pornographic materials. The definition of obscenity remained, for the most part, objectively understood in a society that made clear moral distinctions pertaining to sexual conduct. However, in the wake of the sexual revolution in the 1960s these standards became less clear, more subjective, and thus no longer associated with a universal moral consensus.

Beginning in the 1960s, First Amendment protections were invoked by pornographers claiming that any restriction of obscene material was a violation of free speech. The words of philosopher Søren Kierkegaard seem an appropriate response here, "People demand freedom of speech as is compensation for the freedom of thought, which they seldom use." Nonetheless, necessary steps had to be taken to further define obscenity. In the *Miller v. California* case of 1973 the current definition and legal prohibitions against obscene material were put in place having been upheld by the U.S. Supreme Court.

> *"Since the founding of America there has always been some form of legal prohibition against obscene or pornographic materials."*

The U.S. Supreme Court affirmed that, "this much has been categorically settled by the Court, that obscene material is unprotected by the First Amendment." However, the Court then went on to provide additional qualifications in an effort to clarify the legal definition of obscenity. The Court provided the following three-prong constitutional criteria for federal and state laws and court adjudications of obscenity:

(1) whether the average person, applying contemporary adult community standards, would find that the material, taken as a whole, appeals to a prurient interest in sex (i.e., an erotic, lascivious, abnormal, unhealthy, degrading, shameful, or morbid interest in nudity, sex, or excretion); *and*

(2) whether the average person, applying contemporary adult community standards, would find that the work depicts or describes, in a patently offensive way, sexual conduct (i.e, ultimate sex acts, normal or perverted, actual or simulated; masturbation; excretory functions; lewd exhibition of the genitals; or sadomasochistic sexual abuse); *and*

(3) whether a reasonable person would find that the work, taken as a whole, lacks serious literary, artistic, political, or scientific value.

While there remains some room for interpretation, obscenity was nonetheless defined and the Supreme Court affirmed that such material was NOT protected by the First Amendment.

From then until 1992 obscenity was successfully and vigorously prosecuted by both Federal and State governments. Then in 1992 under the [Bill] Clinton administration, the Justice Department led by Janet Reno virtually abandoned the prosecution of obscenity. . . .

"More and more children are being exposed to pornography."

With the advent of the Internet in the early 90s coupled with an absence of fear from prosecution, the pornography industry found and capitalized on the perfect medium of distribution—affordable, accessible, and anonymous. Every previous barrier to pornography (including child pornography, bestiality, sadomasochistic and every perverse expression imaginable) was suddenly eliminated.

Children Have Unprecedented Access to Pornography

This condition alone should raise universal concern over pornography given the often unrestricted access of children to these materials and worse, the unrestricted access of pornographers to children. In fact, in June 2000, the National Center for Missing and Exploited Children released "Online Victimization: A Report on the Nation's Youth." The survey revealed that 25% of the 5001 surveyed had received "unwanted exposure to pictorial images of naked people or people having sex." The study says this represents an estimated 5.4 to 6.4 million children.

Every person, whether they be liberal or conservative, religious or atheistic, is compelled by conscience to protect the most innocent among us: children. Clearly this is a crisis not only affecting children but in fact *targeting* children in many cases.

It has long been known that Internet pornographers have utilized deceptive and unscrupulous marketing methodologies targeting children. In the past, pornographers have incorporated "key words" and "meta-tags" into their websites such as "Nintendo", "Disney", and "doll" so that children entering these words into Internet search engines might inadvertently click on a link in the search results and be led to a porn site.

What possible interest could pornographers have in marketing their "products" to an audience with little or no means to generate revenue except to cultivate future consumers? Very clearly pornographers understand the addictive nature of their product in much the same way that the tobacco companies do. We are outraged and take legislative steps to stop the tobacco industry from targeting children [and in many cases adults also] and yet any attempts to protect children from exposure to pornography are met with resistance for fear of infringing upon some perceived constitutional right of pornographers to do as they please regardless of harm.

Consequently, more and more children are being exposed to pornography with the inculcation of its disintegrated view of sexuality and relationships occurring at an earlier and more vulnerable age. Dr. Mark Laaser, a nationally known psychologist specializing in sexual addiction, testified before a joint Congressional Committee in May 2000 that the average age of initial exposure to pornography for boys is now age 5. Prior to the advent of the Internet this figure was placed at around 15–16 for males and this was mostly *Playboy*-type publications.

Given the current trends it is safe to say that if steps are not taken to stem the tide of pornographic materials we will likely see a generation of young men incapable of normal, healthy sexuality and relationships, creating, in turn, an era of unprecedented family dissolution, sexual dysfunction, and abuse.

Pornography Has a Negative Effect on Society

Pornography has been in existence since the earliest civilizations; its presence and effects remained minimal up until this point. The convergence of these two factors—prosecutorial neglect along with an ubiquitous and cheap distribution channel—provided the unabated flow of pornographic material into society producing an ever increasing demand and with it, a host of devastating societal consequences.

As we have already seen, pornography very clearly affects individuals and those in relationship to them. We have addressed the question of supply versus demand, the legalities surrounding pornography, and of course the risk to children. Let us return to the question of pornography's broader societal impact.

As we have learned, pornographic images are capable of provoking powerful psychological and physiological responses in people that engender a specific view of sexuality that I have termed *dis*integrated. This disintegrated view then alters how one views relationships, themselves, and in particular the opposite sex.

"Scientifically proving cause and effect in pornography is virtually impossible because, ethically, researchers cannot conduct the necessary research."

Furthermore, we have seen how this altered view never edifies or builds up but rather dehumanizes persons and breaks down relationships.

It is logical to conclude that such persons so affected will project those attitudes on others in sometimes destructive or anti-social behaviors. The research in this area appears to overwhelmingly confirm this. For example, the Los Angeles Police Department's Sexually Exploited Child Unit examined the relationship between extra familial (outside the family) child sexual abuse and pornography in their cases over a ten year period from 1980–1989. Pornography was directly involved in 62% of the cases and actually recovered in 55% of the total cases. The study's author concluded: "Clearly, pornography, whether it be adult or child pornography, is an insidious tool in the hands of the pedophilic population . . . The study merely confirms what detectives have long known: that pornography is a strong factor in the sexual victimization of children."

In another study of adult sex offenders the researchers found that 86 percent of convicted rapists said they were regular users of pornography, with 57 percent admitting direct imitation of pornographic scenes they enjoyed in the commission of their rapes.

In 1979, a U.S. Department of Justice study in Phoenix, Arizona, found that neighborhoods with a pornography business experienced 40 percent more property crime and 500 percent more sexual offenses than similar neighborhoods without a pornography outlet. Michigan state police detective Darrell Pope found that of the 38,000 sexual assault cases in Michigan (1956–1979), in 41 percent of the cases pornographic material was viewed just prior to or during the crime. This agrees with research done by psychotherapist David Scott who found that "half the rapists studied used pornography to arouse themselves immediately prior to seeking out a victim.". . .

Proponents of pornography will argue that these are extreme cases involving a number of other factors which are ignored, such as socioeconomic, early family conditions, mental illness, etc. They argue that attempts to isolate pornography as a contributing cause of so many sex-related incidents is wishful thinking on the part of pornography opponents.

Some proponents argue that pornography actually performs a positive function in society by acting like a "safety-valve" for potential sexual offenders. Aristotle put forth a similar theory with regard to violence stating that "the witnessing of violence will calm the spectator." Of course, today there is an abundance of research evidence refuting such theoretical conjecture.

Ironically, this perspective is based almost exclusively on the work of Berl Kutchinsky, a criminologist at the University of Copenhagen. His famous study on pornography found that when the Danish government lifted restrictions on pornography, the number of sex crimes decreased. His theory was that the availability of pornography siphons off dangerous sexual impulses. But when the data for his "safety valve" theory was further evaluated, many of his research flaws began to show.

For example, Kutchinsky failed to distinguish between different kinds of sex crimes (e.g., rape, indecent exposure, etc.) and instead merely lumped them together. This effectively masked an increase in rape statistics. He also failed to take into account that increased tolerance for certain crimes (e.g., public nudity, sex with a minor) may have contributed to a drop in the reported crimes.

Proponents of pornography will argue that there are no empirical studies demonstrating a direct cause and effect, and, of course, they are correct; however, scientifically proving cause and effect in pornography is virtually impossible because, ethically, researchers cannot conduct the necessary research. Dolf Zillman, a leading researcher in this field, points out, "Men cannot be placed at risk of developing sexually violent inclinations by extensive exposure to violent or nonviolent pornography, and women cannot be placed at risk of becoming victims of such inclinations." But this does not mean that the current body of research offering a correlation between pornography and the aforementioned effects can be completely dismissed either. In fact, a 1994 review of 81 original peer-reviewed research studies concluded that "the empirical research on the effects of aggressive pornography shows, with fairly impressive consistency, that exposure to these materials has a negative effect on attitudes toward women and the perceived likelihood to rape."

In the absence of "empirical" scientific evidence, we are forced to rely upon logic and reason, along with a plethora of anecdotal evidence, which clearly demonstrates that pornography does indeed produce changes in attitudes and values. With this in mind we must conclude that pornography is, in essence, sex education of the worst possible kind, capable of reorienting our natural sexuality into unnatural and unhealthy behaviors both personally and socially.

Again, "If there is some suspicion that the drinking water is contaminated and people are getting sick after drinking it the burden of proof shifts to proving it is safe—rather than having final conclusive proof that it is indeed toxic." Clearly people are getting "sick" and only the person who refuses to recognize the obvious relationship of pornography to its effects insists that the "water is safe."

Flag Burning Is a Legitimate Expression of Dissent

by Ralph G. Neas and Marge Baker

About the author: Ralph G. Neas is the president of People for the American Way (PFAW), a nonprofit organization committed to the values of pluralism, individuality, and freedom of thought. Marge Baker is policy director for PFAW and is the former president of the National Institute for Dispute Resolution.

On behalf of the more than 600,000 members and supporters of People for the American Way, we write in opposition to S.J. Res [Senate Joint Resolution] 4, which would amend the U.S. Constitution to authorize Congress to prohibit the physical desecration of the American flag. We believe that amending the Bill of Rights to censor unpopular speech dishonors the flag and the freedoms that it represents.[1]

Flag Burning Is a Legitimate Expression of Dissent

Freedom of expression is at the very heart of our democracy. At a time when we are working across the globe to secure the right of everyone to be free from totalitarian regimes, it is all the more important that we distinguish ourselves from countries that fear political dissent and imprison dissenters for expressing their views. In contrast, banning flag desecration would put America in the unwelcome league of repressive regimes such as The People's Republic of China, the former Soviet Union, Cuba, and Saddam Hussein's Iraq, all of which do (or did) imprison their citizens for desecrating their national flags.

While most Americans find desecration of the flag offensive and distasteful, the unique strength of our nation lies in our ability to tolerate dissent and free

---

1. The anti-flag-burning amendment did not pass.

speech even when—especially when—we disagree.

Former Vietnam POW and U.S. Marine Corp Major James Warner wrote eloquently about this difference in an article for *The Retired Officer* magazine in which he described an exchange in a Viet Cong prison with one of his captors:

> I remember one interrogation where I was shown a photograph of some Americans protesting the war by burning a flag. "There," the officer said, "People in your country protest against your cause. That proves you are wrong." "No," I said, "That proves that I'm right. In my country we are not afraid of freedom, even if it means that people disagree with us." The officer was on his feet in an instant, his face purple with rage. . . . While he was ranting I was astonished to see pain compounded by fear in his eyes.

Unlike totalitarian regimes, we have never needed to coerce patriotism or respect for our national symbols in America. In fact, in the wake of the September 11th [2001] terrorist attacks, we have seen outpouring of patriotic sentiment as well as support for the flag and public displays of the flag.

Arguments for an Amendment Are Unfounded

Proponents of the flag desecration amendment have tried to inflate the number of unpunished incidents of flag desecration as well as obscure the amendment's impact on free expression in those rare cases where it does occur. These arguments are demonstrably false based on the very examples and statistics constantly cited by pro-amendment organizations and individuals.

First, proponents of the Amendment argue that the amendment is necessary because flag desecration cannot be punished under current law. This is simply not the case. Of the 122 incidents of flag desecration identified by the Citizens Flag Alliance (CFA) on their website, at least two-thirds (76) involved crimes that are already covered by local criminal statutes—including theft, vandalism, destruction of property, trespassing, disorderly conduct or public disturbance. In many of the very cases that CFA cites, for example, an arrest was made on multiple charges. But even this understates the case. At least some of the remaining incidents cited, some of which are clearly acts of political expression, may still involve conduct that violates the law—such as creating a disturbance or violating local fire codes.

Second, these statistics highlight the rarity of flag desecration, incidents of political expression which are protected by the First Amendment. Analysis of the incidents cited by CFA show, at most, only 34 of the 122 incidents could be considered acts of political expression—the behavior targeted by the proposed amendment. Therefore, it is only those extremely rare incidents of political speech—only about two per year between 1989 and 2003—that lead proponents to conclude that we need to pass a constitutional amendment restricting our Bill of Rights.

Third, while flag desecration is very rare, there is no question that on occasion it is done to express a point of view, as the proponents' own materials make clear. The few incidents they cite which clearly are protected speech actually illustrate why our First Amendment protection for free expression is so important. The following are two examples taken verbatim from CFA's website which illustrate this point:

- October 7, 1996, Fort Smith, AR: a flag bearing a swastika and the word 'abortion' was displayed hanging upside down outside a house here. The home's owner said he had displayed the upside-down flag as a statement protesting the failure to overturn President [Bill] Clinton's veto of a bill that would have outlawed partial-birth abortions.
- January 24, 2001, Harrisonburg, VA: More than 300 people watched as two students at James Madison University burned the American flag on the school commons. The flag burning was largely in response to the inauguration of President George W. Bush. The flag never became engulfed in flames, although it did catch fire for a short time.

While many would disagree with the sentiments these individuals were trying to communicate, it's clear that they are political statements. Proponents of the amendment cannot have it both ways. They cannot cite examples of political speech as incidents they would like to ban, while simultaneously claiming they are not trying to bar certain political expression.

Flag Amendment Threatens First Amendment Rights

Finally, proponents of the Constitutional amendment try to minimize the dramatic impact of their proposal on First Amendment rights by arguing that for over 200 years flag protection statutes were constitutional under the First Amendment, until the Supreme Court allegedly changed that in the 1989 *Texas v. Johnson* case. However, this argument is riddled with inaccuracies, both as to the history of flag desecration statutes and the decades of Supreme Court case law that naturally led to the *Johnson* and 1990 *U.S. v. Eichman* decisions.

The First Amendment was not applied to judge the constitutionality of state laws until 1925 (in the U.S. Supreme Court case of *Gitlow v. New York*), so the first flag statutes were not and could not have been challenged under the First Amendment. In fact, the first state flag statute itself was not even enacted until 1897, and the first federal flag statute was not enacted by Congress until 1968. After 1925, when federal courts first began to apply the First Amendment to state flag statutes, the U.S. Supreme Court repeatedly and consistently struck down convictions under different flag statutes for the same fundamental First Amendment principles cited in its 1989 and 1990 flag rulings. The 1989 and 1990 flag rulings directly cite and rely upon this unbroken chain of legal precedent. Contrary to amendment proponents' claims, if the Supreme Court had not struck

> *"While flag desecration is very rare, there is no question that on occasion it is done to express a point of view."*

down the convictions in the 1989 and 1990 flag cases, involving non-verbal, peaceful use of the flag as a form of political protest, it would have been a radical departure from well-established, fundamental First Amendment law.

Surrendering to a handful of offensive individuals by limiting the very freedoms that make us a beacon of liberty for the rest of the world does not honor the flag. In a letter sent to Senator Patrick Leahy in May 1999, General Colin Powell, now Secretary of State, wrote "The First Amendment exists to insure that freedom of speech and expression applies not just to that with which we agree or disagree, but also that which we find outrageous. I would not amend that great shield of democracy to hammer a few miscreants. The flag will be flying proudly long after they have slunk away."

We urge you to protect our First Amendment freedoms by rejecting S.J. Res 4.

Speech Codes Threaten the Free Exchange of Ideas on College Campuses

by Eugene Volokh

About the author: *Eugene Volokh teaches First Amendment law at the University of California at Los Angeles and was a clerk for Justice Sandra Day O'Connor on the Supreme Court.*

Harvard Law School is considering drafting a new speech code, the *Boston Globe* tells us. More nonsense from the P.C. forces, many say. Haven't people realized that campus speech must remain free? It turns out, though, that the issue is more complex and more interesting than that.

The Harvard discussion is partly about a general speech code, which would control speech throughout campus; there the standard free-speech and academic-freedom objection is indeed sound. But there's also discussion of (in the *Boston Globe*'s words) "banning harassing, offensive language from the classroom." And in the classroom, speech certainly isn't free.

Students may not talk in class until they're called on, a necessary prior restraint. The instructor may cut them off, even based on their viewpoints, if he thinks their arguments are unsound. (Sometimes you want students to keep talking, so you can explore the error with the class, but sometimes you just need to clearly explain the right answer and move on.) And the instructor may and should reprimand rude students who swear, hiss, or personally insult their classmates. In my classroom, I would surely clamp down on "harassing, offensive language," vague as that concept may be.

Instructor speech in the classroom has traditionally been freer, because law schools are generally run by the faculty, and give professors wide authority over their classes. But I don't think that a professor's academic freedom entitles him to, for instance, personally insult or belittle students, or even gives him unlimited latitude to present material in a way that's needlessly inaccessible or alienating to students. Such behavior generally makes the professor an ineffective teacher, and schools may deny tenure or promotions to ineffective teachers. Students pay good money to schools, and schools pay good money to faculty, for quality teaching. Students and administrators are entitled to get professional, pedagogically effective behavior from teachers in return.

Speech Codes in the Classroom

So classroom speech—unlike speech in other parts of campus—has to be controlled. Speech codes, though, are the wrong way to control it.

Under the current system of instructor control, students already realize that if they say something rude, the instructor may reprimand them. The threat of such embarrassment generally prevents rudeness—really offensive classroom speech is rare at law schools (certainly at my own school, UCLA, but also to my knowledge at Harvard).

Likewise, if a teacher gets far enough out of line, his dean and his colleagues will talk to him; no professor likes that. Students will grumble, in hallways, in student newspapers, and on evaluations—most professors don't want that, either. Not a perfect system for deterring genuinely rude behavior by teachers, but a decent one.

> *"Speech codes risk deterring even reasoned, polite argument."*

"Fighting bad speech with good speech," the civil libertarian's classic remedy, is highly effective in this sort of closed environment, much more so than in society at large. Students pay close attention to what the instructor, the administration, and other students say. If the professor or the dean condemns genuinely offensive speech, this will powerfully deter such speech in the future. And such a public response (which, incidentally, can be used as to gross rudeness outside class, too) should also help make the victim feel vindicated. When we're insulted, what we usually want is for others to speak up to support us, and to condemn the wrongdoer.

How Speech Codes Harm Classroom Discussion

Speech codes can do little to improve on this system; and they can do much to worsen it.

To begin with, speech codes risk deterring even reasoned, polite argument. Especially when faced with a vague standard such as "harassing" or "offensive," wise students tend to avoid anything that might get them suspended or expelled, or might lead to a notation on their records. Even the accusation of "harassment," with its echoes of tortious or criminal conduct, may itself be a serious threat. This will interfere with in-class discussion—and with student spontaneity—much more than instructor control alone would.

As to faculty members, a speech code will actually weaken collegial-control mechanisms. Instead of a friendly admonition about poor judgment, there'll be an accusation that the professor violated an official rule, which will require a formal hearing and a legalistic debate about the rule's precise boundaries.

Collegial compromise will become harder. Sincere apologies will become harder, too, since any apology could be used as evidence against the teacher. And many disputes will become intra-faculty battles, which could sour faculty relations and faculty self-government for years.

All this exposes three fundamental flaws in the proposal. The first lies in the implicit assumption that formal law is better than informal social control (Jonathan Rauch's "hidden law"). In some contexts, enforceable rules are better than discretionary judgments and social pressure. Here, they're much worse.

The second flaw is still more dangerous: Speech codes lead people to see offensive speech not just as bad manners, but as a violation of their rights. Legalistic responses, after all, are society's way of responding to rights violations (for instance, to assaults or thefts), not to rude conduct.

Once offensive speech becomes seen as a rights violation, then people experience it as only more offensive—"not only did that jerk insult me, but he harassed me and discriminated against me." A demand for legalistic action becomes almost compulsory: Ignoring insults is a sign of fortitude, but ignoring injury to one's rights is often seen as a sign of weakness. The zone of "harassing [and] offensive language" grows, since whenever one word is officially condemned as offensive, more words become seen as offensive by analogy. And the result is more felt offense, not less.

Finally, what do young lawyers need? On the one hand, they need a good education, and people generally do learn better in a relatively (though not perfectly) friendly environment; but social controls can supply that.

On the other hand, young lawyers also need education in the habit of equanimity in the face of hostility; in the skill of mustering social pressure to fight those battles for which law is inapt or too expensive; in the decency and courage to speak up on behalf of those who are being treated rudely, and thus to themselves become part of the social-control mechanisms. The most-serious flaw of speech codes is that they undermine this education, rather than supporting it.

Limiting Hate Speech Threatens Legitimate Debate

by Ira H. Mehlman

About the author: *Ira H. Mehlman is the media director for the Federation for American Immigration Reform (FAIR), a nonpartisan organization dedicated to improving border security, stopping illegal immigration, and promoting immigration levels consistent with the national interest.*

America has become very wary of hate speech, and rightfully so. Notwithstanding what you may have learned on the playground, words can be very harmful and what we say often carries greater consequences than what we do.

The problem we face in dealing with hate speech is that it is often difficult to define. Everyone can recognize the ravings of neo-Nazis or Louis Farrakhan, which extol the superiority of one race and demonize another race, for what they are.

Increasingly, however, hate speech is being defined by the reaction of the listener, rather than by the clear and unambiguous motives of the speaker. Consequently, the line between hate speech and legitimate free speech is becoming blurred.

As America becomes more diverse, the gap between the intent of the speaker and the interpretation of the listener is widening.

As we all know, communication among people who all speak the same language and share a common culture is difficult enough, which is not entirely bad because it forces us to think before we speak. But if we have to stop and think about the unique sensitivities of too many people, there is an even greater peril that communication will cease all together.

Society has a legitimate interest in suppressing hate speech through intense social censure—rather than through government censorship—of those who spew it.

At the same time, society must be vigilant that the moral indignation of a particular segment of society to a message they don't like, or may even find offensive, does not lead to suppression of legitimate free speech.

Incidents of Hate

In the past, we have wrestled with questions of where to draw the line on matters such as sexual harassment and taunting among schoolkids. . . .

We have seen calls from responsible community and academic leadership to limit some forms of political speech in response to the tragic shooting at a Jewish community center in Los Angeles.

Earlier this summer [1999], New York City resident Craig Nelsen bought space on several billboards overlooking the city's (usually jammed) highways that asked motorists to consider the implications of an immigration policy that results in an additional 6,000 people settling in the United States every day.

Gaps of Logic

The billboards were immediately denounced by some as a form of hate speech and there were calls from community activists and local politicians that they be removed. City Councilman Guillermo Lanares went so far as to link the sentiments on Nelsen's billboards with the bloody assault on the Jewish community center and murder of a Filipino-American postal worker by white supremacist Buford Furrow.

> *"If we have to stop and think about the unique sensitivities of too may people . . . communication will cease altogether."*

Lest one write off Lanares' rhetoric as the hyperbole of a politician seeking to ingratiate himself with an important constituency, consider a recent op-ed in *USA Today*, written by Samuel G. Freedman, a journalism professor at Columbia University.

Freedman's op-ed, titled "Wave of hate crimes reflects a war against immigrants," categorically asserts that efforts to limit immigration are responsible for the hate crimes perpetrated by Furrow and Benjamin Smith in the Chicago area a few weeks earlier.

Citing California's Proposition 187 and 1996 congressional legislation as catalysts, Freedman states, "No legitimate figure should labor under the delusion that put a weapon in the hands of Buford Furrow, that America should once again bar its gates."

Limiting Speech Threatens Legitimate Debate

Even if we assume that Freedman is correct, that the twisted minds of Furrow and Smith interpreted calls for restrictions on immigration as a license to hunt immigrants (though, ironically, only one of their collective victims was actually an immigrant), should we halt political debate about this area of public policy?

Can we blame the political debate over Social Security reform with the growing phenomenon of elder abuse? Are those who call for cuts in AFDC [Aid to Families with Dependent Children] responsible for child abuse?

Most Americans are capable of discerning the difference between a billboard that asks whether it is good public policy to add 6,000 people to our population every day, and hate speech.

Those who can't will surely find some other pretext for spraying bullets, even if political speech is suppressed.

An even greater danger than a madman with an assault rifle is the cynicism of those who use the rubric of hate speech to silence the opinions of those with whom they disagree politically.

Both are insidious forms of intolerance.

The Government Should Not Define Obscenity for Its Citizens

by Jeffrey Rosen

About the author: *Jeffrey Rosen is a professor of law at the George Washington University Law School. He is also the author of* The Naked Crowd: Reclaiming Security and Freedom in an Anxious Age.

This June [2004], in *Ashcroft v. ACLU* [American Civil Liberties Union] *II,* the Supreme Court called into question the constitutionality of the Child Online Protection Act (COPA). This was the Court's third encounter with congressional attempts to regulate Internet pornography, and COPA represented Congress's latest effort to address judicial objections raised to an earlier version of the law. As written, COPA imposed up to six months in prison and a $50,000 fine on those who posted online, for commercial purposes, obscene material that is "harmful to minors." The law explicitly protected Internet publishers from liability if they attempted to prevent underage access by requiring the use of a credit card or "any other reasonable measures that are feasible under available technology." But in *Ashcroft v. ACLU II,* the five-to-four majority expressed skepticism about Congress's solution, arguing that alternative technologies might more effectively protect minors from Internet pornography without forcing adults to identify themselves. They sent the case back to the lower court with instructions to hold hearings about whether Internet filtering, blocking software, and other technologies might be less threatening to free speech.

Civil libertarians, liberals, and libertarian conservatives hailed the *Ashcroft* decision, but their celebrations were premature. In each of its three decisions about Internet pornography, the Supreme Court has focused on the peripheral question of whether there are effective technologies for restricting underage access to obscenity. But the justices have so far dodged the more fundamental question: Is there a coherent category of speech on the Internet that can be regulated as obscene? For it is increasingly obvious, as lower courts have recognized, that the exploding demand for Internet pornography and the impossibility of restricting it to any geographic area makes the Supreme Court's traditional tests for defining obscenity incoherent. Rather than encouraging Congress to search for more effective technologies for controlling obscene speech, the Court will eventually have to recognize that the effort to regulate obscenity has been doomed by culture, by technology, and by the Court's own increasingly expansive embrace of individual autonomy as the highest good.

Attempts to Regulate Internet Pornography Have Been Flawed

Congress's first attempt to regulate Internet pornography was the Communications Decency Act of 1996 (CDA), which prohibited the knowing transmission of obscene or indecent messages over the Internet to any recipient under 18 years old. The CDA exempted those who attempted in good faith to restrict underage access, such as websites that required the use of a verified credit card or adult access code. But in 1997, the Supreme Court struck down the CDA in *Reno v. ACLU*. The Court held that Congress, in its eagerness to protect children, had restricted speech that adults had a constitutional right to receive, because "existing technology" did not provide any effective way for purveyors of pornography to prevent minors from accessing indecent communications without also denying access to pornography-seeking adults. The Court also chastised Congress for failing to define the terms "indecent" and "patently offensive," thereby proscribing "large amounts of non-pornographic material with serious educational or other value," including discussions of artistic nudes or the risqué card catalogue of the Carnegie Library.

> *"The Court held that Congress . . . had restricted speech that adults had a constitutional right to receive."*

In response to *Reno*, Congress went back to the drawing board. In the Child Online Protection Act, it tried to refine the definition of material harmful to minors along the lines that the Court had suggested. To protect private users of e-mail or users of public resources like the Carnegie Library, it targeted only communications made for "commercial purposes." And instead of prohibiting "indecent and patently offensive communications," it identified a narrower category of "material that is harmful to minors":

- "any communication, picture, image, graphic image file, article, recording, writing, or other matter of any kind that is obscene or that—
- "(A) the average person, applying contemporary community standards, would find, taking the material as a whole and with respect to minors, is designed to appeal to, or is designed to pander to, the prurient interest;
- "(B) depicts, describes, or represents, in a manner patently offensive with

respect to minors, an actual or simulated sexual act or sexual contact, an actual or simulated normal or perverted sexual act, or a lewd exhibition of the genitals or post-pubescent female breast; and

• "(C) taken as a whole, lacks serious literary, artistic, political, or scientific value for minors."

Precedents Set Flawed Standards

This wording was adapted from the Supreme Court's notorious three-pronged test for obscenity, set forth in *Miller v. California* (1973). Even in 1973, the Miller test was hard to fathom. As Martha Nussbaum notes in her recent book *Hiding from Humanity: Disgust, Shame, and the Law*, Chief Justice Burger conflated two ideas—the obscene and the pornographic. In a footnote, he discussed the etymology of "obscene" from the Latin caenum, for filth, and cited the *Oxford English Dictionary*'s definition of "obscene" as "offensive to the senses, or to taste or refinement, disgusting, repulsive, filthy, foul, abominable, loathsome. "But he went on to note that the materials at issue in *Miller* are "more accurately defined as "pornography," whose etymology derives from the Greek term for "harlot," and which *Webster*'s dictionary defines as "a depiction of licentiousness or lewdness; a portrayal of erotic behavior designed to cause sexual excitement." Burger's odd conflation of the obscene and the pornographic resulted in a definition of obscenity that required the material to be both patently offensive and appealing to the prurient interest. This meant, as Kathleen Sullivan of Stanford Law School has observed, that the material had to "turn you on and gross you out" at the same time.

In 1973, at the dawn of the explosion of commercial pornography, there were at least the remnants of a practical consensus about what kind of material could be banned as obscene and what kind of material could be restricted as harmful to minors. Hard-core material could be banned as obscene and soft-core magazines could be limited to adults in order to avoid harm to minors. By the early 1980s, however, this practical consensus had already broken down. In light of the proliferation of hard-core movies and magazines, a federal court held ten years after *Miller* that "detailed portrayals of genitalia, sexual intercourse, fellatio, and masturbation" are not obscene "in light of community standards prevailing in New York City."

> *"Chief Justice Burger conflated two ideas—the obscene and the pornographic."*

Chief Justice Burger had also argued in *Miller* that community standards should be defined locally rather than nationally, in order to avoid imposing on "Las Vegas or New York City" the standards of the people of "Maine or Mississippi." But as the distribution of pornography became increasingly nationalized with the advent of the video cassette recorder, the attempt to define obscenity with reference to local community standards confounded lower courts. In a 1985 case called *Brockett v. Spokane Arcades, Inc.*, the Supreme Court tried to clarify the question of what qualifies as an "appeal to the prurient interest" by distinguishing "a good, old fashioned, healthy interest in sex," which should be protected, from "a shameful or morbid interest in nudity, sex, or excretion," which could be banned. (Wasn't an old fashioned interest in sex supposed to be shameful?) But the attempt to distinguish between "normal" and "shameful" hard-core material only

> *"With the arrival of the Internet, purveyors of pornography couldn't restrict the destination of their wares."*

confused matters further—once the distinction between hard- and soft-core sex was abandoned, no jury could predict what community standards required. The Court even suggested that in evaluating material targeted at "deviant" groups, jurors might need the help of expert testimony, since they couldn't rely on their own sexual responses.

Because of the complexity of applying community standards in an age when community standards were breaking down, the *Miller* test seemed moribund in practice by the early 1990s, despite a few failed attempts to ban the work of Robert Mapplethorpe and other salacious artists. With the arrival of the Internet, purveyors of pornography couldn't restrict the destination of their wares even if they wanted to. For this reason, lower courts evaluating the new COPA held that the community standards test was too vague to be applied to the World Wide Web, since it might allow the most censorious communities to set the standards for everyone else.

No National Standard for Obscenity Exists

But the lower court's finding didn't daunt the Supreme Court. In its second encounter with Internet pornography in *Ashcroft v. ACLU I* (2002), the high court argued that community standards for identifying obscene speech on the Internet should be national rather than local. Five justices—Clarence Thomas, William H. Rehnquist, Antonin Scalia, Sandra Day O'Connor, and Stephen Breyer—seemed unconcerned that juries in different parts of the country might interpret community standards differently. In separate statements, Justices Breyer and O'Connor emphasized that Congress, in passing COPA, intended to adopt a national standard for identifying material on the Internet that is harmful to minors. If the nation agreed about the nature of such material, Breyer emphasized, then there was nothing wrong with criminally prosecuting it or restricting it across the board.

But neither Breyer nor O'Connor provided any specific guidance for what sort of material they thought (or Congress believed) might violate national standards against obscenity. And they did not confront the awkward fact that the idea of a national consensus about obscenity is a fantasy. In 2001, for example, Frank Rich reported in *The New York Times Magazine* that the American pornography industry—much of it hard-core—generated at least $10 billion per year in revenues for more than 70,000 websites, pornography networks, pay-per-view and rental movies, cable and satellite television, and magazine publishers. Indeed, three years ago, when a local video retailer in Utah was prosecuted for peddling hard-core pornography, he successfully argued that his products were consistent with what his neighbors were watching on pay-per-view: In an age of nationally distributed hotel pornography, there was little difference between the consumption habits of hotel guests in Salt Lake City or Las Vegas. Pornography is everywhere, suggesting that there is no national consensus against it and no vast disparity from one locale to another.

On the Internet, pornography consumption statistics are even starker. According to the Internet Filter Review, an industry group advocating pornography filtering, Internet pornography now accounts for $2.5 billion of the $57 billion worldwide pornography market. The Review estimates that in 2003 there were 4.2 million pornography Web sites—12 percent of the global total—allowing access to 72 million worldwide visitors every year, with 40 million of them Americans. One fourth of the search engine requests every day (68 million) are for pornographic material. And according to the Employment Law Alliance, nearly a quarter of Americans polled this year [2004] said they or their colleagues use computers at work to engage in sexually explicit online activity, from visiting X-rated websites to joining explicit chat rooms. Most of these lascivious Internet users, of course, are men: according to Hitwise, men make up 65 percent of visitors to X-rated sites in the U.S., spending an average of five minutes during each session. Moreover, 15 percent of teens (ages 12 to 17) and 25 percent of older boys (ages 15 to 17) have lied about their age to access an Internet site, according to the Pew research center. And although there are global variations in the consumption of Internet pornography—steamy Spain leads the pack with 40 percent of users visiting an adult site, compared with only 25 percent of British users and 19 percent of Swedes—there is no country in which consumption of hard-core pornography could plausibly be said to be "patently offensive" to the average person by applying contemporary community standards.

> *"The state should not attempt to define the boundaries of sexual choices."*

Courts Should Not Allow Prosecution for Sexually Explicit Speech

The enforcement of obscenity laws has always depended on a social consensus about what is obscene. And now that this social consensus has collapsed, any attempt to resurrect the informal definition on which American obscenity law has long relied—namely, that hard-core material could be banned and soft-core material had to be protected, except for minors—is an exercise in futility.

Ever since hard-core pornography became a multi-billion dollar industry, the idea that it clearly violates national community standards is a hypocrisy that can no longer be sustained in light of clickstream data and consumption statistics. And any attempt to suppress fringe subsets of hard-core material seems to miss the point: How can a particular fetish be singled out as especially shameful in a world where anything goes? For this reason, Justice John Paul Stevens is right to argue, in his concurring opinion in Ashcroft II, that the Court should get out of the business of allowing criminal prosecution for sexually explicit speech. As the justice put it:

> COPA's criminal penalties are . . . strong medicine for the ill that the statute seeks to remedy. To be sure, our cases have recognized a compelling interest in protecting minors from exposure to sexually explicit materials. . . . As a parent, grandparent, and great-grandparent, I endorse that goal without reservation. As a judge, however, I must confess to a growing sense of unease when the interest in protecting children from prurient materials is invoked as a justification for using criminal regulation of speech as a substitute for, or a simple backup to, adult oversight of children's viewing habits.

But there is an additional reason that the Court will feel pressure to reexamine its obscenity jurisprudence. In *Lawrence v. Texas*, the case that invalidated American sodomy laws [in] June [of 2003], Justice Anthony Kennedy embraced a sweeping vision of sexual autonomy that seemed to spell the end of morals legislation. Quoting his own paean to liberty in *Casey v. Planned Parenthood*, the case that reaffirmed *Roe v. Wade* in 1992, he declared: "At the heart of liberty is the right to define one's own concept of existence, of meaning, of the universe, and of the mystery of human life." Liberty, Kennedy added, "gives substantial protection to adult persons in deciding how to conduct their private lives in matters pertaining to sex." He noted that the state should not attempt to define the boundaries of sexual choices "absent injury to a person or abuse of an institution the law protects." He quoted with approval Justice Steven's proposition from his dissenting opinion in *Bowers v. Hardwick:* "the fact that the governing majority in a State has traditionally viewed a particular practice as immoral is not a sufficient reason for upholding a law prohibiting the practice." In response, Justice Scalia was quick to declare that "this effectively decrees the end of all morals legislation." If "the promotion of majoritarian sexual morality is not even a legitimate state interest," Scalia lamented, then presumably "criminal laws against fornication, bigamy, adultery, adult incest, bestiality, and obscenity" would have to fall as well.

Absent Common Morality, Obscenity Legislation Is Useless

In fact, laws against bigamy, adultery, and adult incest might be defended in the interest of preventing harm to others. And the Court has made clear that the state isn't powerless to protect vulnerable minors as long as it doesn't impinge on the free speech rights of adults: child pornography can and should be prosecuted, and panderers who attempt to sell pornography directly to children can be regulated as well. But obscenity laws rest on no other foundation than (presumed) majoritarian disapproval of the sexual tastes and preferences of individuals in private. As a doctrinal matter, I don't find the Court's attempt to constitutionalize John Stuart Mill's harm principle (which holds that private behavior cannot be regulated absent harm to others) especially convincing. But now that a majority of the Court has embraced it in principle, the foundations of its obscenity jurisprudence are on extremely shaky ground. The community standards approach—whether defined at the national or local level—rested on Lord Devlin's traditional vision of the relationship between moral disapproval and the law. "A common morality is part of the bondage" that holds society together in "invisible bonds of common thought," Devlin wrote. He argued that it is "no more possible to define a sphere of private morality than it is to define one of private subversive activity," and that "there can be no theoretical limits to legislation against immorality."

But this is precisely the vision that the Supreme Court has now rejected. Now that moral disapprobation is not considered a constitutionally rational reason for restricting behavior, no definition of obscenity that relied on communal disapproval could easily pass constitutional scrutiny, unless one could demonstrate a clear harm to others. There may be some hard questions on the margins about whether harm to others should be defined broadly or narrowly—what about incest between consenting adults using birth control, for example—but on the central question of whether moral disapproval alone can justify criminal punishment, the battle may soon be over.

Helping parents protect their children from Internet pornography remains a serious national problem, and Congress is not powerless to address it. Just as it has denied funding to libraries that fail to adopt filtering software, so it could create financial incentives for Internet service providers to provide and refine filtering mechanisms as well. But the attempt to define and punish a category of speech as obscene is an atavistic vestige from a distant era. For better or worse, the Court should get out of the attempt to define obscenity, where it has largely embarrassed itself rather than shielding the rest of us from embarrassment.

The Government Should Not Censor Art

by the American Civil Liberties Union

About the author: *The American Civil Liberties Union (ACLU) is a nonprofit, nonpartisan organization dedicated to preserving and defending the Bill of Rights.*

In the late 1980s, state prosecutors brought a criminal obscenity charge against the owner of a record store for selling an album by the rap group, *2 Live Crew*. Although this was the first time that obscenity charges had ever been brought against song lyrics, the *2 Live Crew* case focused the nation's attention on an old question: should the government ever have the authority to dictate to its citizens what they may or may not listen to, read, or watch?

American society has always been deeply ambivalent about this question. On the one hand, our history is filled with examples of overt government censorship, from the 1873 Comstock Law to the 1996 Communications Decency Act. Anthony Comstock, head of the Society for the Suppression of Vice, boasted 194,000 "questionable pictures" and 134,000 pounds of books of "improper character" were destroyed under the Comstock Law—*in the first year alone*. The Communications Decency Act imposed an unconstitutional censorship scheme on the Internet, accurately described by a federal judge as "the most participatory form of mass speech yet developed."

On the other hand, the commitment to freedom of imagination and expression is deeply embedded in our national psyche, buttressed by the First Amendment, and supported by a long line of Supreme Court decisions.

Provocative and controversial art and in-your-face entertainment put our commitment to free speech to the test. Why should we oppose censorship when scenes of murder and mayhem dominate the TV screen, when works of art can be seen as a direct insult to people's religious beliefs, and when much sexually explicit material can be seen as degrading to women? Why not let the major-

American Civil Liberties Union, "Freedom of Expression in the Arts and Entertainment," www.aclu.org, February 27, 2002.

ity's morality and taste dictate what others can look at or listen to?

The answer is simple, and timeless: a free society is based on the principle that each and every individual has the right to decide what art or entertainment he or she wants—or does not want—to receive or create. Once you allow the government to censor someone else, you cede to it the power to censor you, or something you like. Censorship is like poison gas: a powerful weapon that can harm you when the wind shifts.

Freedom of expression for ourselves requires freedom of expression for others. It is at the very heart of our democracy.

Sexual Speech

Sex in art and entertainment is the most frequent target of censorship crusades. Many examples come to mind. A painting of the classical statue of Venus de Milo was removed from a store because the managers of the shopping mall found its semi-nudity "too shocking." Hundreds of works of literature, from Maya Angelou's *I Know Why the Caged Bird Sings* to John Steinbeck's *Grapes of Wrath*, have been banned from public schools based on their sexual content.

A museum director was charged with a crime for including sexually explicit photographs by Robert Mapplethorpe in an art exhibit.

American law is, on the whole, the most speech-protective in the world—but sexual expression is treated as a second-class citizen. No causal link between exposure to sexually explicit material and anti-social or violent behavior has ever been scientifically established. In spite of many efforts to do so. Rather, the Supreme Court has allowed censorship of sexual speech on moral grounds—a remnant of our nation's Puritan heritage.

This does not mean that all sexual expression can be censored, however. Only a narrow range of "obscene" material can be suppressed; a term like "pornography" has no legal meaning. Nevertheless, even the relatively narrow obscenity exception serves as a vehicle for abuse by government authorities as well as pressure groups who want to impose their personal moral views on other people.

Is Media Violence a Threat to Society?

Today's calls for censorship are not motivated solely by morality and taste, but also by the widespread belief that exposure to images of violence causes people to act in destructive ways. Pro-censorship forces, including many politicians, often cite a multitude of "scientific studies" that allegedly prove fictional violence leads to real-life violence.

There is, in fact, virtually no evidence that fictional violence causes otherwise stable people to become violent. And if we suppressed material based on the actions of unstable people, no work of fiction or art would be safe from censorship. Serial killer Theodore Bundy collected cheerleading magazines. And the work most often cited by psychopaths as justification for their acts of violence is the Bible.

But what about the rest of us? Does exposure to media violence actually lead to criminal or anti-social conduct by otherwise stable people, including children, who spend an average of 28 hours watching television each week? These are important questions. If there really were a clear cause-and-effect relationship between what normal children see on TV and harmful actions, then limits on such expression might arguably be warranted.

What the Studies Show

Studies on the relationship between media violence and real violence are the subject of considerable debate. Children have been shown TV programs with violent episodes in a laboratory setting and then tested for "aggressive" behavior. *Some* of these studies suggest that watching TV violence may temporarily induce "object aggression" in some children (such as popping balloons or hitting dolls or playing sports more aggressively) but not actual criminal violence against another person.

Correlational studies that seek to explain why some aggressive people have a history of watching a lot of violent TV suffer from the chicken-and-egg dilemma: does violent TV cause such people to behave aggressively, or do aggressive people simply prefer more violent entertainment? There is no definitive answer. But all scientists agree that statistical correlations between two phenomena do not mean that one causes the other.

> *"Only a narrow range of 'obscene' material can be suppressed; a term like 'pornography' has no legal meaning."*

International comparisons are no more helpful. Japanese TV and movies are famous for their extreme, graphic violence, but Japan has a very low crime rate—much lower than many societies in which television watching is relatively rare. What the studies reveal on the issue of fictional violence and real world aggression is—not much.

The only clear assertion that can be made is that the relationship between art and human behavior is a very complex one. Violent and sexually explicit art and entertainment have been a staple of human cultures from time immemorial. Many human behavioralists believe that these themes have a useful and constructive societal role, serving as a vicarious outlet for individual aggression.

What Does Artistic Freedom Include?

The Supreme Court has interpreted the First Amendment's protection of artistic expression very broadly. It extends not only to books, theatrical works and paintings, but also to posters, television, music videos and comic books—whatever the human creative impulse produces.

Two fundamental principles come into play whenever a court must decide a case involving freedom of expression. The first is "content neutrality"—the government cannot limit expression just because any listener, or even the majority of a community, is offended by its content. In the context of art and entertainment, this means tolerating some works that we might find offensive, insulting, outrageous—or just plain bad.

The second principle is that expression may be restricted only if it will clearly cause *direct and imminent* harm to an important societal interest. The classic example is falsely shouting fire in a crowded theater and causing a stampede. Even then, the speech may be silenced or punished only if there is no other way to avert the harm.

Where Do the Experts Agree?

Whatever influence fictional violence has on behavior, most experts believe its effects are marginal compared to other factors. Even small children know the difference between fiction and reality, and their attitudes and behavior are shaped more by their life circumstances than by the books they read or the TV they watch. In 1972, the U.S. Surgeon General's Advisory Committee on Television and Social Behavior released a 200-page report, "Television and Growing Up: The Impact of Televised Violence," which

> *"The only clear assertion that can be made is that the relationship between art and human behavior is a very complex one."*

concluded, "The effect [of television] is small compared with many other possible causes, such as parental attitudes or knowledge of and experience with the real violence of our society." Twenty-one years later, the American Psychological Association published its 1993 report, "Violence & Youth," and concluded, "The greatest predictor of future violent behavior is a previous history of violence." In 1995, the Center for Communication Policy at UCLA, which monitors TV violence, came to a similar conclusion in its yearly report: "It is known that television does not have a simple, direct stimulus-response effect on its audiences."

Blaming the media does not get us very far, and, to the extent that it diverts the public's attention from the real causes of violence in society, it may do more harm than good.

Which Media Violence Would You Ban?

A pro-censorship member of Congress once attacked the following shows for being too violent: *The Miracle Worker, Civil War Journal, Star Trek 9, The Untouchables*, and *Teenage Mutant Ninja Turtles*. What would be left if all these kinds of programs were purged from the airwaves? Is there good violence and bad violence? If so, who decides? Sports and the news are at least as violent as fiction, from the fights that erupt during every televised hockey game, to the videotaped beating of Rodney King by the LA Police Department, shown over and over again on prime time TV. If we accept censorship of violence in the media, we will have to censor sports and news programs.

Individual Rights, Individual Decisions

The First Amendment is based upon the belief that in a free and democratic society, individual adults must be free to decide for themselves what to read, write, paint, draw, see and hear. If we are disturbed by images of violence or sex, we can change the channel, turn off the TV, and decline to go to certain movies or museum exhibits.

We can also exercise our *own* free speech rights by voicing our objections to forms of expression that we don't like. Justice Louis Brandeis' advice that the remedy for messages we disagree with or dislike in art, entertainment or politics is "more speech, not enforced silence," is as true today as it was when given in 1927.

Further, we can exercise our prerogative as parents without resorting to censorship. Devices now exist that make it possible to block access to specific TV programs and internet sites. Periodicals that review books, recordings, and films can help parents determine what they feel is appropriate for their youngsters. Viewing decisions can, and should, be made at home, without government interference.

Pornographic! Indecent! Obscene!

Justice John Marshall Harlan's line, "one man's vulgarity is another's lyric," sums up the impossibility of developing a definition of obscenity that isn't hopelessly vague and subjective. And Justice Potter Stewart's famous assurance, "I know it when I see it," is of small comfort to artists, writers, movie directors and lyricists who must navigate the murky waters of obscenity law trying to figure out what police, prosecutors, judges and juries will think.

> *"The Supreme Court has held that indecent expression is entitled to some constitutional protection, but that indecency in some media may be regulated."*

The Supreme Court's current definition of constitutionally unprotected Obscenity, first announced in a 1973 case called *Miller v. California*, has three requirements. The work must 1) appeal to the average person's prurient (shameful, morbid) interest in sex; 2) depict sexual conduct in a "patently offensive way" as defined by community standards; and 3) taken as a whole, lack serious literary, artistic, political, or scientific value.

The Supreme Court has held that indecent expression—in contrast with "obscenity"—is entitled to some constitutional protection, but that indecency in some media (broadcasting, cable, and telephone) may be regulated. In its 1978 decision in *Federal Communications Commission v. Pacifica*, the Court ruled that the government could require radio and television stations to air "indecent" material only during those hours when children would be unlikely listeners or viewers. Broadcast indecency was defined as: "language that describes, in terms patently offensive as measured by contemporary community standards for the broadcast medium, sexual or excretory activities or organs." This vague concept continues to baffle both the public and the courts.

"Pornography" is not a legal term at all. Its dictionary definition is "writing or pictures intended to arouse sexual desire." Pornography comes in as many varieties as the human sexual impulse and is protected by the First Amendment unless it meets the definition for illegal obscenity.

What Is Censorship?

Censorship, the suppression of words, images, or ideas that are "offensive," happens whenever some people succeed in imposing their personal political or moral values on others. Censorship can be carried out by the government as well as private pressure groups. Censorship by the government is unconstitutional.

In contrast, when private individuals or groups organize boycotts against stores that sell magazines of which they disapprove, their actions are protected by the First Amendment, although they can become dangerous in the extreme. Private pressure groups, not the government, promulgated and enforced the infamous Hollywood blacklists during the McCarthy period [the early 1950s]. But these private censorship campaigns are best encountered by groups and individuals speaking out and organizing in defense of the threatened expression.

Chapter 2

Is Free Speech Threatened?

Current
CONTROVERSIES

Chapter Preface

Military service was a hotly debated issue in the 2004 presidential election. It was not, however, service in the war on terror, the war in Afghanistan, or even the war in Iraq that was the focus of controversy, but of military service during the Vietnam War. Two political advocacy groups launched attacks on the presidential candidates and their Vietnam War service records. A liberal group known as MoveOn took aim at President George W. Bush, issuing ads questioning whether or not he had served his full term in the Texas Air National Guard in the 1970s. To counter, a group known as Swift Boat Veterans for Truth (SBVFT) launched ads claiming that the Democratic nominee, Senator John Kerry, had exaggerated the extent of his accomplishments as a soldier in Vietnam. In the midst of this firestorm of debate over Vietnam War service, some political commentators questioned whether MoveOn and SBVFT had the legal right to create and distribute these ads in the first place. At question was whether or not their activities could be considered protected speech. In debates about whether free speech should ever be restricted, issues surrounding elections—most notably campaign finance rules—often rise to the fore.

Ever since 1976, the Supreme Court has recognized that spending money on political campaigns is a form of expression protected by the First Amendment. Many experts contend that this decision carries with it the inherent assumption that, if spending money is equivalent to exercising free speech, the poor will always have less say in the political marketplace than the rich. Campaign finance legislation since 1976 has attempted to limit campaign contributions from wealthy donors to avoid undue influence on political candidates. The 2004 presidential election was the first major election following the implementation of the Bipartisan Campaign Reform Act (BCRA) of 2002, which banned soft money (unregulated money donated to political parties) contributions to federal candidates and national political parties. This ban on soft money inadvertently prompted the rise of "527" groups, so named for the section of the federal tax code that describes them. MoveOn and the SBVFT are 527s. These groups may raise as much money as they like for political advocacy, but they may not endorse specific candidates and may not be affiliated with political parties.

As the advertising efforts of both MoveOn and the SBVFT intensified late in the summer of 2004, a debate erupted over whether or not campaign finance reform had really worked to control the influence of unregulated money during campaigns. Even President Bush seemed torn on the issue. As the MoveOn campaign mounted against him gained strength in August of 2004, he said, "I think [527s] ought to be outlawed . . . we have billionaires writing checks, large checks, to influence the outcome of this election." When he signed the BCRA in 2002, however, he had said, "I believe individual freedom to participate in elections should be expanded, not diminished; and when individual freedoms are restricted, questions arise under the First Amendment."

The debate over campaign finance reform is just one of the issues discussed in the following chapter. Other topics addressed include Internet filters and media consolidation. In each case, limitations placed on speech are considered reasonable and necessary by some and as excessive and detrimental by others.

Media Consolidation Threatens Free Speech

by Robert W. McChesney

About the author: *Robert W. McChesney is a professor at the University of Illinois and the cofounder of Free Press, a nonpartisan organization devoted to increasing public participation in media policy debates. He is the author of eleven books, including* Rich Media, Poor Democracy.

Our press system is failing in the United States, and we must be clear about why it is failing. The problem is not with poorly trained or unethical journalists; in fact, I suspect this may well be as talented and ethical as any generation of journalists in memory. Nor is the problem nefarious or corrupt owners.

Even if Rupert Murdoch and Sumner Redstone were to quit their jobs, change their names, and move off to New Mexico to do yoga and share a bong all day in a mountain cabin, the operations of the News Corporation and Viacom, respectively, would not change appreciably. Whoever replaced them would follow the same cues, with more or less success. But the logic of the system would remain intact.

That system is set up to maximize profit for a relative handful of large companies. The system works well for them, but it is a disaster for the communication needs of a healthy and self-governing society. So if we want to change the content and logic of the media, we have to change the system. And following my logic, we must change media content radically if we are going to have a viable self-governing society and transform this country for the better. As former Federal Communications Commission [FCC] member Nicholas Johnson likes to put it: When speaking to activists and progressives, whatever your first issue of concern, media had better be your second, because without change in the media, progress in your primary area is far less likely.

Let's begin with the obvious question: Where does our media system come from? In mythology, it is the result of competition between entrepreneurs duk-

Robert W. McChesney, "Waging the Media Battle," *The American Prospect*, vol. 15, July 2004.

ing it out in the free market. In reality, our media system is the result of a wide range of explicit government policies, regulations, and subsidies. Each of the 20 or so giant media firms that dominate the entirety of our media system is the recipient of massive government largesse—what could be regarded as corporate welfare. They receive (for free) one or more of: scarce monopoly licenses to radio and television channels, monopoly franchises to cable- and satellite-TV systems, or copyright protection for their content. When the government sets up a firm with one of these monopoly licenses, it is virtually impossible to fail. As media mogul Barry Diller put it, the only way a commercial broadcaster can lose money is if someone steals from it.

> "We need to have widespread, informed public participation in media policy-making."

If policies establish the nature of the media system, and the nature of the media system determines the nature and logic of media content, the nucleus of the media atom is the policy-making process. And it is here that we get to the source of the media crisis in the United States. Media and communication policies have been made in the most corrupt manner imaginable for generations. Perhaps the best way to capture the media policy-making process in the United States is to consider a scene from the 1974 Oscar-winning film *The Godfather II*. Roughly halfway through the movie, a bunch of American gangsters, including Michael Corleone, assemble on a Havana patio to celebrate Hyman Roth's birthday. This is 1958, pre–Fidel Castro, when Fulgencio Batista and the Mob ruled Cuba. Roth is giving a slice of his birthday cake, which has the outline of Cuba on it, to each of the gangsters. As he does so, Roth outlines how the gangsters are divvying up the island among themselves, then triumphantly states how great it is to be in a country with a government that works with private enterprise.

That is pretty much how media policies are generated in the United States. But do not think it is a conspiracy through which the corporate interests peacefully carve up the cake. In fact, as in the *Godfather II*, where the plot revolves around the Corleone-Roth battle, the big media trade associations and corporations are all slugging it out with one another for the largest slice of the cake. That is why they have such enormous lobbying arsenals and why they flood politicians with campaign donations. But, like those gangsters in Havana, there is one crucial point on which they all agree: It is their cake. Nobody else gets a slice.

Solving the Media Crisis

The solution to the media crisis now becomes evident. We need to have widespread, informed public participation in media policymaking. This will lead to better policies and a better system. There are no magic cure all systems, and even the best policies have their weaknesses. But informed public participation is the key to seeing that the best policies emerge, the policies most likely to serve broadly determined values and objectives.

Imagine, for example, that there had been a modicum of public involvement when Congress lifted the national cap on how many radio stations a single company could own in 1996. That provision was written, as far as anyone can tell, by radio-industry lobbyists. It sailed through Congress without a shred of discussion and without a trace of press coverage. It is safe to say that 99.9 percent of Americans had no clue. As a result, radio broadcasting has become the province of a small number of firms that can own as many as eight stations each in a single market. The notorious Clear Channel owns more than 1,200 stations nationally.

As a result of this single change in policy, competition has declined, local radio news and programming have been decimated (too expensive and much less competitive pressure to produce local content), musical playlists have less nutrition and variety than the menu at McDonald's, and the amount of advertising has skyrocketed. This is all due to a change in policy—not to the inexorable workings of the free market. "There is too much concentration in radio," John McCain said on the Senate floor in 2003. "I know of no credible person who disagrees with that." Radio has been destroyed. A medium that is arguably the least expensive and most accessible of our major media, that is ideally suited for localism, has been converted into a Wal-Mart-like profit machine for a handful of massive chains. This can only happen when policies are made under the cover of night. Welcome to Havana, Mr. Corleone.

> *"The corporate media political lobby is extraordinarily powerful and is used to having its way on both sides of the aisle in Congress."*

Radio is instructive also because it highlights the propagandistic use of the term "deregulation." This term is often used to describe the relaxation of media ownership rules, even by opponents of rules relaxation. The term deregulation implies something good: that people will be less regulated and enjoy more liberty. Who could oppose that? Radio broadcasting is the classic case of a deregulated industry. But just how deregulated is it? Try testing this definition of deregulation by broadcasting on one of the 1,200 channels for which Clear Channel has a government-enforced monopoly license. If you persist, you will do many years in a federal penitentiary. That is very serious regulation. In fact, all deregulation means in radio is that firms can possess many more government-granted and government-enforced monopoly licenses than before.

As the radio example indicates, we have a very long way to go to bring widespread and informed public participation to media-policy debates. The immediate barrier is the standard problem facing democratic forces in the United States: The corporate media political lobby is extraordinarily powerful and is used to having its way on both sides of the aisle in Congress. Moreover, corporate media power is protected from public review by a series of very powerful myths. Four of these myths in particular need to be debunked if there is going to be any hope of successfully infusing the public into media policy debates.

The first myth is that the existing profit-driven U.S. media system is the American way, and that there is nothing we can do about it. The Founders, this myth holds, crafted the First Amendment to prevent any government interference with the free market. In fact, this could hardly be more inaccurate. Freedom of the press was seen more as a social right belonging to the entire population than as a commercial right belonging to wealthy investors. The establishment of the U.S. Post Office provides a dramatic case in point. In the first generations of the republic, newspapers accounted for between 70 percent and 95 percent of post-office traffic, and newspapers depended upon the post office for the distribution of much of their circulation. A key question facing Congress was what to charge newspapers to be mailed. No one at the time was arguing that newspapers should pay full freight, that the market should rule; the range of debate was between those who argued for a large public subsidy and those who argued that all postage for newspapers should be free, to encourage the production and distribution of a wide range of ideas. The former position won, and it contributed to a massive flowering of print media in the United States throughout the early 19th century. What is most striking about this period, as, [Princeton professor of sociology] Paul Starr argues in his new book, *The Creation of the Media*, is that there wasn't rhetoric about free markets in the media, nor about the sacrosanct rights of commercial interests. That came later.

Profits Influence the News

The second myth is that professional practices in journalism will protect the public from the ravages of concentrated private commercial control over the news media—and that therefore we need not worry about the media system or the policies that put it into place. The notion of professional journalism dates to the early 20th century, by which time the explicit partisanship of American newspapers had come to resemble something akin to the one-party press rule of an authoritarian society. The solution to this problem was to be professional autonomy for journalism. Trained professional journalists who were politically neutral would cover the news, and the political views of the owners and advertisers would be irrelevant (except on the editorial page). There were no schools of journalism in 1900; by 1920 many of the major schools had been established, often at the behest of major publishers.

Professional journalism was far from perfect, but it looked awfully good compared with what it replaced. And at its high-water mark, the 1960s and '70s, it was a barrier of sorts to

> *"Media content comes marinated in commercialism."*

commercial media ownership. But the autonomy of journalists was never written into law, and the problem today is that as media companies have grown larger and larger, the pressure to generate profit from the news has increased. That has meant slashing editorial budgets, sloughing off on expensive investigative and international coverage, and allowing for commercial values to play a larger role in determining inexpensive and trivial news topics. In short, the autonomy and integrity of U.S. journalism has been under sustained attack. This is why journalists rank among the leading proponents of media reform. They know first-hand how the media system is overwhelming their best intentions, their professional autonomy. And unless the system changes, there is not hope for a viable journalism.

The Complexities of Supply and Demand

The third myth is probably the most prevalent, and it applies primarily to the entertainment media, though with the commercialization of journalism, it is being applied increasingly there, too. This is the notion that as bad as the media system may seem to be, it gives the people what they want. If we are dissatisfied with media content, don't blame the media firms; blame the morons who demand it. This is such a powerful myth because it contains an element of truth. After all, what movie studio or TV network intentionally produces programming that people do not want to watch? The problem with it, as I detail in *The Problem of the Media*, is that it reduces a complex relationship of audience and producers to a simplistic one-way flow. In oligopolistic media markets, there is producer sovereignty, not consumer sovereignty, so media firms give you what you want, but only within the range that generates maximum profits for them. Supply creates demand as much as demand creates supply.

> *"If we wish to change the nature of media content, we have to change the system."*

And some things are strictly off-limits to consumer pressure. Media content comes marinated in commercialism although survey after survey shows that a significant percentage of Americans do not want so much advertising (65 percent, according to an April 2004 survey by Yankelovich Partners, believe they are "constantly bombarded with too much" advertising). But don't expect a mad dash by media corporations to respond to that public desire. It is difficult if not impossible, to use the market to register opposition to hypercommercialism—that is, to the market itself. Further, the media system clearly generates many things that we do not want. Economists call these externalities—the consequences of market transactions that do not directly affect the buyer's or seller's decision to buy or sell but have a significant effect, and can level massive costs, upon society.

Media generate huge negative externalities. What we are doing to children with hypercommercialization is a huge externality that will almost certainly bring massive social costs. Likewise, dreadful journalism will lead to corrupt and incompetent governance, which will exact a high cost on all of our lives, not just those who are in the market for journalism. The long and short of it is

72

that the market cannot effectively address externalities; it will require enlightened public policy.

Policies, Not Workers Drive Internet Growth

The fourth myth is that the Internet will set us free. Who cares if Rupert Murdoch owns film studios and satellite-TV systems and TV stations and newspapers? Anyone can launch a blog or a Web site and finally compete with the big guys. It is just a matter of time until the corporate media dinosaurs disappear beneath the tidal wave of new media competition.

The Internet and the digital-communications revolution are, in fact, radically transforming the media landscape, but how they do so will be determined by policies, not by magic. The Internet itself is the result of years of heavy public subsidy, and its rapid spread owed to the open-access "common carrier" policy forced upon telecommunications companies. How the Internet develops in the future will have everything to do with policies, from the copyright and the allocation of spectrum to open wireless systems to policies to assist the production of media content on the Internet. The one point that is already clear is that merely having the ability to launch a Web site does not magically transform media content. That will require public policy.

Changing Media's Content Means Changing the System

So, again, the moral of the story is clear: If we wish to change the nature of media content, we have to change the system. If we wish to change the media system, we need to change media policies. And if we wish to change media policies, we have to blast open the media policy-making process and remove it from the proverbial Havana patio.

My sense is that the more widespread public participation there is in media policy making, the more likely we are to have policies to encourage a more competitive and locally oriented commercial media system, as well as a much more prominent and heterogeneous nonprofit and noncommercial media sector. But if there is a legitimate public debate, I will certainly live with the results, what ever they might be.

From the emergence of the corporate media system more than a century ago to the present, the dominant commercial interests have done everything within their considerable power to keep people oblivious to the policies made in their name but without their informed consent. There have been a handful of key moments when media policy making became part of the public dialogue. For example, in the Progressive Era, the corruption, sensationalism, and pro-business partisanship of much of commercial journalism produced a crisis that led to widespread criticism of capitalist control of the press, and even to movements to establish municipal or worker ownership of newspapers. In the 1930s, a fairly significant movement arose that opposed the government secretly turning over all the choice monopoly radio channels to owners affiliated with the two huge national chains—NBC and CBS—and calling for the establishment of a dominant noncommercial broadcasting system. I will not keep you in suspense: These movements failed.

But following World War II, media policy-making has increasingly gravitated to the Havana patio. As a result, our media system is increasingly the province of a very small number of large firms, with nary a trace of public-service marrow in their commercial bones. Regulation of commercial broadcasting degenerated to farcical proportions, as there was no leverage to force commercial broadcasters to do anything that would interfere with their ability to exploit the government granted and enforced monopoly licenses for maximum commercial gain.

The prospects for challenging the corrupt policy-making process seemed especially bleak by the 1990s with the ascension of neoliberalism. Even many Democrats abandoned much of their long-standing rhetoric about media regulation in the public interest and accepted the "market uber alles" logic.

Public Interest on Media Issues Is Key to Reform

So when the FCC announced it would review several of its major media-ownership rules in 2002, nearly everyone thought it was a slam dunk that the commission would relax or eliminate the rules. After all, a majority of the FCC's members were on record as favoring the media firms getting bigger— even before they did any study of the matter. The media giants hated these rules and were calling in all their markers with the politicians so they could get bigger, reduce competition and risk, and get more profitable—and it didn't look as if anything could prevent them from winning.

But over the course of 2003, the FCC's review of media-ownership rules caused a spectacular and wholly unanticipated backlash from the general public. Literally millions of Americans contacted members of Congress or the FCC to oppose media concentration. By the end of 2003, members of Congress were saying that media ownership was the second-most discussed issue by their constituents, trailing only the invasion and occupation of Iraq. It is safe to say that media issues never had cracked the congressional "top 20" list in decades. What was also striking was how much of the opposition came from the political right, as well as a nearly unified left. In September 2003, the Senate overturned the FCC's media rules changes by a 55-to-40 vote. . . .

"Surveys showed that the more people understood media as a policy issue, the more they supported reform."

But what drove millions of Americans to get active on media ownership in 2003 was not a belief that the status quo is quite good, or that the problem with rules changes is that they will remove the media from its exalted status. To the contrary, the movement was driven by explicit dissatisfaction with the status quo and a desire to make the system better. Years of frustration burst like an enormous boil when Americans came to the realization that the media system was not "natural" or inviolable but the result of explicit policies. Surveys showed that the more people understood media as a policy issue, the more they supported reform. Once that truth is grasped, all bets are off.

Coming off the media-ownership struggle, there is extraordinary momentum. Scores of groups have emerged over the past few years—local, national, and even global in scope—organized around a wide range of issues. In the coming few years, expect to see major progressive legislation launched to restore more competitive markets in radio and television; to have antitrust law applied effectively to media; to have copyright returned to some semblance of concern for protecting the public domain; to have viable subsidies put in place that will spawn a wide range of nonprofit and noncommercial media; to have a wireless high-speed Internet system that will be superior and vastly less expensive than what Mr. Roth and Mr. Corleone (the cable and telephone companies) have in mind; to have real limitations on advertising and commercialism, especially that aimed at children; to have protection for mediaworkers, so they can do their work without onerous demands upon their labor by rapacious owners. The list goes on and on.

All of these measures would have been unthinkable just a year or two ago. Now they are in play. One of the exciting developments [from 2003 to 2004] has been the recognition that media activism is flexible politically. Unlike campaign-finance reform, where anything short of fully publicly financed elections leaves open a crack that big money exploits to destroy the reforms, media activism allows for tangible piecemeal reforms. We may well get several hundred additional noncommercial FM stations on the dial this year, largely as a result of sustained activism. Those stations will be a tangible demonstration to people of what they can achieve, and they will spur continued activism. And media reform allows for a broad array of alliances, depending upon the issue, as the 2003 media-ownership fight demonstrated. Indeed, media activism might just be the glue to sustain a progressive democratic vision for the nation's politics.

But it will not be an easy fight, not at all. This is a longterm struggle, a never-ending one. What we know is that it is impossible to have a viable democracy with the current media system, and that we are capable of changing this system. The future depends upon our being successful.

Library Internet Filters Block Access to Vital Information

by the Kaiser Family Foundation

About the author: *The Kaiser Family Foundation is an independent, national health philanthropy dedicated to providing information and analysis on health issues to policy makers, the media, and the general public.*

Concern has been raised as to whether Internet filters block young people's access to non-pornographic health information. Despite prolonged and impassioned debate about the potential impact of blocking software, there is surprisingly little empirical evidence regarding blocking errors, particularly as they might affect access to health information. Most reports have been anecdotal rather that systematic in nature and have not focused on health searches in particular.

The study reported here is a large-scale, scientific study designed to help determine whether Internet filters are likely to block young people's access to non-pornographic health information. The study simulates young people's online health information searches and measures the impact of seven different filtering products on those searches, looking at both the effectiveness of the filters at blocking pornography and the rate at which they also block non-pornographic health information.

The basic design of the study is to:

- Run searches on a variety of youth-oriented health topics on six of the search engines that are most popular among young people.
- Test the thousands of health URLs resulting from these searches against six different filtering products commonly used in schools and libraries, and one product widely used in the home; and
- Run searches on a variety of porn search terms, and test the hundreds of URLs resulting from those searches against the same filtering products.

Victoria Rideout, Caroline Richardson, and Paul Resnick, "See No Evil: How the Internet Filters Affect the Search for Online Health Information," *Executive Summary #3294*, December 2002. Copyright © 2002 by The Henry J. Kaiser Family Foundation. Reproduced by permission.

Importantly, most filtering software allows system administrators to specify blocking configurations, giving individual schools and libraries the ability to tailor the blocking to local community standards. The effect of different configurations is examined closely in this report.

While there is no good data on how the different school districts or libraries have decided to configure their filters, an informal survey conducted for this study indicated a wide range in approaches.

Accordingly, the study tests a "least restrictive," "intermediate," and "most restrictive" configuration for each filtering product.

Concerns Over Blocking Pornography vs. Access to Information

Over the past few years, there has been an explosion in Internet use among young people in this country. According to the U.S. Census Bureau, three out of four teenagers (14–17 years old) used the Internet in 2001, up from half of teens in 1998. Overall, the Census Bureau reports that nearly 60% of all school-aged children (5–17) used the Internet in 2001.

As access to the Internet expands, more and more young people are turning to the Web as a source of health information. Teenagers in particular face a host of sensitive health issues—from substance abuse to birth control to eating disorders—and the confidentiality and convenience of the Web make it a popular destination for those seeking information and guidance on those topics. Indeed, earlier studies indicate that more than 70% of 15- to 17-year-olds say they have used the Internet to look up health information. Some of the most common topics searched include sexual health issues such as pregnancy, birth control, HIV/AIDS, or other sexually transmitted diseases (40% have researched one of these subjects); problems with drugs or alcohol (25%); and depression or mental illness (17%).

At the same time, concerns about young people's exposure to online pornography and other adult content led to the passage of the Children's Internet Protection Act (CIPA) in December 2000. CIPA requires schools and libraries receiving federal funds to block access to inappropriate Internet content through the use of "technology protection measures"—i.e., Internet blocking software. The CIPA requirement for *libraries* was struck down in Spring 2002 by a circuit court on the

> *"The law requires blocking of sites that are obscene, contain child pornography, or are 'harmful to minors.'"*

grounds that it violates the First Amendment, although that decision [was] appealed to the U.S. Supreme Court [and upheld]. Meanwhile, the CIPA requirements for *schools* have *not* been challenged in the courts, and 73% of schools already employ filters of some kind. The law requires blocking of sites that are obscene, contain child pornography, or are "harmful to minors"—a standard it leaves up to the local community to set.

In addition to filters at school, many parents use some sort of filtering product at home as well. In earlier studies, a third of teens with home Internet access have reported that there is a filter in place at their home. While the primary purpose of this study is to review the filters most commonly used in schools or libraries, the most common home product, AOL Parental Controls, was also tested. . . .

Key Findings of the Study

At the least restrictive or intermediate configurations, the filters tested do not block a substantial proportion of general health information sites; however, at the most restrictive configuration, one in four health sites are blocked. When set at the *least restrictive* level of blocking ("pornography only"), filters block an average of 1.4% of all health sites; this figure is the average across all six of the institutional filters tested, and across all of the various health topics studied. When set at the *intermediate* level of blocking, filters block an average of 5% of all health sites. When set at the *most restrictive* configuration, 24% of all non-pornographic health sites are blocked.

> *"Some health topics are much more likely to be blocked, even at the least restrictive or intermediate blocking levels."*

Some health topics are much more likely to be blocked, even at the least restrictive or intermediate blocking levels. Even when set at their *least restrictive* blocking configurations, filters block an average of about one in ten non-pornographic health sites resulting from searches on the terms "condoms," "safe sex," and "gay." At the *intermediate* level of blocking, a substantial proportion of health sites resulting from searches on some sensitive topics are blocked:

- Condoms <27% of health sites were blocked>
- Ecstasy <25% of health sites were blocked>
- Gay <24% of health sites were blocked>
- Safe sex <20% of health sites were blocked>

The proportion of *pornographic* sites blocked *does not* increase substantially based on how the filters are configured. At the *least restrictive* setting, the filtering products block an average of 87% of all pornographic sites; at the *intermediate* level, an average of 90% of porn sites are blocked, and at the *most restrictive* configuration, 91% of porn sites are blocked.

The proportion of *non-pornographic* health sites blocked *does* increase substantially based on how the filters are configured, especially on topics related to sexual health. As noted, across all health topics studied, the proportion of non-pornographic sites blocked averaged 1.4% at the *least restrictive* blocking level, 5% at the *intermediate* blocking level, and 24% at the *most restrictive* blocking level. Similar results emerge for the "recommended" health sites listed on the teen health sections of the online directories at Yahoo! and Google. At the *least restrictive* setting, an average of 0.5% of these sites (on a variety of health topics) were blocked, at the *intermediate* setting an average of 2.8% were blocked, and at the *most restrictive* setting an average of 24% were blocked. The increase in blocked health content is especially pronounced on searches related to *sexual health.* For example, for a search on "safe sex," on average about one in ten health sites (9%) is blocked at the *least restrictive* level of blocking, one in five (21%) at the *intermediate* level, and one in two (50%) at the *most restrictive* level.

Incidental exposure to pornography during health information searches does not appear to be a substantial problem; filters can further reduce but not eliminate such incidental exposure. Across the 24 health-related searches conducted on six different search engines, 1% of the results contained pornographic content. At the minimal blocking configurations, the products blocked an average of 62% of these "inadvertently" retrieved porn sites. Thus, the products were noticeably worse at identifying pornography resulting from health searches than from deliberate searches for pornography (87% blocking rate).

The different filtering products vary somewhat in the proportion of health sites they blocked, especially at the more restrictive settings. At the *least restrictive* setting, the percentage of health sites blocked by the different filters ranged from 0.6% to 2.3%; at the *intermediate* level the range between products was 2.8% to 7.6%; and at the *most restrictive* level the range was 15.1% to 35.4%.

Many Web sites of health organizations that provide online content for youth are being blocked by one or more filtering products. In the previous findings, we have been examining the filters' performance by looking at the average rate of over- or under-blocking for any one of the six products studied. For example, when set at the intermediate level, on average any one filter blocks 5% of health sites. However, cumulatively, the six filters in this study blocked a total of 16% of all health sites at the intermediate level. Therefore, 16% of all health sites would be blocked by one filtering product or another, when set at the intermediate level. Across all of the health topics studied, 5% of all health sites were blocked by at least one of the filtering products studied when set at the *least restrictive* configuration, 16% were blocked by at least one filtering product at the *intermediate* configuration, and 63% were blocked by at least one filter at the *most restrictive* configuration. Organizations providing information on *sexual health* are even more likely to have their Web sites blocked by some filtering product. For example, one in every three of the safe sex health sites studied (33%) were blocked by at least one filtering product at the *least restrictive* setting, one in two (49%) were blocked by at least one filter at the *intermediate* level, and

> *"Filters incorrectly blocked about one in ten sites on safe sex, condoms, or health issues pertaining to gays."*

more than nine in ten (91%) were blocked at the *most restrictive* setting.

Internet users seeking health information can avoid some blocking by using alternate search terms.

Sexual health sites associated with certain search terms—such as "safe sex" or "condoms"—were much more likely to be blocked than sites that resulted from alternate search strings, such as "birth control," "STD," or "herpes" (for example, 28% of health sites from the "condom" search were blocked at intermediate blocking levels, compared to 5% of sites from a search on "birth control").

Filters Block Information Along with Pornography

The extent to which Internet filters may adversely impact young people's access to online health information depends in large measure on how the filters are configured by the schools or libraries installing them. Indeed, how a specific filtering product is configured is more important in avoiding inadvertent blocking of health information than is the choice between different products. The major filtering products on the market allow administrators a great deal of leeway in determining how much material will be blocked. At their least restrictive settings, overblocking by filters has a negligible impact on access to general health information—especially when compared to other factors that can affect search results, such as spelling errors, limited search skills, and uneven quality of search engines. However, even at their least restrictive settings, filters could have a modest impact on those seeking information on sexual health issues; on average, filters incorrectly blocked about one in ten sites on safe sex, condoms, or health issues pertaining to gays. A determined searcher would likely still find the information he or she was searching for, particularly by altering search terms slightly: far fewer health sites were improperly blocked on terms such as "birth control," "STD," or "herpes."

The use of Internet filters could have a major impact on access to health information if administrators at schools and libraries configure them to block additional categories of content beyond just pornography: one in every four health sites was blocked, on average, at the most restrictive settings, and for topics related to sexual health, the rates were as high as one in every two sites. While using a more restrictive setting for the filters results in a significant increase in blocking of health sites, it yields only a marginal increase in effectiveness at blocking pornography (the percentage of health sites blocked increases from 1.4% to 24%, while the percent of porn sites blocked increases from 87% to 91%).

Inadvertent exposure to pornography occurs relatively infrequently during health searches—just 1% of the time—and none of the filters tested was particularly effective at blocking these sites (62% were blocked, on average). Young people who *proactively* seek out pornographic Web sites will find the filters more of an obstacle, but those who are determined to find such content will be able to do so eventually, even at the most restrictive levels of blocking: if nine out of ten porn sites are blocked, there will still be those students who pursue and find the one in ten that gets through.

Organizations that provide online health information for adolescents need to be aware of the potential impact of Internet filters on their efforts, given that nearly two out of three health sites are blocked by at least one of the filtering products when set at their most restrictive levels. For those providing sexual health information, the issue is quite serious: one in three "safe sex" health sites are blocked by at least one of the filters even when set at their *least* restrictive settings.

In sum, the results of this study indicate that Internet filters reduce but do not prevent inadvertent exposure to pornography during searches for health information, something that is an infrequent occurrence to begin with. They make it substantially harder for, but do not entirely prevent, young people from *proactively* seeking out pornographic content. The filters do not significantly impede searches for general health information when they are set at low levels of blocking, but they do have a modest impact on searches for sexual health information even at these settings. Filters do interfere with general health searches at higher levels of configuration, and have an especially serious impact on searches for *sexual health* information at these levels, blocking many non-pornographic sites.

Setting Internet filters to more restrictive levels does not significantly increase their effectiveness at blocking pornography, but does not significantly increase overblocking of non-pornographic health content. Some schools or libraries may decide that they wish to block additional content categories beyond pornography, but this should be a conscious decision by policymakers rather than an inadvertent one by those who install the filter software; and this decision should be made with an awareness of the impact on young people's access to health information.

Campaign Finance Reform Limits Political Expression

by John Samples

About the author: *John Samples is the director for the Center for Representative Government at the Cato Institute. He is also the author of* James Madison and the Future of Limited Government.

[In early 2002] Congress . . . passed extensive new restrictions on campaign finance. The proponents of these new limits—Reps. Christopher Shays (R-Connecticut) and Martin Meehan (D-Massachusetts), along with Sens. John McCain (R-Arizona) and Russell Feingold (D-Wisconsin)—say their law will clean up and reform American politics. The new law—dubbed Shays-Meehan—has two major provisions: a ban on "soft money" and restrictions on broadcast advertising. Far from reforming American politics, these restrictions ensure the continuation of the status quo and its powers-that-be: incumbent officeholders and the establishment media.

Campaign Finance Reform Is a Recent Development

For most of our history, Americans have enjoyed a relatively unregulated system of campaign finance. These freedoms, like many others, began to erode in the 1960s and early 1970s as powerful groups pushed restrictions on the right to spend money on political advocacy.

In 1974, Congress passed the Federal Election Campaign Act (FECA), which set tight limits on overall campaign spending, imposed ceilings on contributions, continued existing prohibitions on contributions from corporations and labor unions in federal elections, and established government funding of presidential campaigns. The law was immediately challenged as a violation of the rights of Americans.

The Supreme Court's decision in *Buckley v. Valeo* in 1976 partially struck down FECA. The majority set forth the tight connection between freedom of speech and money:

Virtually every means of communicating ideas in today's mass society requires the expenditure of money. The distribution of the humblest handbill or leaflet entails printing, paper, and circulation costs. Speeches and rallies generally necessitate hiring a hall and publicizing the event. The electorate's increasing dependence on television, radio, and other mass media for news and information has made these expensive modes of communication indispensable instruments of effective political speech.

Limits on political spending thus limit political speech "by restricting the number of issues discussed, the depth of their exploration, and the size of the audience reached." Any limits on political spending, the Court concluded, violated the First Amendment.

The tight link between money and speech would appear to apply to all political spending, including campaign outlays and contributions. After all, if I give money to a candidate, I'm expressing a position on politics and policy.

However, the *Buckley* decision did not give campaign contributions the same First Amendment protections it afforded other spending on politics. Contributions could be limited, the justices said, to advance the state's compelling interest in preventing "corruption or the appearance of corruption." With these concepts in hand, we can judge Shays-Meehan.

Soft Money Raises the Question of Undue Influence

Hard money comprises campaign contributions regulated by the FECA. Soft money contributions have not been regulated by federal law until now. In the late 1970s, Congress and the Federal Election Commission exempted soft money contributions to the political parties, which they could spend on voter registration, some campaign materials, and voter turnout programs. Far from a nefarious loophole in election law, soft money began life as an attempt to strengthen the parties and raise voter turnout.

Debates about soft money necessarily concern large sums that are often labeled "obscene" by those seeking new regulations. The total soft money raised in the 2000 election—$490 million—is a large sum in anyone's book. Yet absolute numbers easily mislead. Campaign spending in general, and soft money specifically, pale beside the $2.5 trillion spent by federal, state, and local governments annually. The soft money total for 2000 is less than $3 per eligible voter in the United States. Moreover, soft money accounts for only 15 percent of all money spent on campaigns.

"Political scientists have found that campaign contributions have little effect on legislative votes."

Advocates of new campaign finance regulations might argue that their real concern is not the numbers but how soft money affects politics and policy. They might point to the numerous scandals and suggestions of impropriety that haunted President [Bill] Clinton and Vice President [Al] Gore from 1995 onward. Supporters of Shays-Meehan believe soft money corrupts American politics. Are they right?

Campaign Contributions Do Not Constitute Corruption

What is corruption? First, there is direct bribery. Public officials are certainly corrupt when they provide political favors in exchange for bribes. This kind of corruption of American national politics is already illegal and rare—judging by the relatively few indictments and convictions of members of Congress.

Some say legislators are corrupt if they cast their votes in Congress to advance the interests of their contributors. Such indirect bribery is difficult to prove. After all, most contributors give to candidates whose policy views they share. Contributors don't corrupt a legislator who would have voted the same on an issue in the absence of the contribution. In any case, "Political scientists have found that campaign contributions have little effect on legislative votes.'"

The idea of indirect bribery is based on the false premise that the need for campaign funds is the most important influence on legislators. In contrast, political scientists assume officeholders give primacy to being reelected. Being reelected requires a majority of votes, not the greatest success in fund-raising.

If corruption is defined as direct or indirect bribery, the case for regulating core First Amendment activities such as campaign contributions seems weak. Even advocates of new regulations do not contend that much direct bribery exists. We also have little hard evidence that indirect bribery is a big problem. Why so much talk about corruption and campaign finance?

Advocates of campaign finance regulations equate corruption with what they see as the "undue influence" of contributors. They argue that large contributions "distort" the legislative process and prevent representatives from advancing the true interest of the American people. Absent money, the advocates argue, members of Congress would help "the people, not the powerful." More often than not, this means they believe Congress would enact a left-wing agenda if private campaign contributions were restricted or banned.

All political participation, including campaign contributions, tries to influence policy choices. The Constitution does not contain a matrix enabling us to distinguish "proper" and "improper" influence. It does forbid restricting fundamental freedoms to achieve equality of influence.

As the Supreme Court noted in *Buckley v. Valeo:* "The concept that government may restrict the speech of some elements of our society in order to enhance the relative voice of others is wholly foreign to the First Amendment." Moreover, the advocates are incorrect that "big money" prevents Congress from passing leftist legislation. Scholars have found that Americans, including those of modest means, believe deeply in the American dream of individual freedom, responsibility, and social mobility. Congress does not enact the Left's agenda because Americans reject it, not because of campaign contributions.

Chapter 2

The Consequences of Banning Soft Money

The history of campaign finance regulation is filled with unintended consequences. Congress enacted contribution limits in the FECA to get average Americans involved in politics, but these limits reinforced the power of established groups and encouraged the candidacies of wealthy individuals.

Trade unions fought hard to make sure political action committees (PACs) had a special status under federal election law only to discover that the PAC strategy worked better for their opponents than it did for them. Low contribution limits aimed at freeing officials from special interests ended up forcing legislators to spend much of their time raising money. What are the likely consequences of McCain-Feingold-Cochran's ban on soft money? Will those consequences be good for America?

Incumbent members of Congress are almost always reelected. Challenging an incumbent is tough. Members of Congress supply themselves at public cost with significant resources to pursue reelection, including salary, travel, office, staff, and communication allowances that are estimated to be worth $1 million annually to House members and several times that for Senators. In particular, taxpayers now support unlimited trips by House members back to their districts.

"In a democracy, elected officials are not allowed to prohibit criticism."

In 1999, members of Congress had 11,488 full-time staffers, many of whom focused on helping constituents with their problems, thereby generating support in the home district. Members also possess the "franking privilege" which allows them to send mail to constituents free of charge. By the time an election rolls around, incumbents have much higher name recognition among voters than potential challengers. Such advantages of office are not governed or limited by the FECA.

To overcome the incumbent's advantage, challengers must raise significant sums of money. In 1996 and 1998, for example, challengers who defeated House incumbents raised on average well over $1 million; in the Senate, successful challengers raised many times that sum. Banning or limiting contributions of any kind makes it harder for challengers to be competitive.

Prohibiting soft money particularly hurts challengers. Parties direct soft money toward close races, thereby making elections more competitive. A recent scholarly analysis showed that PACs tend to donate to incumbents, while parties concentrate equally on vulnerable incumbents and credible challengers. The Shays-Meehan law bans the kind of money most useful to challengers and leaves unmolested the kind of money most useful to incumbents.

The law will hurt American politics in other ways. Political scientists Stephen Ansolabohere and James Snyder Jr. found that soft money supported numerous activities, including get-out-the-vote drives, broadcast advertising, and day-today campaign operations. Based on their analysis of how state and local parties use soft money, they argue that a soft money ban would force parties to cut direct campaign expenditures by 20 percent. Given that it costs $15–35 to get every new voter to the polls, Ansolabohere and Snyder believe banning soft money would reduce turnout by about 2 percent.

Banning Political Ads Limits Speech

Shays-Meehan will not drive money out of politics. Government affects all aspects of life, and citizens will find new ways to influence elections and lawmaking. In recent elections, labor unions, some businesses, and interest groups have bought advertising during elections that often attacked sitting members of Congress. With soft money banned, these groups may spend more on such advertising. That possibility alarmed Congress so much that Shays-Meehan prohibited labor unions and corporations from running such ads 60 days before an election. Interest groups may still buy such advertising, but they must fully disclose where they get the money for the effort.

The ban on ads follows several unpleasant experiences of members of Congress. In 1996, for example, the AFL-CIO carried out a $35 million television advertising campaign that ran in dozens of congressional districts with vulnerable Republican incumbents. The ads attacked incumbents' voting records on such issues as Social Security, Medicare, and education. In the election of 2000, labor was at it again. Rep. Clay Shaw, a Republican congressman from Florida who was a target, drew a revealing lesson from his experience: "After you've been a victim of soft money [ads], you realize the magnitude of the problem, I'm determined to address this problem when we come back. It's really ripping at the fabric of our nation's political structure."

Congress has now addressed Shaw's "problem." Their solution is banning such ads or making them more difficult by requiring disclosure of the donors supporting the ads. The coming elections will be freer of ads criticizing incumbent members of Congress. But being criticized, even unfairly, goes with the territory of being an elected official. In a democracy, elected officials are not allowed to prohibit criticism. . . .

Campaign Finance Reform Hurts Citizens

Senator McCain believes restrictions on campaign finance will heal American democracy: "This is a system that has become dominated by the special interests, and the average American citizen is no longer represented, and everybody knows it's got to be fixed." Similarly, House Democratic Leader Richard Gephardt (D-Missouri) said, "Democrats believe the time has come to give our democracy back to the people. We need to reduce the power of special interests and money in the political process." In truth, Shays-Meehan will benefit two powerful special interests: incumbent officeholders and the media.

We have already seen how Shays-Meehan helps incumbents. Prohibiting soft money makes electoral challenges difficult, if not impossible. Banning advertising frees incumbents from criticism just prior to an election. Yet another kind of incumbent also benefits from "reform": incumbent speakers in the established media.

Fighting elections depends on access to the mass media, which costs money. Any regulation that restricts contributions or expenditures on election campaigns makes it harder to gain access to the public square. Such restrictions, however, serve the interests of the incumbent media—conservative, liberal, and in between—who already have a platform from which to speak out on public issues. Looked at another way, Shays-Meehan restricts competition to the existing media during elections. After campaign finance "reform" goes into effect, the voices of the established media will be louder and more powerful than ever.

In the end, campaign finance "reform" depends on a false and undemocratic premise. McCain, Feingold, Shays, and Meehan all believe that elections belong to the government, which has the right to decide who participates, and on what terms. In the United States, however, elections belong to the people, who elect a government that should be their servant.

Freedom of the Press Is Threatened

by Charles Lewis

About the author: *Charles Lewis is the founder of the Center for Public Integrity, a nonprofit, nonpartisan organization that does investigative reporting and research on public policy issues. He has written for several newspapers and written or cowritten many books, including* The Buying of the President.

The tension between power and the press, between spinning and searching for truth, between disinformation and information, is of course endemic to the human condition itself. And in trying times like these, when it occasionally looks like things are going to hell, it is strangely consoling to recall that actually others before us also have traveled on what must have seemed to be the road to perdition.

The Case of the Pentagon Papers

For example, [in the early 1970s] a President and his administration were prosecuting a difficult, unpopular war thousands of miles away on foreign soil, keenly attempting without great success to control the media's access to information, particularly of the unfavorable kind. Two newspapers, the *New York Times* and the *Washington Post*, each began publishing a leaked, secret Defense Department history of the Vietnam War that dramatically revealed government deception and incompetence. The Nixon administration went into federal court against the two news organizations, separately, and, citing national security and charging treason, managed to halt publication of the "Pentagon Papers" until the U.S. Supreme Court, on June 30, 1971, sided with the First Amendment by a vote of 6-3.

While *Washington Post* executive editor Ben Bradlee was, among others, understandably exultant and relieved, he also recognized, as Bradlee later recalled in his memoir, *A Good Life*, that he had just stared into the abyss, "For the first time in the history of the American republic, newspapers had been restrained by the government from publishing a story—a black mark in the history of democracy. . . . What the hell was going on in this country that this could happen?"

Certainly a common refrain among many journalists *these* days as well, but to finish the flashback, the Pentagon Papers episode obviously was just the beginning. Bradlee at the time did not know the answer to his own question, except that "the Cold War dominated our society, and . . . the Nixon-Agnew administration was playing

> *"It is not difficult to understand the current, wholesale assault on openness and government accountability today."*

hardball." While Vietnam wore on for a few more years, Richard Nixon seethed and the White House siege mentality worsened.

Two days before the historic Supreme Court case, the whistleblower who had leaked the Pentagon Papers, Daniel Ellsberg, was indicted on federal charges of conspiracy, espionage, theft of government property and the unauthorized possession of "documents and writing related to the national defense." The day after the high court decision, White House Special Counsel Charles Colson asked former CIA operative E. Howard Hunt whether "we should go down the line to nail the guy [Ellsberg] cold."

The Pentagon Papers obsession spawned the White House Special Investigations Unit, the infamous "Plumbers" unit, who, among other misadventures, weeks later broke into Ellsberg's psychiatrist's office, looking for dirt. And the poisonous paranoia didn't stop there but extended to other burglaries, including the Democratic Party national headquarters at the Watergate complex, electronic surveillance, misuse of confidential tax return information against perceived political enemies, mail fraud, obstruction of justice and an astonishing array of other illegal government abuses of power, ultimately exposed, prosecuted and culminating in the *only* resignation of a sitting U.S. president.

Implications for the War on Terror

The Pentagon Papers case and the Watergate scandal still represent U.S. history's high-water mark in the longstanding struggle between raw political power and democratic values, poignantly affirming the public's right to know about its government. They still represent the bleakest moments and the loftiest triumphs of journalism in contemporary America, an invaluable perspective today as we ponder the future and assess the tectonic damage to our long-cherished freedoms of speech and information in the . . . disquieting years in the wake of the devastating, unimaginable carnage of [the September 11, 2001, terrorist attacks].

Suddenly, despite living in the most powerful nation on earth, we all faced a shattering if all-too-familiar realization of our own human vulnerabilities, including the quite palpable fear for our own personal safety, indelibly seared into our collective consciousness. While the Vietnam and Watergate era was quite extraordinary, most Americans, including journalists, *never* had the sense that their physical well-being was potentially at risk. Juxtapose our pervasive sense of insecurity and the patriotic and visceral, survival-related instinct to do anything to thwart "terrorism," with a President and administration which assumed power with a well-documented predisposition to tightly manage and control information, and it is not difficult to understand the current, wholesale assault on openness and government accountability today.

Indeed, let us not forget the hard-wiring, lifelong sensibility that Watergate and the Nixonian animosity and adversarial culture toward the news media unavoidably had to have on three rising Republicans: George W. Bush, Donald Rumsfeld and Dick Cheney. Bush's father, George H.W. Bush, was personally close to Nixon and was chairman of the Republican National Committee at the time of the resignation. Rumsfeld and Cheney not only served in the Nixon administration, but the two men were also in President Gerald R. Ford's White House, as successive chiefs of staff.

As defense secretary in the first Bush administration, Cheney was one of the architects of the controversial Persian Gulf War media restrictions, as [investigative reporter] Jacqueline Sharkey documented in a 1992 Center for Public Integrity report, *Under Fire: U.S. Military Restrictions on the Media from Grenada to the Persian Gulf.* From the military and public relations debacle of Vietnam, Cheney and others in the Pentagon and White House recognized the usefulness of trying "to hide the true face of war by controlling the images of the conflict," including caskets at Dover Air Force Base in Delaware. In the U.S. military conflicts in Grenada, Panama and the Persian Gulf during the 1980s and early 1990s, the media thus was constrained from the actual field of action, thereby substantially preventing those Vietnam-reminiscent pictures of body bags in American TV living rooms.

> *"The American people unfortunately are not as informed, concerned, or supportive about this deepening crisis as they ought to be."*

Prewar Foundations of Information Control

In the weeks and months *prior* to September 11, 2001, the secrecy obsession and aggressive control tactics by the new Bush administration had already become apparent. For example, instead of turning his gubernatorial papers over to the Texas State Library and Archives, as tradition would have it, Gov. Bush, in his last hours, tried to shelter his official records inside his father's presidential library at Texas A&M University, outside the jurisdiction of the strong Texas public information law. He was overruled by the state attorney general and they fortunately are accessible to the public.

In the summer of 2001, Vice President Cheney refused to release basic information about meetings he and other administration officials had held—on government time and property—with energy company executives to help formulate federal policies, a position on which he remains steadfastly adamant.

And a month before September 11, the Justice Department secretly subpoenaed Associated Press reporter John Solomon's home telephone records. As Solomon, the AP deputy Washington bureau chief, told me, "The Justice Department has indicated to us that they were actually trying to stop the publication of a story that I was working on and tried to find out who I was talking to and cut off the flow of information. So it does get into the issue of prior restraint along with First and Fourth amendment issues."

Information Control Immediately Following September 11, 2001

As we all know too well, in the weeks immediately following September 11th, the Bush administration obtained passage of the USA Patriot Act, with no public debate or amendments, among other things, giving federal authorities more power to access email and telephone communications. The federal government detained hundreds of people indefinitely without releasing the most basic information about them. Attorney General John Ashcroft described the news blackout in Orwellian fashion, "It would be a violation of the privacy rights of individuals for me to create some kind of list." Usually open U.S. immigration proceedings were closed to the public, and separately, the Attorney General sent a chilling, unprecedented directive throughout the government, "When you carefully consider FOIA [Freedom of Information Act] requests and decide to withhold records, in whole or in part, you can be assured that the Department of Justice will defend your decisions. . . ." And President Bush quietly signed Executive Order 13233, overriding the post-Watergate 1978 Presidential Records Act and sharply reducing public access to the papers of former presidents, including his father's.

In the war in Afghanistan, journalists were severely limited in their access to field of action. As the Reporters Committee on Freedom of the Press noted in its excellent report, *Homeland Confidential*, "In effect, most American broadcasters and newspaper reporters scratched out coverage from Pentagon briefings, a rare interview on a U.S. aircraft carrier or a humanitarian aid airlift, or from carefully selected military videos or from leaks. . . . The truth is, the American media's vantage point for the war has never been at the frontlines with American troops."

Indeed, who can forget December 6, 2001, when Marines locked reporters and photographers in a warehouse to prevent them from covering American troops killed or injured north of Kandahar, Afghanistan? And while embedded reporters enjoyed far greater access—and danger—in Iraq, many news organizations, including the *New York Times* and the *Washington Post*, have recently been introspective or even mildly apologetic for their over-reliance on official statements in the lead-up to the war.

But, meanwhile, it is hard to overstate the fear and paranoia of an entire, terrorized nation. Within six months of September 11th, in 300 separate instances, federal, state and local officials restricted access to government records by executive order, or proposed new laws to sharply curtail their availability, according to the National Conference of State Legislatures. More recently, sunshine activists are most alarmed about the Homeland Security Act, especially its Protected Critical Infrastructure Information (PCII) section. Former *Miami Herald* managing editor Pete Weitzel recently described it in the *American Editor* as a "black hole" for almost boundless censorship. The ranking Democrat on the Senate Judiciary Committee, Patrick Leahy, called the move—which would create an entirely new level of secrecy and a system of binding nondisclosure agreements effectively muzzling millions of state and local officials and private contractors—"the single greatest rollback of FOIA in history."

Public Fear and Lack of Information

The American people unfortunately are not as informed, concerned, or supportive about this deepening crisis as they ought to be. A national poll sponsored by the *Chicago Tribune* on First Amendment issues in late June found that roughly half of the public believe there should have been some kind of "press restraint" on coverage of the Abu Ghraib prison abuse scandal in Iraq—somewhat ironic considering that the chairman of the Joint Chiefs of Staff, General Richard Myers, personally had implored CBS's *60 Minutes II* to keep its exposé off the air in the name of national security, which the network actually did voluntarily until learning that investigative reporter Seymour Hersh would be publishing the story in the *New Yorker.* In general, according to Charles Madigan, editor of the *Tribune*'s Perspective section, fifty or sixty percent of the public "would embrace government controls of some kind on free speech, particularly when it has sexual content or is heard as unpatriotic."

This ambivalence in which at least half of the country equates draconian security and secrecy measures with their own safety is quite serious and very possibly insurmountable. Tom Blanton, executive director of the National Security Archive in Washington wrote in *National Security and Open Government*, "The government has successfully framed the debate after 9/11 as terrorism fighters versus civil libertarians, as soldiers versus reporters, as hawks versus doves. In wartime, the poundage of the former will always outweigh the latter. . . . We need to place openness where it belongs, not only at the center of our values, but also at the center of our strategy for security."

> *"Nothing resonates more with the American people than the straight skinny itself about the powers that be."*

Both the Congressional September 11th investigation and the 9/11 Commission appointed by President Bush separately documented extensive "intelligence hoarding" and petty bureaucratic turf wars inside the government, excessive secrecy for all the wrong reasons and the dire consequences of not sharing information. But beyond that, the ignorance of the body politic was anything but blissful. The 9/11 Commission concluded, "We believe American and international public opinion might have been different—and so might the range of options for a president—had they [the American people] been informed of [the growing al Qaeda (terrorist group) danger]."

A Free Press Is Key to Upholding Democracy

It is a powerful message still substantially untold but essential to understanding and preserving freedom of the press as we know it. Indeed, the situation is so foreboding that the Associated Press has taken the unusual step of proposing an industry-wide lobby to "identify and oppose legislation that puts unreasonable restrictions on public information." AP stepped forward after seven national journalism groups and the National Freedom of Information Coalition had already joined to form the Coalition of Journalists for Open Government.

The Center for Public Integrity has found that nothing resonates more with the American people than the straight skinny itself about the powers that be. When the CPI obtained a secret draft of the Domestic Enhancement Security Act of 2003, better known as "Patriot II," it was posted in its 100-plus page entirety on the Web site, www.publicintegrity.org, over the objections of the Justice Department. Because of the public furor over some of its controversial provisions—including internal GOP frustration on Capitol Hill that the secretive Attorney General and his staff had kept them in the dark for nearly half a year—the draft bill was dead within months (although the Bush administration has been trying to push a few provisions separately).

Or, noticing that no one was terribly helpful or definitive about the awarding of billions of dollars in government contracts in Iraq and Afghanistan, the CPI decided to go to work, filing 73 FOIAs [Freedom of Information Act requests] and, when necessary, successfully suing the State Department and the Army for the contracts. Six months later, a report, Windfalls of War, revealed all of the major known contractors and contracts, and the fact that Vice President Cheney's former company, Halliburton, and its subsidiaries had gotten by far the most taxpayer money, some of them with no other bidders. Our approach now on any issue is to push back and appeal on any stonewalling that elevates our blood pressure. In other words, appeal early and often—it's the principle of the thing, and you just might win.

Besides educating the American people about the Vietnam War, the greatest result of courageous publication of the Pentagon Papers was the confidence it imbued in newsrooms all across America. Inside the *Washington Post*, years later Bradlee recalled, "a sense of mission and agreement on new goals, and how to attain them. . . . After the Pentagon Papers, there would be no decision too difficult for us to overcome together."

And Solicitor General Erwin Griswold, who argued the government's case against the *Post* and the *Times* before the Supreme Court, later acknowledged in an op-ed what many had suspected all along, "I have never seen any trace of a threat to the national security from the Pentagon Papers' publication."

As Supreme Court Justice Potter Stewart wrote in the Pentagon Papers case, words we should all remember, "In the absence of governmental checks and balances present in other areas of our national life, the only effective restraint upon executive policy and power in the areas of national defense and international affairs may lie in an enlightened citizenry—in an informed and critical public opinion which alone can here protect the values of democratic government."

Campaign Finance Reform Could Enhance Political Expression

by John Kerry

About the author: *John Kerry is a U.S. Senator. He ran as the Democratic candidate in the 2004 presidential election, which he lost to George W. Bush.*

Today we take an important first step toward reforming our campaign finance system. After an election in which $3 billion was spent in an effort to elect or defeat candidates, we are finally taking action to attempt to make our campaign finance laws meaningful. However, there are predictable consequences from this legislation that will not be positive and will require further attention to the issue of campaign finance reform.

The money spent on the 2000 election should come as a surprise to no one. Soft money [money given to political parties for voter registration, some campaign materials, and voter turnout programs], an important target of this bill, has increased at a remarkable pace. Year after year, there has been a steady and dramatic increase in the amount of money raised and spent on elections. For example, in 1992, Democrats raised $30 million in soft money. In 1996, the Democrats more than tripled that amount and raised $107 million in soft money. In 2000 Democrats raised $243 million in soft money.

The Republican party has consistently proven itself to have even more fundraising prowess than the Democrats, but the trends are exactly the same, with substantial increases year after year. In 1992, the Republican party raised $45 million in soft money. In 1996, they raised $120 million in soft money. And in 2000, the Republican party raised $244 million in soft money. The American people have become almost numb to these kinds of staggering figures, and they have come to expect fund-raising records to be broken with each election cycle. And, what is far worse for our Democracy is that the public also believes that

John Kerry, "Kerry Statement on McCain-Feingold Campaign Finance Reform Victory," http://kerry. senate.gov, March 20, 2002.

this money buys access and influence that average citizens don't have.

In addition to the overwhelming amounts of soft money that were raised and spent in 2000, hundreds of millions of dollars were also spent on so-called issue ads. Now, I'm not talking about television ads that truly discuss the issues of the day. I'm talking about ads that air just before an election that show candidates, surrounded by their families, American flags waving in the background, that tell of the candidates' service to the nation, or heroic actions during a war. Anyone who sees an ad like this believes it is a campaign ad. But, because of a quirk in the law, even these most blatant of campaign ads are called issue ads. As such, the contributions that pay for them are unlimited and relatively undisclosed. Yet, in many cases, these ads shape the debate in a race, and they most certainly are intended to shape the outcome.

Those ubiquitous television ads are purchased by all kinds of organized special interests to persuade the American people to vote for or against a candidate. These ads—usually negative, often inaccurate—are driving the political process today. Do they violate the spirit of the campaign finance laws in this country? They certainly do. But, don't take my word for it. Listen to the Executive Director of the National Rifle Association's Institute for Legislative Action, who said, "It is foolish to believe there is a difference between issue advocacy and advocacy of a political candidate. What separates issue advocacy and political advocacy is a line in the sand drawn on a windy day." The bill that we are sending to the President [the Shays-Meehan bill, also referred to as McCain-Feingold, which passed in 2002] takes a step toward reform. It is important to know that it is also firmly rooted in prior laws. Federal law has prohibited corporations from contributing to federal candidates since 1907. Labor unions likewise have been barred from contributing to candidates since 1943. In addition, the post-Watergate campaign finance law caps individual contributions at $25,000 per calendar year, and permits individuals to give no more than $20,000 to a national party, $5,000 to a political action committee, and $2,000 to a candidate. These limits were put in place after the country learned a hard lessen about the corrupting influence of money in politics.

Nowhere in these laws are there any provisions for soft money. That aberration came into play in 1978 when the Federal Election Commission [FEC] gave the Kansas Republican State Committee permission to use corporate and union funds to pay for a voter drive benefitting federal as well as state candidates. The costs of the

> *"The Supreme Court . . . held that limits on individual campaign contributions do not violate the First Amendment."*

drive were to be split between hard money raised under federal law and soft money raised under Kansas law. The FEC's decision in the Kansas case gives parties the option to spend soft money any time a federal election coincides with a state or local race. A creation not of Congress, but of a weak, politically motivated federal agency, soft money is a loophole to our system that is long overdue for eradication. . . .

Despite what the foes of this bill claim, banning soft money contributions does not violate the Constitution. The Supreme Court in *Buckley v. Valeo* held that limits on individual campaign contributions do not violate the First Amendment. If a limit of $1000 on contributions by individuals was upheld as constitutional, then a ban on contributions of $10,000, $100,000 or $1 million is also going to be upheld. *Buckley*, too, said that the risk of corruption or the appearance of corruption warranted limits on individual campaign contributions. Soft money contributions to political parties can be limited for the same reason. Like soft money, issue advocacy has a history that defies the intent of campaign finance laws. In what remains the seminal case on campaign finance, *Buckley*, the Supreme Court held that campaign finance limitations applied only to "communications that in express terms advocate the election or defeat of a clearly identified candidate for federal office." A footnote to the opinion says that the limits apply when communications include terms "such as 'vote for,' 'elect,' 'support,' 'cast your ballot for,' 'Smith for Congress,' 'vote against,' 'defeat,' 'reject.'" The phrases in the footnote have become known as the "magic words" without which a communication, no matter what its purpose or impact, is often classified as issue advocacy, thus falling outside the reach of the campaign finance laws.

> *"Less money might actually improve the quality of discourse, requiring candidates to more cautiously spend their resources."*

Until the 1992 election cycle, most for-profit, not-for-profit, and labor organizations did not attempt to get into electoral politics via issue advocacy. That year, one advocacy group pushed the envelope and aired what was, for all intents and purposes, a negative campaign ad attacking Bill Clinton. Because the ad never used *Buckley*'s "magic words," the Court of Appeals decided that the ad was a discussion of issues related rather than an exhortation to vote against Clinton in the upcoming presidential election.

That ad and others like it opened the flood gates to more so-called issue advocacy in 1996, when countless special interests started overwhelming the airwaves with millions of dollars in ads that looked like campaign ads, but, because they avoided those magic words, were deemed issue ads.

Opponents of this proposal will also argue that any effort to control or limit sham issue ads would violate the First Amendment. They argue that as long as you don't use the so-called "magic words" in *Buckley*—such as "vote for" or "vote against"—you can say just about anything you want in an advertisement. But that is simply not what the Supreme Court said in *Buckley*. It said that one way to identify campaign speech that can be regulated is by looking at whether it uses words of express advocacy. But the Court never said that Congress was precluded from adopting another test so long as it was clear, precise and narrow.

A final argument opponents of reform like to make is that we spend less on campaigns than we do on potato chips or laundry detergent. But I would ask the proponents of this argument whether what we are seeking in our democracy is electioneering that has no more depth or substance than a snack food commercial. Despite the ever-increasing sums spent on campaigns, we have not seen an improvement in campaign discourse, issue discussion or voter education. More money does not mean more ideas, more substance or more depth. Instead, it means more of what voters complain about most. More thirty-second spots, more negativity and an increasingly longer campaign period. Less money might actually improve the quality of discourse, requiring candidates to more cautiously spend their resources. It might encourage more debates—as was the case in my own race against Bill Weld in 1996—and it would certainly focus the candidates' voter education efforts during the period shortly before the election, when most voters are tuned in, instead of starting the campaign 18 months before election day.

Shays-Meehan takes an important step that begins to tackle the problems of soft money and issue advocacy. I support this legislation that has been championed by two very able colleagues, but I would note one serious shortcoming of the bill. It won't curb the rampant spending that drives the quest for money. Unfortunately, we all recognize that creating spending limits is not a simple proposition. In the 1976 *Buckley* case, the Supreme Court struck spending limits as an unconstitutional restriction of political speech. An important caveat to its decision is that spending limits could be imposed in exchange for a public benefit. I wish we had at our disposal a number of bargaining chips—public benefits that we could trade in exchange for spending limits. However, unless the Supreme Court reverses itself—something I am certainly not expecting in the near future—we must accept that if we want to limit the amounts spent on campaigns, we must provide candidates with some sort of public grant.

I realize that a lot of my colleagues aren't ready to embrace public funding as a way to finance our campaigns. But it is, in my opinion, the best constitutional means to the important end of limiting campaign spending and the contributions that go with it. Ultimately, I would support a system that provides full public funding for political candidates. I will continue to support Clean Money as the ultimate way to truly and completely purge our system of the negative influence of corporate money. I would also support a partial public funding system as a way to wean candidates from their reliance on hard money and get them used to campaigning under generous spending limits. . . . I recognize that we are a long way away from enacting such a program. Nevertheless I will continue to support and work for that type of reform as a way to end the cycle of unlimited money being raised and spent on our elections. . . .

This bill is a way to break free from the status quo. However, as with any reform measure, there are always going to be possibilities for abuse. The fact that some people will try to skirt the law is not a reason for us to fail to take this incremental movement towards repairing the system. But, it does mean we must ensure that this is the first, rather than the last, step for fundamental reform. I have supported campaign finance reform for eighteen years and I believe that even legislation that takes only a small step forward is necessary to begin to restore the dwindling faith the average American has in our political system. We can't go on leaving our citizens with the impression that the only kind of influence left in American politics is the kind you wield with a checkbook. I believe this bill reduces the power of the checkbook and I will therefore support it.

Filters and Ratings Systems Are Protecting Free Speech

by Jeffrey Cole

About the author: *Jeffrey Cole is the director of the Center for Communication Policy at the University of California at Los Angeles.*

The Internet is well on its way to becoming the most important means of communication since the development of the printing press in the 15th century. There is almost no human activity that will not be affected by this technology and most activity will be transformed. . . . In this critical period of the Internet's maturation as a medium for all people, it is essential that governments encourage Internet growth and provide support, and it is even more essential that governments stay out of the regulatory business.

The history of mass communications demonstrates clearly and repeatedly that self-regulation, rather than governmental control, is the most effective means of sustaining growth and nurturing content in the media. Self-regulation moves the burden of regulating content from the government to where it properly belongs: in the hands of users. During this important transformational stage of the Internet, particularly when non-users are overly aware of harmful content and less aware of the beneficial content (and non-users are the majority), there is great pressure for governments to regulate. Politicians can grab quick headlines by proposing to "do something" about this unappealing content, especially pornography and hate speech. Once a governmental effort to "clean up" begins, it becomes politically difficult for anyone to oppose the legislation, lest they appear to be supporting such awful content. In the United States, even though many legislators opposed the Communications Decency Act (CDA) both because of first amendment grounds and because it was overly broad and difficult to enforce, many of these opponents were forced to "support" the CDA for political reasons. It fell to the courts, designed by the constitution to be immune to political pressure, to overturn the legislation. Ironically, the very same Congress that passed the CDA would have violated its own law (had it not been overturned) in September 1998 when it released the salacious details of the Starr Report on President [Bill] Clinton onto the Internet.

Clearly all industry committed to regulating itself with the support of government and a people willing to take the time to learn the methods of self-regulation is, by far, the best method of dealing with content problems in the media. However, before self-regulation can become truly effective, there are several important issues that must be understood by all parties, i.e., the industry, the government and parents.

Self-Regulation Does Not Censor Content

With very few exceptions, self-regulation does not eliminate "bad" content; it merely labels it and places it into proper categories.

The exceptions are content that is clearly illegal such as "child pornography" to which everyone must be committed to eliminate. If self-regulation is to work, all sides must understand that content that they find objectionable will survive and may flourish under this system. This means that people will have to accept the notion that occasionally they will be offended by the content they see on the Internet just as they are occasionally offended by what they see in the movies or on television. Filters and labeling will allow most people to keep unacceptable content (to them) away from their eyes and especially from the eyes of their children. Not all content will be labeled the way people want and from time to time they will see things they would rather not see. This is the price people must be willing to pay to participate in a free society. The alternative is for some governmental agency to screen everything before it is distributed (prior restraint) and eliminate anything that might offend anyone. This would ensure an Internet devoid of vitality and one so bland that it would quickly pass into oblivion.

In the United States the presence of an industry-applied rating system for film and television does not eliminate any content whatsoever (although some people are afraid that producers censor themselves or are censored by their companies to keep programming within acceptable ratings or limits). Tasteless films and television programs are still made, but are labeled with a rating that provides guidance to parents about the content. Many critics in government and advocacy groups are unhappy with ratings systems for the very reason that they do not eliminate "bad" content. Many would prefer to get this programming out of theaters, off the air or off the Internet. An authoritarian system where someone censors "inappropriate" content according to his or her standards is not a feature of self-regulation.

Parents Must Be Internet Savvy

Parents must educate themselves about how labeling and filtering systems work.

None of these self-regulatory systems work if parents do not learn how to use them. If parents do not make the effort to learn this technology, the only systems that can result are ones that block everything or one that blocks nothing. It falls to the makers of filtering or labeling systems to make the technology as transparent as possible and the concepts of the system as easy to learn as possible.

In 1968, the Motion Picture Association of America (MPAA) devised a set of film ratings to provide guidance to parents about the appropriateness of films their children might want to see. The original system contained four ratings beginning with the tame G, and running through the harsher M, R and X. Today that system has evolved into five categories of G, PG, PG-13, R and NC-17.

Each film and all advertisements for the film contain these ratings. The only part of the system that is passive for parents is that children under 17 are blocked (in theory) from seeing a film rated R (unless with a parent or guardian) or NC-17. For the ratings to work, parents must learn the system and through experience learn the practical application of each rating symbol. This does seem to have happened rather well over the past 30 years.

It is less clear what is happening in the television world. After close to a year of turmoil over the design of the system, three of the four American broadcast television networks and almost all cable networks agreed to label programming with a TV-G, TV-PG, TV-14 and TV-MA (with additional ratings for programs created for children). In addition to these ratings, content descriptors of S (sex), V (violence), L (language) and D (dialogue) were added to the age-based ratings. The importance of this system is that it will ultimately trigger the use of the V-chip that will allow parents to block programming that exceeds the level they wish their child to see. In this way, the V-chip is analogous to the use of filtering systems on the Internet when applied by the user. Although the ratings have been on television programs for [sometime] it is not clear whether parents are learning what the labels mean and using the system. Furthermore, there is a serious question as to whether parents will learn how to program a V-chip and block the programming they select. Without parents taking the time to learn these systems, self-regulation simply does not work effectively.

> *"Filters and labeling will allow most people to keep unacceptable content (to them) away from their eyes."*

When talking about the Internet, parents have an additional responsibility in a self-regulatory environment: they must, to the best of their ability, learn a little bit about how computers and the Internet work. This was never a problem in the television world because any parent knows how to turn a television on or off and how to change a channel. While computers and the Internet are almost as easy to use, a psychological barrier exists for some that are afraid of the technology. Of course, this will disappear as a problem in 20 years when today's 8-year-olds become parents. Until then, if parents are to apply filters and use labels, they must understand both the filtering systems and a little bit about the technology. . . .

Self-regulation can and will work on the Internet. But to work effectively, an added burden is placed on parents to be more than passive figures. The easiest system for parents is one in which the government or an ISP [Internet Service Provider] merely decides what is acceptable and blocks the rest. This would be tragic in stifling what is turning out to be the world's most open, international and interactive means of communication. For the system to thrive, parents must be willing to take on the added burdens of occasionally being offended, learning how the technology and filtering systems work and, most important of all, sharing the experience of going on-line with their children.

Media Consolidation Does Not Threaten Free Speech

by Adam Thierer

About the author: *Adam Thierer is the director of telecommunication studies at the Cato Institute and is the author of* Media Myths: Making Sense of the Debate over Media Ownership.

The debate over media ownership is being driven more by myth than reality. That is, while critics of media liberalization have had great success employing heated rhetoric and extremely emotional rationales for media regulation, claims about a lack of "diversity," the end of "localism," or the supposed "death of democracy" simply do not square with reality.

Objective facts reveal that such rhetoric and claims are baseless. Indeed, by all impartial measures, citizens are better off today than they have ever been before. Regardless of what the underlying business structures or ownership patterns look like, the real question in this debate must be this: "Do citizens have more news, information, and entertainment choices at their disposal today than in the past?" The answer to that question is unambiguously "yes."

There are 7 leading myths about modern media. I'll quickly summarize each one for you.

Debunking the Media Myths

The first, and probably most commonly repeated myth, is that diversity will disappear absent extensive government regulation of the media. The reality, however, could not be more different. Today's media environment is more diverse than ever before and is characterized by information abundance, not scarcity. Citizens enjoy more news and entertainment options than at any other point in history. To the extent there is a media diversity problem today, it is that citizens suffer from "information overload." The number of media options has become so overwhelming that most of us struggle to manage all the information

Adam Thierer, testimony before the U.S. Senate Committee on Commerce, Science and Transportation, Washington, DC, September 28, 2004.

at our disposal. Consider that in 1979 most households had 6 or fewer local television stations to choose from, but today the average U.S. household receives 7 broadcast television networks and an average of 102 cable or satellite channels per home. Also, the number of radio stations in America has roughly doubled from about 6,700 in 1970 to almost 13,500 today. And there are more magazines and periodicals being produced now than at any time in our nation's history. In 2003, there were 17,254 magazines produced up from 14,302 in 1993.

A second common myth is that "localism" in media is disappearing. The truth is, while we do not really know exactly how much local fare citizens demand, citizens still receive a wealth of information about developments in their communities. That is, although citizens are increasingly opting for more sources of national news and entertainment, local information and programming are still popular and will not disappear in a deregulated media marketplace.

The third myth concerns concentration and the mistaken belief that only a few companies control the entire media universe. Contrary to this widely circulated myth, the media marketplace is vigorously competitive and not significantly more concentrated than in past decades. A McKinsey & Company analyst recently noted that "There are more than 100 media companies worldwide . . . and entertainment and media are still fragmented compared with other industries such as pharmaceuticals and aerospace." An FCC [Federal Communications Commission] survey of various media markets across America from 1960 to 2000 also showed that, "Collectively, the number of media outlets and owners increased tremendously over the 40-year period," with an average of a 200 percent increase in the number of outlets and a 140 percent increase in the number of owners. Media expert Eli Noam of Columbia University has nicely summarized why we must understand that "bigness" is a relative term in media: "While the fish in the pond have grown in size, the pond did grow too, and there have been new fish and new ponds." But, in any event, competition and concentration are not mutually exclusive. Citizens can have more choices even as the ownership grows slightly more concentrated as it has in some sectors in recent years.

> *"The media marketplace is vigorously competitive and not significantly more concentrated than in past decades."*

The fourth myth involves assertions about the future of our democracy somehow being at risk. These arguments strike me as quite preposterous since increased media availability and communications connectivity have given Americans the ability to learn and debate more about our democracy than ever before. More importantly, civil discourse and a healthy democracy are the product of a free and open society unconstrained by government restrictions on media structures or content. If government can simply ordain any ownership structures or business arrangements it wishes in the name of serving "democracy," then it raises serious censorship concerns.

A fifth myth is that regulation is needed to preserve high quality journalism and entertainment. I find these arguments very troubling since, at root, media quality is a subjective matter. Government should have no say over, or even attempt to influence the quality of news or entertainment in America. The good news, however, is that with so many media outlets available today, citizens have a wide range of options from which to choose, meaning they can decide for themselves what level of "quality" they desire.

A sixth myth is that the First Amendment justifies extensive media ownership controls, or can be used as a regulatory tool to mandate access to media outlets. This is, without doubt, the most dangerous of all the media myths. In reality, the First Amendment was not written as a constraint on private speech or actions, but rather as a direct restraint on government actions as they relate to speech. If the First Amendment is to retain its force as a bulwark against government control of the press, it cannot be used to justify ownership rules or "media access" mandates.

> *"The First Amendment . . . cannot be used to justify ownership rules or 'media access' mandates."*

A seventh and final myth is that new technologies or media outlets, including the Internet, have little bearing on this debate or cannot be used as justification for relaxing existing media ownership rules at all. To the contrary, new technologies and outlets do have an important relationship to this debate and call into question the wisdom of existing media ownership restrictions. In particular, the rise of the Internet and the World Wide Web is radically changing the nature of modern media. . . . With 72% of Americans now online and spending an average of nine hours weekly on the Internet surfing through the 170 terabytes of information available online—which is seventeen times the size of the Library of Congress print collections—I do not see how anyone can seriously argue that the Internet is not fundamentally transforming our media universe.

More Choices than Ever

More generally, my research finds that all media compete in a broad sense and that citizens frequently substitute one type of media for another. What else explains cable stations stealing so much audience share from traditional broadcasters, or that 88% of Americans now subscribe to cable and satellite TV even though "free, over-the-air" television remains at their disposal? What else explains how satellite radio, an industry that did not even exist prior to December 2001, today boasts over 2 million subscribers and is rapidly eating into traditional radio's market share? Or the fact that millions of Americans purchase daily editions of national newspapers such as *USA Today*, *The Wall Street Journal* and *The New York Times*? In fact, 49 percent of *The New York Times*' daily circulation is now outside the New York area and it offers home delivery in 275 markets. Such statistics reveal a healthy, competitive market at work; a market in which citizens exercise their right to be as finicky as they want in substituting one media option or outlet for another.

Our media world has changed, and changed in almost every way for the better. To the extent there was ever a "Golden Age" of American media, we are living in it today. There has never been a time in our nation's history when citizens had access to more media outlets, more news and information, or more entertainment. This conclusion is supported by a solid factual record. Advocates of media regulation, by contrast, continue to base their case for government regulation on emotional appeals and baseless "Chicken Little" doomsday scenarios.

In such an age of abundance, the question of who owns what, or how much they own, is irrelevant. No matter how large any given media outlet is today, it is ultimately just one of hundreds of sources of news, information and entertainment that we have at our disposal. "Indeed," as the FCC concluded when revising these rules, "the question confronting media companies today is not whether they will be able to dominate the distribution of news and information in any market, but whether they will be able to be heard at all among the cacophony of voices vying for the attention of Americans."

Chapter 3

Does the War on Terror Threaten Free Speech?

Chapter Preface

During wartime, civil liberties have occasionally been suspended in order to protect the population, and many commentators contend that the war on terrorism is no exception. Indeed, the main tool for fighting domestic terrorism, the Patriot Act, has become the center of an intense controversy. The act was signed into law by President George W. Bush on October 26, 2001, following the terrorist attacks on New York City and Washington, D.C., on September 11. The Patriot Act, which greatly expanded the powers of domestic law enforcement, was broadly touted as necessary to defend the United States against terrorism. While many in the Department of Justice, including Attorney General John Ashcroft, maintained that the act was an essential law enforcement tool in the new war on terror, the Patriot Act raised concern among many civil libertarians and civil liberties organizations. In a letter to the U.S. Senate, the American Civil Liberties Union (ACLU) expressed its fear that "the USA Patriot Act gives the Attorney General and federal law enforcement unnecessary and permanent new powers to violate civil liberties that go far beyond the stated goal of fighting international terrorism."

A particular portion of the Patriot Act, Section 215, has generated First Amendment concerns for civil liberties groups. Section 215 allows the FBI to seek an order "for any tangible things for an investigation to protect against international terrorism or clandestine activities." This means that, under the Patriot Act, the FBI can seize books, records, papers, or documents, including library, bookstore, or charitable organization records. According to the ACLU, fear of the Patriot Act has caused a marked decline in charitable contributions to Muslim groups and memberships at U.S. mosques. Americans clearly feel that any association with Islamic organizations will make them suspect, the ACLU maintains.

The Justice Department, however, maintains that the Patriot Act is necessary to combat terrorism, and that its provisions have not been used to stifle First Amendment freedoms. Barbara Comstock, director of Public Affairs for the U.S. Department of Justice, said in a July 30, 2003, statement that "Section 215 goes to great lengths to preserve the First Amendment rights of libraries, bookstores and other affected entities and their patrons. FBI agents are prohibited from using a suspect's exercise of First Amendment rights as a pretext for seeking records or information."

As the war on terror progresses, the right to free speech will almost certainly continue to be tested under the Patriot Act. The following chapter addresses this as well as issues such as the role of the press and the value of political dissent during wartime.

Free Speech Is Often Restricted During Wartime

by David Hudson

About the author: *David Hudson is a research attorney at the First Amendment Center, which works to preserve and protect First Amendment freedoms through information and education.* He has authored several books, including The Bill of Rights: The First Ten Amendments of the Constitution.

The terrorist strikes of Sept. 11 [2001] led to many casualties, including thousands at the World Trade Center in New York City. Those concerned with civil liberties worry that constitutional freedoms may be the latest victim of the attacks and the resulting war on terrorism.

Perhaps the most obvious threat to civil liberties in the wake of Sept. 11 was Congress' quick passage of the so-called USA Patriot Act—a behemoth 342-page law that provides great powers to law enforcement officials.

To some, this new law epitomizes the assault on our nation's civil liberties. The law allows the government to search a person's home without immediately listing the object of the search. The law also allows the attorney general to deport individuals who engage in any nonviolent activity on behalf of any group deemed a terrorist organization.

Georgetown law professor David Cole writes: "This provision in effect resurrects the philosophy of McCarthyism, simply substituting 'terrorist' for 'communist.'"

A related provision allows the attorney general to detain and lock up aliens whom he suspects of association with terrorists. The federal government has already detained more than 1,200 people. Cole says, "Never in our history has the government engaged in such a blanket practice of secret incarceration."

Other provisions expand wiretapping capabilities for federal law enforcement officials. Still other parts of the law allow the police to obtain information about private Internet communications under a relaxed standard of review. The statute also allows the government to obtain private information, including student records, without judicial review.

"This new law is clearly the latest in a long tradition of government overreaction in times of crisis," said civil liberties attorney and author Ronald Weich in a telephone interview. "It is part of the same strain of thinking that led to earlier overreactions in times of war and should be a cause of concern for all Americans."

Critics say the USA Patriot Act is not the only example of intolerance to First Amendment freedoms. The

> *"The American tradition suggests that civil liberties take a backseat during times of war."*

news media have been restricted in accessing the war effort in Afghanistan. Educators have been punished for a range of activities, from allegedly making anti-Islamic comments to criticizing the American war effort. A public high school student in Ohio was suspended for posting a pro-war poster on his locker. Attorney General John Ashcroft has said that critics of the war effort "give aid and comfort to the enemy."

History and the First Amendment

Justice Oliver Wendell Holmes once wrote that a "page of history is worth a volume of logic." The American tradition suggests that civil liberties take a backseat during times of war. "History shows us that in times of crisis, the suppression of dissension occurs," said Erwin Chemerinsky, a constitutional law professor at the University of Southern California, in a telephone interview.

Sanford Levinson, a law professor at the University of Texas, writes: "It is difficult to read our constitutional history . . . without believing that the Constitution is often reduced at best to a whisper during times of war."

The First Amendment is no exception. Attorney Michael Linfield, author of *Freedom Under Fire: U.S. Civil Liberties in Times of War*, writes: "Rather than being an exception, war-era violations of civil liberties in the United States are the accepted norm for our government."

War and Suppression of Freedom

During times of conflict, federal and state officials often have passed laws or engaged in practices that violate civil liberties.

For example, during the Revolutionary War, the state of New Hampshire passed a law defining treason as believing in the authority of the king of England. Many local officials harassed those loyal to the Crown (called loyalists) and required citizens to take loyalty oaths supporting the colonists' efforts for independence.

Only seven years after the ratification of the Bill of Rights in 1791, the federal government passed four laws designed to punish internal dissent during a time of conflict with France. The fourth and final law was the infamous Sedition Act of 1798. This law made it a crime to "write, print, utter or publish . . . any false, scandalous, and malicious" statements against the government, Congress or president of the United States.

The Federalist Party used the law to attempt to silence leading Democratic-Republican politicians and editors. Federalists used the Sedition Act, or related common-law sedition laws, to arrest Benjamin Bache, editor of the Philadelphia, *Aurora*, and John Daly Burk, editor of the *Times Piece*. Prosecutors also charged Republican Matthew Lyon for his critical comments against President John Adams. Lyon allegedly referred to the president's "unbounded thirst for ridiculous pomp, foolish adulation and selfish avarice."

Free Speech During the Civil War

The Civil War witnessed a similar assault on press freedoms and civil liberty. President Abraham Lincoln seized the telegraph lines, suspend habeas corpus [or the right of a prisoner to challenge detainment] and issued an order prohibiting the printing of war news about military movements without approval. People were arrested for wearing Confederate buttons and for singing Confederate songs.

Government officials shut down the *Chicago Times* for excessively criticizing the Lincoln administration. Editors were arrested, papers closed and correspondents were banned from the fields of battle. A military governor with the approval of Secretary of War

> *"Congress became concerned with internal dissent."*

Edwin Stanton destroyed the office of the Washington, D.C., newspaper, the *Sunday Chronicle*.

Prominent Democratic politician Clement L. Vallandingham was arrested for making an anti-war political speech at a party rally in Mount Vernon, Ohio. After his conviction by a military tribunal, he was sentenced to prison. However, President Lincoln changed the punishment to banishment to the Confederate states.

Several congressmen attempted to expel Ohio Rep. Alexander Long from Congress for an unpatriotic speech made on the House floor. One congressman stated: "A man is free to speak so long as he speaks for the nation . . . [but not] against the nation on this floor."

The First Amendment During World War I

The First Amendment and other civil liberties suffered greatly during World War I. Paul Murphy writes in his book *World War I and the Origin of Civil Liberties:* "A deliberately planned program of federal suppression was underway and was about to be expanded, in the form of opinion molding, Americanization, homogenization, the coercing of patriotic support, and the rooting out of disloyalty."

Congress became concerned with internal dissent, particularly with those whom they suspected of sympathizing with the Germans and the Russians. It passed the Espionage Act of 1917, which has been described as an "overt assault upon First Amendment freedoms."

The law criminalized attempting to cause insubordination to the war effort, willfully attempting to cause insurrection and obstructing the recruiting or enlistment of potential volunteers. Another section of the law gave the postmaster general the power to ban from the mail any material "advocating or urging treason, insurrection, or forcible resistance to any law of the United States."

Congress passed an amendment to the Espionage Act—called the Sedition Act of 1918—which further infringed on First Amendment freedoms. The law prohibited:

> Uttering, printing, writing, or publishing any disloyal, profane, scurrilous, or abusive language intended to cause contempt, scorn . . . as regards the form of government of the United States or Constitution, or the flag or the uniform of the Army or Navy . . . urging any curtailment of the war with intent to hinder its prosecution; advocating, teaching, defending, or acts supporting or favoring the cause of any country at war with the United States, or opposing the cause of the United States.

Famed labor organizer and Socialist Eugene Debs was prosecuted under this law for a speech in Canton, Ohio, criticizing the war effort. [Author and activist] Rose Pastor Stokes was prosecuted, in part, for writing to a newspaper: "I am for the people and the government is for the profiteers."

Excess patriotic zeal resulted in a draconian crackdown on free expression, including:

- Authorities in Pittsburgh banned music by the German composer Ludwig van Beethoven during the course of the war.
- The Los Angeles Board of Education prohibited all discussions of peace.
- An Ohio farmer, John White, was imprisoned for stating that soldiers in American camps were "dying off like flies" and that the "murder of innocent women and children by German soldiers was no worse than what the United States' soldiers did in the Philippines."
- A Minnesota man was arrested under a state espionage law for criticizing women knitting socks for soldiers, saying: "No soldier ever sees these socks."
- Twenty-seven South Dakota farmers were convicted for sending a petition to the government objecting to the draft and calling the conflict a "capitalist war."

World War II and the Korean War

The pattern of government overreaction continued during the second World War and the Korean War. During this time, the government committed perhaps the greatest civil liberties violation in the history of the country since slavery— the internment of 110,000 Japanese-Americans in concentration camps.

The day after the attack on Pearl Harbor, President Franklin D. Roosevelt gave FBI Director J. Edgar Hoover emergency authority to censor all news and control all communications in and out of the country.

Before the start of World War II, Congress passed the country's first peace-time sedition law, called the Alien Registration Act of 1940. Title I of this law was called the Smith Act after its sponsor, Rep. Howard W. Smith of Virginia.

The law prohibited advocating or teaching the "propriety of overthrowing or destroying any government in the United States by force or violence" and the printing or publishing of any material advocating or teaching the violent over-throw of the country.

The act was used to harass and punish members of the Communist Party. In its 1951 decision *Dennis v. United States*, the U.S. Supreme Court upheld the conviction of 12 people for Communist Party activity. The court wrote: "To those who would paralyze our Government in the face of impending threat by encasing it in a semantic straitjacket we must reply that all concepts are relative."

The government also infringed on civil liberties during the course of the Vietnam War. Many historians characterize this era as one in which citizens actively demonstrated for social change and brought about civil rights and civil liberties advances. Unfortunately, the period was also marked by repression.

> *"Only a free and unrestrained press can effectively expose deception in government."*

Linfield writes: "While the civil rights movement did make great strides and the Supreme Court did extend the legal framework of civil liberties, this era was one of a massive, continual and conscious program of war-time repression by the federal, state and local governments."

The violence that erupted when police clashed with protesters outside the 1968 Democratic National Convention in Chicago showed that tolerance for dissent was running quite low. In 1965, the Georgia Legislature refused to allow civil rights activist Julian Bond to take his elected seat in the state House because he made comments critical of the war effort Bond stated in a press release: "I think it is sort of hypocritical for us to maintain that we are fighting for liberty in other places and we are not guaranteeing liberty to citizens inside the continental United States.

In the famous Pentagon Papers case, the government sought to prohibit *The New York Times* and *The Washington Post* from publishing a series of articles about some highly classified documents about the U.S. government and the Vietnam War.

Then-Attorney General John Mitchell sought injunctions to prohibit the newspapers from publishing such information. The case eventually reached the U.S. Supreme Court, which in 1971 ruled 6-3 in favor of the press. In his opinion, Justice Hugo Black wrote: Only a free and unrestrained press can effectively expose deception in government. And paramount among the responsibilities of a free press is the duty to prevent any part of the government from deceiving the people and sending them off to distant lands to die of foreign fevers and foreign shot and shell."

First Amendment Fears for the Future

History shows that fears of a fragile First Amendment during times of crisis are well founded. The famous adage "History repeats itself" appears to be true in the aftermath of Sept. 11. For example, the traditional separation between church and state has been ignored in some public schools where administrators have posted religious messages and lead students in prayer. The First Amendment right of free association has been severely compromised, particularly for those connected with Muslim organizations that the government believes supports anti-American causes.

Experts warn that anonymous speech on the Internet, once a staple of the democratic new medium, could become a thing of the past. The Internet has already been blamed for other tragedies, such as the Columbine High School shooting in Littleton, Colo., and the Oklahoma City bombing. Terrorists do communicate using anonymous online speech—but so do many millions of innocent Americans.

Government officials will likely restrict access to information that they consider related to the war on terrorism. For example, several civil liberties groups have filed a lawsuit, *Center for National Security Studies v. Department of Justice*, contending that the government must turn over information regarding the more than 1,000 detainees since Sept. 11.

The suit alleges that the groups and the public have both a common law and a First Amendment right of access to "records concerning judicial proceedings."

Experts disagree on what effect the war on terrorism will have on First Amendment freedoms. Some constitutional experts say the most egregious affronts to the Constitution have occurred in the Fourth Amendment arena. But many believe that freedom of speech will be curtailed.

"I am very worried that there will be more efforts to suppress speech if the war on terrorism drags on," says Chemerinsky.

Perhaps [free speech author and historian] Nat Hentoff says it best: "This will be one of our severest tests yet to rescue the Constitution from our government."

Criticisms of the War on Terror Are Being Suppressed

by Alisa Solomon

About the author: *Alisa Solomon is a staff writer at the* Village Voice *and a professor of English at Baruch College of the City University of New York.*

At a lecture in Cleveland in March [2003], Supreme Court Justice Antonin Scalia told the audience. "Most of the rights that you enjoy go way beyond what the Constitution requires." The government can legitimately scale back individual rights during wartime, he explained, since "the Constitution just sets minimums." For an increasing number of Americans, it seems, even such minimums are excessive. [In] August [2002], the Freedom Forum's annual First Amendment survey showed that 49 percent of those polled said the Amendment goes too far in the rights it guarantees, a ten-point jump since the last survey, conducted just before [the September 11, 2001, terrorist attacks]. . . .

While we've seen a flood of antiwar activity [in late 2002 and early 2003], we've also witnessed a powerful countercurrent of political repression. From shopping malls to cyberspace, Hollywood to the Ivy League, Americans have taken it upon themselves to stifle and shame those who question the legitimacy of the Administration or the [2003] war on Iraq. When we read a story here or there about the arrest of a man wearing a "Peace on Earth" T-shirt in an upstate New York mall, or about country music fans crushing Dixie Chicks CDs because the lead singer said she was ashamed of the President, each may seem like an anomalous episode. But taken as a whole, the far-flung incidents of bullying, silencing and even threats of violence reveal a political and cultural shift that recalls some of America's darkest days.

Like any avalanche, this one started at the top, and likely dates back to the moment after 9/11 when President [George W.] Bush warned the world's nations, "Either you are with us or you are with the terrorists." From Bush on down, in the months that followed, government officials drew limits around acceptable speech. White House spokesperson Ari Fleischer told Americans to "watch what they say." Such words gained force when the Patriot Act gave the government extensive new powers to spy, interrogate and detain. When civil libertarians began to protest the curbing of constitutional rights, Attorney General John Ashcroft offered a forbidding rejoinder: "To those who scare peace-loving people with phantoms of lost liberty, my message is this: Your tactics only aid terrorists." These kinds of remarks from our government's top leaders, says Anthony Romero, executive director of the ACLU [American Civil Liberties Union], have granted ordinary people license "to shut down alternative views." The Administration has fashioned a domestic arm of its new doctrine of pre-emption.

Dissent in Wartime

Rashes of American conformity and nativism have broken out before during periods of war, social strain and insecurity over national self-definition. During World War I, the McCarthy period and the COINTELPRO program of three decades ago, dissenters lost their jobs, went to jail and endured mob violence or government smears. Today's crackdowns do not match the force and scale of those shameful times, or take the same forms. History rarely repeats precisely those excesses, which have since been declared dishonorable or unconstitutional. Though [talk show host] Phil Donahue was recently fired for his views, and charities have been canceling events with antiwar celebrities such as Susan Sarandon and Tim Robbins, the Hollywood blacklist itself, says historian Howard Zinn, could not happen again. Still, while the government expands its power even as it loosens constitutional limitations on it, the public acquiescence—and participation—in suppression threatens American democracy anew.

Henry Foner, a longtime labor organizer who lost his state teaching license to the Red Scare, remembers the "tremendous terror" he felt in the McCarthy period, as "FBI agents were all over the place, visiting people's neighbors." Now, that fear is being experienced by Muslim and Arab immigrants, who are regarded as dangerous regardless of their political beliefs. Immigrant neighborhoods like Midwood, Brooklyn, home to more than 100,000 Pakistanis, have been decimated by the loss of thousands of men who were deported or who have fled. Many still languish in detention for minor visa violations or for donations to the wrong charity. Businesses have failed as customers have been afraid to venture out even to buy their groceries.

"From Bush on down, . . . government officials drew limits around acceptable speech."

But if Arab and Muslim immigrants are enduring fear levels reminiscent of the McCarthy period, dissenters are experiencing a chill, according to historian

Blanche Wiesen Cook, "more along the lines of the total repression during World War I, though we're not all the way there yet." The government has not revived, precisely, the Espionage Act of 1917, which barred from the mails any material . . . "advocating or urging treason, insurrection, or forcible resistance to any law of the United States"; or the Sedition Act of 1918, which outlawed virtually all criticism of the war and the government. Under that law, a man was sentenced to twenty years for stating in a private conversation that he hoped the "government goes to hell so it will be of no value." Today's

> *"Patriotic vigilantism has broken out . . . across the nation."*

clampdown, though far less systematic, is reminiscent: In February [2003] a former public defender, Andrew O'Conner, was arrested in Santa Fe for "threatening the president" and subjected to five hours of interrogation by special agents because he'd said, in an Internet chat room, "Bush is out of control." Glenda Gilmore, a professor of US history at Yale, sees significant parallels with that period, especially in the "nationalist hysteria that was in the streets and in the air." Egged on by government leaders warning of the presence of German spies and "seditious" antiwar labor activists, Americans joined mob actions to contain and castigate dissenters. Though not as widespread or as violent, patriotic vigilantism has broken out again across the nation. As before, it is often spontaneous, threatening and out of proportion to the action it means to challenge.

Patriotism Can Be Violent

During the First World War, a man was beaten by fellow baseball fans for failing to stand up for "The Star-Spangled Banner." Today's patriotic outbursts are less bloody, though just as emotionally intense. [In 2002], hundreds of merchant marine cadets amassed at a Manhattanville College basketball game to chant "Leave our country!" at senior Toni Smith, who had quietly been turning her back during the national anthem all season. Practically every sports columnist and talk-radio host in the country made sure to get in his licks against the obscure Division III player.

At Wheaton College, a small liberal arts school in Norton, Massachusetts, seven housemates hung an upside-down "distress" flag on their campus house the day the [Iraq] war started. Their neighbors responded by throwing rocks through the students' windows, calling in death threats to their answering machine and strapping a dead fish to their front door, Godfather-style. Restaurants in town stopped serving kids from Wheaton, and bar patrons harassed them. Norton police recommended that for their own safety, the housemates move out for a few days. "I know it's nothing like Baghdad or Palestine," says Geoffrey Bickford, a recent political science graduate and resident of the house. "But being forced to flee from my home, having my voice silenced and living in fear because of my beliefs—that concept is so frightening."

At Yale, when sophomore Katherine Lo also hung an upside-down flag out her window, several men wielding a 2 by 4 tried to enter her room late at night while Lo was home. They left a convoluted note on her door that ended, "Fuck Iraqi Saddam following fucks. I hate you, GO AMERICA."

In the swanky Detroit suburb of Birmingham, Shelli Weissberg recalls sitting down to lunch at a cafe with her 8-year-old daughter and one of the child's friends, when a man she'd never met stomped up and yelled at her for wearing a "No War" button in front of children. The Rev. Joseph Matoush, who led peace vigils in the military town of Twentynine Palms, California, found a letter tacked to his church door with caricatures of Saddam Hussein and Osama bin Laden next to the lines, "These are your friends! Why don't you leave America now."

In Albuquerque, humanities teacher Bill Nevins was suspended because, he told the local press, poetry students he coaches wrote and recited anti-Bush verses at a local slam. (School officials say it's because he failed to supervise the kids correctly.)

ACLU affiliates around the country report cases of students being punished for expressing antiwar views. In Louisville, Kentucky, Sarah Doyle and her two older brothers, inspired by ballplayer Toni Smith, decided to protest the war by staying seated through the daily Pledge of Allegiance. Doyle's seventh-grade teacher made her come up to the front of the room and recite the pledge twice; one of her brothers received in-school suspension. Bretton Barber, 16, was sent home from Dearborn High School in Michigan when he refused to remove a T-shirt labeling George Bush an international terrorist. "I thought it was obvious the T-shirt was protected speech," says Barber, who filed suit against Dearborn High in March [2003]. He says he hopes to "send the message that all high school students have the right to express themselves."

But as the social costs increase, how many people will make use of such rights? Tim Robbins told the National Press Club on April 15 that on a recent trip to Florida for an extended family reunion, "the most frightening thing . . . was the amount of times we were thanked for speaking out against the war. . . . 'Keep talking,' they said. 'I haven't been able to open my mouth.'"

> *"Jingoistic broadcast media have provided Bush with his own 'protective league' by setting the tone for repression."*

A hush has even come over the arts, where free expression is supposed to be paramount. San Francisco's Alliance Francaise, a French language and cultural center, removed a sculpture that poked fun at the Bush Administration from its February [2003] exhibition. The Palestinian-American comedian Maysoon Zayid reports that clubs she plays regularly have taken to declaring certain material beyond the pale: No more jokes, for instance, about [Israeli Prime Minister] Ariel Sharon bragging to [Iraqi President] Saddam Hussein about the Security Council resolutions he's violated. In a joint act of self-censorship, New York's most established Off Broadway theater companies declined to participate in an April day of action called by the downtown group Theaters Against War. According to Mark Russell, executive director of the experimental performance space P.S. 122, people inside the National Endowment for the Arts have let it be known that "we shouldn't even bother to apply this year unless we have a really safe project."

> *"Confronting the right's organized censure, and the patriotic flare-ups it inspires, it's easy to become demoralized."*

This self-censorship extends all the way up to the halls of Congress, where Democrats have assured the President, in the words of Tom Lantos, the ranking Democrat on the House International Relations Committee, of "solid, unanimous support" in the war on terrorism. This silence on the part of the official opposition party serves as a restraining factor, too: Notes political historian Gerald Home. "Americans say to themselves, 'If people with money and power and influence are trimming their sails, why should little old me step forward?'"

Fear Leads to Silence

The September 11 terrorist attacks go a long way toward explaining why so much of the public has shivered quietly under this chill. "The fear in this country since 9/11," says Henry Foner, "is probably more intense than the fear of Communism in the 1950s." Already a nation primed to panic, thanks to sensational broadcast news and the Willie Horton tradition in political campaigns, a real attack on American soil profoundly shook most Americans. We've still not had a chance to recover.

Quite the contrary. Since the Department of Homeland Security began its color-coded alerts [in 2002], it has never designated the United States to be at less than yellow—at "significant" risk of terrorist attack.[1] A shoe-bomber arrest, an orange alert for Christmas, checkpoints on highways and now a simulated bioterror attack in Seattle—a constant drumbeat reminds us of our vulnerability. Facing a shattered economy, the Bush Administration fans these anxieties, sending us to buy duct tape, warning us away from public monuments and scheduling the Republican Party's convention for New York City on the anniversary of 9/11. People who are afraid want to be protected and reassured, explains Barry Glassner, author of *The Culture of Fear*. When the White House tends to those fears by laying out a plan to protect Americans, however misdirected, people do not want to see those leaders undermined.

The events of 9/11 were destabilizing in another way: They forced on many Americans the astonishing recognition that their country is not universally beloved. While some Americans responded with teach-ins or protests, others

1. The color-coded alert system has been abandoned.

have acted out aggressively—think of the 2 by 4, the broken windows, the angry outbursts—to quell the expression of these troubling doubts.

The anti-dissidents don't have to look far for validation—it's available every night from the broadcast media and most days from the halls of government. Fox's Bill O'Reilly criticizes progressive *Los Angeles Times* (and *Nation*) columnist Robert Scheer by hammering him as a "traitor"; defense adviser Richard Perle, objecting to a report on his conflicts of interest, calls [political commentator] Seymour Hersh "the closest thing American journalism has to a terrorist." When [Senator] Tom Daschle lamented the President's failure to find a diplomatic solution in Iraq, it wasn't just [shock jock] Rush Limbaugh who laid into the Senate minority leader, but House Speaker Dennis Hastert too, saying Daschle came "mighty close" to giving "comfort" to the enemy. Joint Chiefs of Staff Chairman Richard Myers even lashed out angrily at former generals who had aired reservations about the war strategy, questioning their "agenda."

[President] Woodrow Wilson officially sponsored vigilantism by forming the American Protective League, citizen security forces that spied on and intimidated war critics. But then he didn't have Fox TV. Jingoistic broadcast media have provided Bush with his own "protective league" by setting the tone for repression. Who needs government censorship when stations owned by Clear Channel, the nation's largest radio chain (reaching, thanks to deregulation, 54 percent of all American adults under age 49), can drop the Dixie Chicks from their playlists, as they did in March [2003]? Clear Channel, facing a Congressional investigation into its business practices, promoted prowar rallies in cities throughout the country.

The Administration Acts to Squash Dissent

As an inflamed public, incited by government hawks and shock jocks, does its best to shut down critical speech, the state has used force to quash expression in the public square. Local police across the country have used barricades and handcuffs to assert that some speech is more free than others.

On October 24 [2002] Brett Bursey tucked a cardboard sign under his arm and headed out to the Columbia, South Carolina, airport, where President Bash was about to touch down and stump for local Republicans. But as soon as Bursey lifted his homemade No War for Oil placard above the cheering throngs, police ordered him to leave the airport access road and take his message to a "free-speech zone" about a mile away.

When Bursey, director of the statewide Progressive Network, pointed out that people with pro-Bush banners were not being asked to move, an officer replied, "It's the content of your sign that is the problem." When Bursey refused to move, he was arrested and now faces federal charges carrying a potential penalty of six months in prison.

In St. Louis in January [2003], where Bush was giving a presentation on his economic stimulus plan, residents lined his motorcade with flags and signs.

Banners proclaiming INSTEAD OF WAR, INVEST IN PEOPLE were selected by the police for removal; WE LOVE YOU, MR. PRESIDENT was allowed to stay. Police in other cities have subjected protesters to mass arrests, questions about their political views and affiliations, and even, in Oakland, rubber bullets. Legislation proposed in Oregon would jail street-blocking demontrators as "terrorists" for at least twenty-five years.

> *"It takes powerful civic institutions . . . and vigorous open debate to make democracy function."*

Just as the range of expression permitted in the public square is constricted, traditional "free-speech zones," such as campuses, find themselves under pressure to hold dissent in check as well. Middle East studies scholars have been targeted in the past year in an aggressive, highly organized campaign attacking their positions not only on the war in Iraq but on the Israeli-Palestinian conflict. Campus Watch, launched [in] September [2002] to "monitor Middle East studies" on campus, has conducted virtual witch-hunts, posting "dossiers" on individual professors, distorting their criticisms of Israeli or US policy to malign them as "apologists for Palestinian and Islamist violence." In April [2003], Bush nominated Campus Watch founder Daniel Pipes to join the board of the United States Institute of Peace, a body designed to promote the peaceful resolution of international conflicts.

Dozens of scholars have been mercilessly harassed and threatened. According to Amy Newhall, executive director of the Middle East Studies Association, some faculty members have had to abandon their e-mail addresses because they received so much anti-Arab hate e-mail—as many as 18,000 messages in a single day. Some have been "spoofed," meaning hackers sent out anti-Semitic diatribes from the professor's own e-mail accounts. Some have received menacing warnings—"Your neighbors have been alerted to your allegiance to Islamic terrorists"—and threats of violence.

No sooner had Yale's Glenda Gilmore published an antiwar op-ed in the campus paper than she received a rush of rape and death threats. It turned out that Andrew Sullivan had set up a link from a blog denouncing her, and Pipes had attacked her in a hyperventilating op-ed titled "Professors Who Hate America."

In an article for *Academe*, Newhall notes that the purpose of these attacks is to stifle debate, and she warns that these efforts "will provide a model for future assaults."

At Columbia University an assistant professor of anthropology received so many death threats after remarks he made at a late March [2003] teach-in that he had to move out of his home and teach under the protection of security guards. The professor, Nicholas de Genova, was quoted by *Newsday* as saying that he hoped Iraq would defeat the United States and that he wished for "a million Mogadishus." An ugly statement, certainly, but not as extreme as [political commentator] Bill O'Reilly's enthusicastic on-air reading of an e-mail from a US soldier who bragged, "You would not believe the carnage. Imagine your street where you live with body parts, knee deep, with hundreds of vehicles burning and the occupants inside." On O'Reilly's remarks? Silence. But dozens of news outlets, from the *Jerusalem Post* to CNN, seized on de Genova's, portraying them as a bloodcurdling cry for American deaths, in an interview with *The Chronicle of Higher Education*, de Genova said he had hoped to "contest . . . the notion that an effective strategy for the antiwar movement is to capitulate to the patriotic pro-war pressure that demands that one must affirm support for the troops."

The debate de Genova meant to provoke, needless to say, was never engaged. In an unprecedented move, 104 Republican members of Congress signed a letter to Columbia president Lee Bollinger demanding de Genova's ouster.

The Defense Mechanisms of Democracy

Confronting the right's organized censure, and the patriotic flare-ups it inspires, it's easy to become demoralized. In the face of such effective pressure, says Gerald Horne, young people like his students at the University of North Carolina—who were born during [Ronald] Reagan's presidency—easily learn to distrust the very idea of dissent out of a feeling that the right always wins. "They have a pragmatic, if not very deep, sentiment that's the political version of 'Nobody ever got fired for buying IBM': If you want to lead a comfortable, hassle-free life and not be a loser, be with the right," he says. "Unlike in the Vietnam period, we've all become sadly familiar with TINA—there is no alternative." In such a univocal world, dissent can seem downright futile.

As the space for dissent constricts, it's global public opinion and our own domestic civic institutions of liberal democracy—the courts, opposition parties, nongovernmental organizations and the media—that have to keep the channels open for alternatives to emerge. An inquisitive and vigorous press is essential, but too much of the mainstream media quickly succumbed to Pentagon spin. NBC fired Peter Arnett for making the obvious points to Iraqi television that war planners had "misjudged the determination of the Iraqi forces" and that there was "a growing challenge to President Bush about the conduct of the war." According to a leaked memo, MSNBC's sacking of Donahue in February [2003] was the result of fear that he might ask guests tough questions about foreign policy; he was replaced by right-wingers like former Republican Congressman Joe Scarborough. *San Francisco Chronicle* technology staff writer Henry Norr was fired in April after taking a sick day to participate in an antiwar protest, and two deejays at Colorado radio station KKCS were suspended in early May for playing a Dixie Chicks tune. Aaron McGruder's acerbic antiwar comic *The Boondocks* was dropped by the *Boston Globe* in late March [2003] when McGruder penned a special antiwar "protest strip."

As for the courts, Ellen Schrecker, who has written several books about the McCarthy period, fears that they won't reverse their trade-off rights for security the way they did some decades ago. By 1957, the Supreme Court had begun to rein in the most restrictive Red Scare laws. "They're feeble now," she says. "Twenty years of Reagan-Bush have really reconfigured the judiciary." The opposition party has also failed to rise to the occasion, leaving us, says Horne, accidental anarchists, with "no electoral vehicle through which to express dissent." What we do have is a small but vibrant alternative press, growing numbers in organizations like the ACLU, more than a hundred city councils that have voted to condemn the Patriot Act or similar measures and an inchoate protest movement that thronged the streets all winter. [Progressive scholar and writer] Howard Zinn regards these outpourings as significant, "a broader shield of protection than we had during the McCarthy period."

One of the spirited chants at the February and March [2003] demonstrations went, "This is what democracy looks like." True enough, the multiracial, intergenerational demos, which brought together Plumbers for Peace and Queers Against War, corporate attorneys, public hospital nurses, students, retirees and Sunday school teachers, reflected the vast diversity and insistent expression of the American polis. But that can't be all that democracy looks like. It takes powerful civic institutions to provide checks and balances, meaningful enfranchisement and vigorous open debate to make democracy function. None other than [Secretary of Defense] Donald Rumsfeld made this point recently. He was talking about Iraq.

In at least one respect, the current situation has the potential to do graver damage than even the McCarthy and Wilson eras. Historically, civil liberties have sprung back to full force when hot or cold wars have ended, thanks in large part to the perseverance, or the resuscitation, of the press, the courts and the opposition party. But in an open-ended "war on terrorism," the day when danger passes may never come. Even if it does, the democratic muscle of the courts, the press and the opposition party—already failing so miserably to flex themselves—may be too atrophied to do the heavy lifting needed to restore our fundamental rights and freedoms.

Anti-Terrorism Policies Threaten First Amendment Protections

by Elizabeth Dahl and Joseph Onek

About the authors: *Elizabeth Dahl is the former director of the Constitution Project, based at Georgetown University's Public Policy Institute, which seeks solutions to difficult legal and constitutional issues. Joseph Onek is the Constitution Project's senior counsel and the director of the Liberty and Security Initiative.*

Since the September 11, 2001, attacks against the United States, the federal government has implemented several laws, regulations and guidelines aimed at the terrorist threat. Many of these measures have important First Amendment implications.

1. Congress enacted the principal piece of anti-terrorist legislation, the PATRIOT Act, on October 26, 2001. In relevant part, the PATRIOT Act expands federal authority to investigate, engage in surveillance of, or seize assets from individuals or organizations suspected of terrorist activity against the United States. The PATRIOT Act revises or supplements several other federal laws on which the federal government relies for authority to seize the assets of or undertake surveillance of suspected terrorists or terrorist organizations.

2. The government has adopted a policy to refuse to release the names and other information concerning individuals who were detained on immigration charges or as material witnesses in the wake of 9/11. It has also closed all the hearings of the immigration detainees.

3. On May 30, 2002, Attorney General John Ashcroft issued a revised version of the Guidelines on General Crimes, Racketeering Enterprise and Terrorism Enterprise Investigations (hereafter referred to as "the Revised Guidelines"). The Revised Guidelines were intended to expand the FBI's authority and capability

to detect and prevent future terrorist activities through such means as authorizing the FBI to enter any place or attend any event that is open to the public so long as the FBI abides by the same rules as the general public; permitting the FBI to use the Internet to investigate individuals or groups who may be involved in criminal activities; authorizing the FBI to use non-profit and commercial data mining services, as well as information voluntarily provided by private organizations, for the purposes of identifying, preventing, and prosecuting criminal activities. The Revised Guidelines replace the guidelines initially drafted in 1976 at the direction of then-Attorney General Edward Levi and subsequently amended in 1983 at the direction of then-Attorney General William French Smith and in 1989 (hereafter referred to as the "Levi-Smith Guidelines").

4. In October 2002, Attorney General Ashcroft issued a memorandum that encouraged federal agencies to withhold more information under the Freedom of Information Act (FOIA) by changing the standard under which the Department of Justice would defend agency decisions to deny FOIA requests?

The [Constitution Project's Liberty and Security] Initiative further recognizes that some important First Amendment values are likely to be implicated by other measures or actions undertaken by federal authorities and state authorities. First, Initiative members have been concerned that, in at least two cases, state prosecutors in the state of New York have arrested and charged people for violating local ordinances even though their primary activity seems to have been engaging in unpopular speech. In one case, officials are prosecuting a man who stood on 42nd Street in Manhattan and screamed that more firefighters and others should have been killed in the terrorist attacks on September 11. Prosecutors have charged this man with inciting a riot, though we fail (at least thus far) to see how this prosecution can be squared with the well-settled principles consistently recognized by the Court as protecting political speech. In a second case, state officials filed but later dismissed charges against a man at the site of the former World Trade Center buildings for displaying a picture of [terrorist leader] Osama Bin Laden. We have been heartened by the outcome of the second case, since we are hard pressed to reconcile this prosecution, like the other, with the

> *"Openness promotes widespread understanding of what our government is doing and thus is indispensable for ensuring an informed citizenry."*

long line of Supreme Court decisions granting considerable latitude for unpopular and disagreeable speech in our society.

The Initiative notes two other circumstances about which the press has reported widely but do not merit, in our judgment, protracted discussion. The first is Attorney General John Ashcroft's suggestion in testimony before the Senate Judiciary Committee that critics of the administration's policies unwittingly give aid and comfort to our enemies. The members of the Initiative view this effort to question the patriotism of administration critics as plainly at odds with our national commitment, recognized explicitly in the First Amendment, to free and robust discourse and disagreement about governmental policies and objectives. A second circumstance is the administration's efforts shortly after September 11, 2001, to pressure national networks not to release certain videotapes of Osama Bin Laden on the grounds that playing the tapes might facilitate communication among terrorists. Initiative members doubt that on this occasion there was an imminent danger warranting such an attempt to inhibit the press. It does not

> *"It is hard to imagine why over a relatively lengthy period of time the national government needs to maintain secrecy."*

appear, however, that the government has repeated the questioning of its critics' patriotism or has sought to censor press coverage. Thus the Initiative deems these actions as unfortunate, quite temporary, lapses.

Anti-Terrorist Measures Must Respect First Amendment Values

The Initiative recognizes three fundamental, related principles of First Amendment law that it strongly recommends the federal government should take, or continue to take, seriously in formulating anti-terrorism measures. These basic principles are (1) openness, (2) robust political dialogue, and (3) freedom of association.

Openness promotes widespread understanding of what our government is doing and thus is indispensable for ensuring an informed citizenry. Openness allows for robust public dialogue about important social and political questions as well as the proliferation of information that makes such dialogue possible. In addition, openness contrasts our values with those of regimes that criminalize public criticism and even put their critics to death and thus is itself a weapon against terrorism.

The Supreme Court has also long recognized that the First Amendment guarantees a right to freedom of association. This freedom extends to non-violent political activity of all kinds and precludes the government from compelling the disclosure of "affiliations with groups engaged in advocacy." This right further requires the government to refrain from harassing or imposing criminal sanctions on individuals because of their political associations.

Initiative members believe that these three principles, which form the bedrock of our democratic system of government, are applicable at all times, including war and periods of national emergency. They believe that, at all times, the government has the heavy burden of justifying restrictions on, or regulation of, speech or speech-related activity. Of course, in exceptional circumstances such as war or times of peril, the government might have less difficulty in meeting this burden, but this does not translate into a presumption that favors governmental regulation of freedom of speech, press, or association. To the contrary, the presumption required by our Constitution favors more rather than less open debate about political issues and more rather than less openness in governmental activities.

Several Anti-Terrorist Measures Violate
or Threaten First Amendment Guarantees

Initiative members believe at least five specific policies and practices of the federal government raise serious First Amendment questions. In this part, we discuss each of the problem areas.

Excessive Secrecy Constitutes a General Threat to First Amendment Values. The Initiative is troubled by the federal government's excessive secrecy since September 11, 2001. This excessive secrecy extends to a wide variety of circumstances, including but not limited to the government's ongoing refusal to release the names of the people detained in the wake of 9/11 and the federal government's blanket closure of immigration hearings for those detainees. Moreover, the federal government's excessive secrecy includes the President's refusal to allow the Director of Homeland Security to testify, even in a closed hearing, before a duly constituted congressional committee.

The Government's Policies to Preclude Disclosure of Information about Detainees and Immigration Hearings Violate the First Amendment. The federal government's closure of allegedly terrorist-related immigration hearings and its refusal to make public information about people detained in the wake of 9/11 raise serious First Amendment questions.

First, the Initiative believes that the First Amendment establishes a presumption that people should not be arrested in secret except under compelling circumstances and, even then, only with a judicial determination of the propriety of the arrest and the secrecy. At present, there is no statute setting forth specific justifications for maintaining secrecy of arrests and detentions and providing for periodic or internal reviews of the ongoing legitimacy or credibility of these justifications. Nevertheless, it is the responsibility of the judiciary under the Constitution to require federal officials to justify on the basis of particularized facts the reasons for secret arrests, arraignments, and/or detentions and to delineate an appropriate range of officials who are responsible for approving and reviewing the written records of and justifications for such arrests and detentions.

In the judgment of the Initiative, one of the most disturbing things about the secrecy regarding the number and names of detainees apprehended in the immediate wake of 9/11 is that this information is still secret [as of June 2003]. The initial justification for secrecy was to prevent terrorist organizations from understanding the extent to which the federal government had penetrated their operations or the direction of federal investigations; such a rationale, if it was ever credible, no longer remains plausible. By now, it is likely that terrorist organizations have developed relatively good information about which if any of their members or sympathizers have been detained by the United States government and about the direction and scope of the government's investigations. Many Initiative members are concerned that federal officials are insisting on secrecy more to cover up the (perhaps necessarily) random nature of the post 9/11 detentions than to protect national security.

Again, the Initiative recognizes that in light of the dangers the nation faces, some secrecy may be in order. There can be circumstances, such as the government's arrest of a close associate of Bin Laden, in which there is an important need for secrecy at the time of the arrest to facilitate other arrests or otherwise to prevent an imminent harm. To the extent the government can make the requisite showing, it would be entitled to maintain the secrecy of a particular arrest, but its burden grows heavier with time. The government has not met the burden of demonstrating why the names of all the post 9/11 immigrant and material witness detainees should be kept secret.

Initiative members agree, therefore, with U.S. District Judge Gladys Kessler's rejection of the Attorney General's interpretation of FOIA and the laws governing grand jury secrecy to support the government's refusal to disclose the names of the post-9/11 detainees. They believe further that, under the circumstances here, disclosure is also required by the First Amendment. Initiative members regard the federal government's order closing all 9/11-related immigration proceedings to the public as also being at odds with the basic First Amendment principles of openness and robust political dialogue. To be sure, members recognize that under the present circumstances more immigration hearings than usual might have to be closed, at least in part. Federal immigration law authorizes a very narrow exception to maintain the secrecy of specific evidence employed in an immigration hearing. The difficulty for the government in justifying secrecy for every aspect of every 9/11-related immigration proceeding is that it could be justified only on the dubious ground that every aspect of such hearing constitutes evidence putting national security at serious risk. It is hard to imagine why over a relatively lengthy period of time the national government needs to maintain the secrecy. Initiative members believe the First Amendment requires at the very least that the government make a specified showing as to why it requires secrecy of all or most aspects of a particular proceeding. They note that there are a variety of mechanisms for protecting classified information without totally closing proceedings.

> *"This change in standards . . . was made without any consultation with the Congress or the public."*

The Initiative recognizes that the federal courts have not ruled uniformly on the legitimacy of the administration's policy of closed immigration proceedings in all 9/11-related cases. One federal appellate court has struck down the policy while another has upheld it. The Supreme Court recently denied certiorari [or a petition to review the case of a lower court] in the case upholding the policy. In its brief opposing certiorari, the government suggested that it was reviewing its policy. The Initiative believes that the government should reverse its position and accept that a particularized showing on a case-by-case basis is required to justify closing particular proceedings in order to protect national security. If the government fails to do so, Congress has the power to require such a particularized case-by-case showing.

> *"Congress should consider enacting legislation requiring the federal government to release the names of all detainees."*

The Weakening of FOIA is Inconsistent with First Amendment Values. The Freedom of Information Act implements First Amendment values by enabling the public and the press to find out "what their government is up to." Since 9/11, the government has weakened FOIA implementation in an important respect.

The Department of Justice has lowered the standard under which it will defend a government agency's failure to comply with a FOIA request. In his memorandum of October 12, 2001, to all agencies, Attorney General Ashcroft stated that the Justice Department would defend an agency as long as its decision to deny a FOIA request rested on a "sound legal basis." The previous standard was that the Justice Department would defend an agency's denial of a FOIA request only when the release of the information would result in "foreseeable harm." This change in standards applies to all FOIA requests, not just those related to war or terrorism, and was made without any consultation with the Congress or the public.

The Changes in the FBI Surveillance Guidelines Raise Serious First Amendment Issues. The recent revisions to the Levi-Smith Guidelines permit FBI field personnel to monitor religious and political gatherings even without a "reasonable indication" that any criminal activity is involved. Initiative members agree with House Judiciary Chairman Sensenbrenner and others that these revisions, because of their First Amendment sensitivity, should not have been made without consultation with Congress and the public.

Initiative members differ, however, about the substance of the revised guidelines. Some members believe that the government may only investigate and collect information about political or religious activities protected by the First Amendment when there is some reasonable indication of criminal activity—either past or contemplated. They are disturbed that the revised guidelines allow the FBI to collect information by monitoring public events and conducting Internet searches with only a hunch that doing so may help to prevent terrorist activity. They are concerned that individuals may be reluctant to communicate freely on the Internet or attend political demonstrations if they fear that the FBI will be monitoring, and may harass or detain them on the basis of their speech or association. They believe further that as a result of the possibility of FBI surveillance (especially undercover surveillance), members of religious organizations, especially Muslims, may be deterred from exercising their religious freedom and going to their places of worship.

On the other hand, some Initiative members believe that the government's motives in expanding the guidelines should not be presumed to be hostile to First Amendment interests and that certain expansions of FBI surveillance activities of essentially public meetings and data are, under the circumstances, justified. They see no sense, for example, in prohibiting FBI agents from going to public meetings or from looking at information available to any person with a computer and they believe that measures can be taken to prevent inappropriate use by the government of the additional information it gathers.

With respect to the use of information, all Initiative members are concerned by the lack of guidance as to how long records will be retained, who will have access to them within the government and how will they be disseminated. If the FBI is going to expand its collection of information about individuals' religious and political activities, it becomes more important than ever to address these questions.

Recommendations for the Executive and Legislative Branches

The Initiative proposes several specific recommendations that would enable the federal government to achieve a better balance between protecting national security and preserving First Amendment guarantees. The members hope that these recommendations will spur public debate, receive careful attention from both executive and legislative officials, and be useful at all times regardless of whether the nation is at war.

There Should Be No Blanket Closure of Deportation Hearings. The Administration should reverse its policy of automatically closing all deportation hearings for immigrants who may conceivably have some connection to terrorism. No compelling case has been made that national security will be jeopardized by having public hearings except when classified or similarly sensitive material is being considered. If the Administration does not reverse its policy, Congress should enact appropriate legislation.

The Government Should Release the Names of All Persons It Detains Except Under Compelling Circumstances as Determined by a Court. The Administration should end its blanket refusal to disclose the names of immigrants and material witnesses detained since 9/11 in connection with the investigation of terrorism. If the government believes there are compelling national security reasons, beyond the very general reasons it has advanced thus far, for withholding some of the names, it should make that argument to the district court. If the court agrees that the government has made the compelling showing required by the First Amendment, it should review the non-disclosure every three months.

Congress should consider enacting legislation requiring the federal government to release the names of all detainees (without the necessity of a FOIA request) except when there are compelling national security reasons not to do so.

The legislation could give the government the burden of going to court when it wishes to withhold the names of detainees and could delineate the circumstances and conditions under which such withholding is authorized. The law could provide, for example, that the government is not entitled to withhold the names of its detainees unless Congress has authorized the use of military force and the need for maintaining secrecy is specifically linked to the use of such force. It could also require, that officials responsible for arrests or detentions make written records in which they particularize the facts justifying secrecy of arrests and detentions and specify a timetable for periodic review of the facts.

The Federal Government Should Adopt More Extensive Guidelines and Tighter Controls for Investigations Implicating First Amendment Values. Although Initiative members differ on the predicate required for initiating government investigations related to terrorism, they agree that the FBI guidelines need to be strengthened in several respects. First, the FBI should reinstate central headquarters supervision over those investigations—*e.g.*, of religious and political—that have First Amendment implications. Such investigations, unlike investigations of flight training schools, should not be left solely to the discretion of field personnel. Second, guidelines should be developed concerning who has access to First Amendment-sensitive records, how long such records will be retained and how they will be disseminated to other agencies. The Attorney General should consult with Congress and the public in the development of these guidelines and Congress should be willing to take legislative action if the guidelines are inadequate.

The Federal Government Should Consult with the Communities Affected by Terrorist-Related Investigations. The FBI and other agencies that are investigating and prosecuting terrorist-related offenses in the United States may sometimes lack a full understanding of the institutions—*e.g.*, mosques, schools and foundations—established by Islamic and Arab communities here. The investigation process may be more effective, and unnecessary investigations avoided, if the agencies engage in broad consultation with representatives of the affected communities.

The Federal Government Should Not Weaken FOIA. The Department of Justice should not defend an agency's denial of a FOIA request unless release of the information would result in "foreseeable harm." The "foreseeable harm" standard is broad enough to protect against disclosures that could assists terrorists and promotes the First Amendment value of openness. If the Administration wishes to change policies related to FOIA in the future, it should first consult the public. A useful model is the informal notice and comment procedure the [Bill] Clinton Administration adopted prior to changing declassification policy.

The Patriot Act Discourages the Free Exchange of Ideas

by Eleanor J. Bader

About the author: *Eleanor J. Bader is a freelance writer and teacher. She is also the coauthor of* Targets of Hatred: Anti-Abortion Terrorism.

Within days of [the September 11, 2001, terrorist attacks], the police and FBI were besieged with tips informing them that several suspects—including one who fit [September 11 terrorist] Mohammed Atta's description—had used public libraries in Hollywood Beach and Delray Beach, Florida, to surf the Internet. Shortly thereafter, a federal grand jury ordered library staff to submit all user records to law enforcement.

The order began a pattern of government requests for information about citizens' reading material that has increased dramatically since [the October 2001] passage of the USA Patriot Act, which amended 15 federal statutes, including laws governing criminal procedure, computer fraud, foreign intelligence, wiretapping, immigration and privacy. The act gives the government a host of new powers, including the ability to scrutinize what a person reads or purchases.

According to a University of Illinois study of 1,020 libraries conducted during the first two months of 2002, government sources asked 85 university and public libraries—8.3 percent of those queried—for information on patrons following the attacks. More detail is unknown since divulging specific information violates provisions of the legislation.

"The act grants the executive branch unprecedented, and largely unchecked, surveillance powers," says attorney Nancy Chang, author of Silencing Political Dissent, "including the enhanced ability to track e-mail and Internet usage, obtain sensitive personal records from third parties, monitor financial transactions and conduct nationwide roving wiretaps."

Eleanor J. Bader, "Thought Police: Big Brother May Be Watching What You Read," *In These Times*, www.inthesetimes.com, November 25, 2002. Copyright © 2002 by the Institute for Public Affairs. Reproduced by permission.

In fact, a court can now allow a wiretap to follow a suspect wherever he or she goes, including a public library or bookstore. That's right: Booksellers can also be targeted. What's more, the government is no longer required to demonstrate "probable cause" when requesting records. "FBI and police used to have to show probable cause that a person had committed a crime when requesting materials," says Chris Finan, president of the American Booksellers Foundation for Free Expression (ABFFE).

> *"The government is no longer required to demonstrate 'probable cause' when requesting records."*

"Now, under Section 215 of the Patriot Act," Finan continues, "it is possible for them to investigate a person who is not suspected of criminal activity, but who may have some connection to a person [who is]. Worse . . . there is a gag provision barring bookstores or libraries from telling anyone—including the suspect—about the investigation. Violators of the gag order can go to jail."

Implications of the Patriot Act

Members of Congress, as well as librarians, booksellers and ordinary citizens, have expressed outrage and concern over the Orwellian reach of the law. On June 12, [2002] the House Judiciary Committee sent a 12-page letter to the Justice Department requesting hard data on the number of subpoenas issued to booksellers and libraries since October [2001]. Two months later, on August 19 [2002], Assistant Attorney General Daniel J. Bryant responded. The figures are "confidential," he wrote, and will only be shared with the House Intelligence Committee. The Judiciary Committee told Bryant the response was unsatisfactory. Finan reports that everyone is "waiting to see what the committee will do next."

Meanwhile, the ABFFE has joined a coalition of booksellers and libraries to denounce Section 215. They have also signed onto a Freedom of Information Act request for information on both the number and content of subpoenas issued. To date [November 2002], there has been no response to their entreaty; though such responses are required by law, they can often take months or even years to complete.

But community activists, librarians and publishers have joined forces to publicize the threat that the act poses to free speech, privacy and civil liberties. The American Library Association, a national alliance of library staff, issued a statement in early 2002 affirming their position: "Librarians do not police what library users read or access in the library. Libraries ensure the freedom to read, to view, to speak, and to participate."

Though the ALA has agreed to cooperate with federal requests within the framework of state law, it has warned local branches not to create or retain unnecessary records, and trained staff to read subpoenas carefully before providing unnecessary information.

Despite this modicum of defiance, everyone agrees that Section 215 has begun to exact a toll. "Right after 9/11, Americans seemed eager to learn more about the world," says Larry Siems, director of International Programs at the PEN American Center. "They were reading, buying and checking out books on Islam. . . . But the administration's overall approach discourages people from seeking information. It is counterproductive. We end up with a society that is more isolated, less able to respond to the rest of the world."

In addition, he states, the Constitution guarantees that Americans have the right to read books, write books, and express their opinions. Even when the ideas expressed are unpopular—even when they're downright unpatriotic or seditious—the government should not be in the business of prohibiting them. Indeed, he cautions, a distinction between acts and ideas is imperative.

Finan and Chang agree, and they are doing their best to ensure that the Patriot Act fades away in October 2005, when it is set to expire. "At the very least," Finan concludes, "we want changes in sections like 215, to exempt libraries and bookstores from scrutiny."

The Right to Dissent Has Not Been Threatened in the War on Terrorism

by Bobby Eberle

About the author: *Bobby Eberle is president and chief executive officer of GOPUSA, a company that provides news, information, and commentary on current events.*

Since the adoption of the Bill of Rights into the U.S. Constitution, there have been few tenets as reliable as our freedom of speech. On playgrounds across the country, children pour forth with epithets such as "pigface" and "goof ball." When told by peers to be quiet, the standard response is: "It's a free country." The target of the verbal barrage would then respond in kind.

Criticism from adults works in much the same way, or at least it did until we were given the Hollywood interpretation of the First Amendment. According to Hollywood, freedom of speech (when used by a "celebrity") also implies freedom from criticism.

Celebrity Criticism

On April 15 [2003], actor Tim Robbins spoke at the National Press Club in Washington and said that a "chill wind is blowing in this nation," referring to the repercussions he says are being felt by people who spoke out against the war [on terrorism]. "A message is being sent through the White House and its allies in talk radio and Clear Channel [Communications Inc.] and Cooperstown [the town in New York where the Baseball Hall of Fame is located]. If you oppose this administration, there can and will be ramifications," Robbins said.

Robbins goes on to say, "Every day, the airwaves are filled with warnings, veiled and unveiled threats, spewed invective and hatred directed at any voice of dissent. And the public, like so many relatives and friends that I saw this weekend, sit in mute opposition and fear."

Robbins, like many on the liberal left, just doesn't get it. For him, it is perfectly fine to exercise his First Amendment rights to criticize the war with Iraq, President George W. Bush and any number of conservative policies just as long as he is not criticized in return. How dare anyone dispute his claims!

In his speech, Robbins goes as far as saying that he and his "wife," [actress] Susan Sarandon, "were told that both we and the First Amendment were not welcome at the Baseball Hall of Fame [for an event celebrating the anniversary of the film *Bull Durham*]." This comment would be laughable if it weren't so scary. Apparently, Robbins and Sarandon find it offensive that the organizers of the Baseball Hall of Fame would exercise their First Amendment rights to say what they want to say and host the kind of event that they want to host. Although it might seem unlikely to some, perhaps the organizers of the Baseball Hall of Fame wanted their event actually to focus on baseball.

> *"Yes, we have a First Amendment right to freedom of speech. But, as often as we want to say it, how many of us actually tell our boss to jump in a lake?"*

Robbins again shows his arrogance when he talks about a friend of his in the music business. "A famous middle-aged rock 'n' roller called me last week to thank me for speaking out against the war, only to go on to tell me that he could not speak himself because he fears repercussions from Clear Channel. 'They promote our concert appearances,' he said. 'They own most of the [radio] stations that play our music. I can't come out against this war,'" Robbins reported.

Statements such as these demonstrate that many liberal "celebrities" live in an isolated fantasy world. Although Robbins' friends might see that people sometimes are held accountable for what they say, many on the left do not. Many not only feel they can say anything they want and not be criticized for it, they also feel that their words and actions do not have consequences.

Freedom of Speech

Yes, we have a First Amendment right to freedom of speech. But, as often as we sometimes want to say it, how many of us actually tell our boss to go jump in a lake? How many of us would actually say "yes" when asked by our wife or girlfriend, "Do I look fat to you?" Why not? Because words are not empty. Words have meaning. Expressing thoughts as spoken words implies a willingness to face the consequences that could happen as a result. In other words, if you can't take the heat, don't open your mouth.

Most Hollywood executives hope that the films they make will be accepted by audiences and make them money. Their motivating factor is the bottom line. So, when faced with circumstances that may affect their bottom line, who can blame them for not taking corrective actions? Who can blame them? The "celebrities" can.

With the public outraged by statements from the likes of [actors] Janeane Garofalo, Martin Sheen and Sarandon, it seems quite logical that film executives would not cast that trio in a feature and honestly think it would be a box-office hit. When faced with thousands of angry phone calls about the [music group] Dixie Chicks,[1] Clear Channel stations could do one of two things: ignore the deluge of calls from its audience or stop playing the Dixie Chicks. In a simple act of protecting its bottom line, Clear Channel chose to pull the songs. Fortunately, Clear Channel seems as much motivated by patriotism as by economics, but the point is that its actions were justified simply from an economic perspective.

The cries of "conspiracy" by the left about being blacklisted for their anti-war/anti-Bush comments also show a complete lack of ability to grasp public opinion. It is not a conspiracy when 80 percent of the people agree that the war to remove [former Iraqi president] Saddam Hussein is a good thing. It is not a conspiracy when phone lines are flooded with callers complaining about the Dixie Chicks criticizing President Bush on foreign soil during a war. The majority of Americans support Bush and the war with Iraq, and for these "celebrities" to be surprised when they receive criticism shows just how out of touch they are.

The Hollywood celebrities on the left think they can do or say whatever they please and face no criticism or consequences. It's time for them to wake up and join the real world. Until then, our First Amendment rights continue to be strong. Just as strong are the consequences for using those First Amendment rights without first using our brain.

---

1. In March 2003, Dixie Chicks member Natalie Maines stated at a concert in London that she was ashamed that U.S. president George W. Bush came from her home state of Texas.

The Patriot Act Does Not Threaten Free Speech

by John Ashcroft

About the author: *John Ashcroft is a former United States senator and former attorney general of the United States.*

Editor's Note: The following viewpoint was originally given as a speech at the Federalist Society Convention on November 15, 2003.

The Federalist Society and its membership have been resolute defenders of our nation's founding ideals: liberty, the rule of law, limited government. It is in this capacity that the Federalist Society is so necessary today.

[From 2001 to 2003], you have been part of the debate about how best to preserve and protect our liberty in the face of a very real terrorist threat.

America has an honored tradition of debate and dissent under the First Amendment. It is an essential piece of our constitutional and cultural fabric. As a former politician, I have heard a few dissents in my time, and even expressed a couple of my own.

The Founders believed debate should enlighten, not just enliven. It should reveal truth, not obscure it. The future of freedom demands that our discourse be based on a solid foundation of facts and a sincere desire for truth. As we consider the direction and destiny of our nation, the friends of freedom must practice for themselves . . . and demand from others . . . a debate informed by fact and directed toward truth.

Take away all the bells and whistles . . . the rhetorical flourishes and occasional vitriol . . . and the current debate about liberty is about the rule of law and the role of law.

The notion that the law can enhance, not diminish, freedom is an old one. [Philosopher] John Locke said the end of law is, quote, ". . . not to abolish or restrain but to preserve and enlarge freedom." George Washington called this, "ordered liberty."

John Ashcroft, "Prepared Remarks of Attorney General John Ashcroft, Federalist Society Convention, Saturday, November 15, 2003," www.usdoj.gov, November 15, 2003.

There are some voices in this discussion of how best to preserve freedom that reject the idea that law can enhance freedom. They think that passage and enforcement of any law is necessarily an infringement of liberty.

Ordered liberty is the reason that we are the most open and the most secure society in the world. Ordered liberty is a guiding principle, not a stumbling block to security.

When the first societies passed and enforced the first laws against murder, theft and rape, the men and women of those societies unquestionably were made more free.

A test of a law, then, is this: does it honor or degrade liberty? Does it enhance or diminish freedom?

The Founders provided the mechanism to protect our liberties and preserve the safety and security of the Republic: the Constitution. It is a document that safeguards security, but not at the expense of freedom. It celebrates freedom, but not at the expense of security. It protects us and our way of life.

Creation of the Patriot Act

Since [the terrorist attacks of] September 11, 2001, the Department of Justice has fought for, Congress has created, and the judiciary has upheld, legal tools that honor the Constitution . . . legal tools that are making America safer while enhancing American freedom.

It is a compliment to all who worked on the Patriot Act to say that it is not constitutionally innovative. The Act uses court-tested safeguards and time-honored ideas to aid the war against terrorism, while protecting the rights and lives of citizens.

Madison noted in 1792 that the greatest threat to our liberty was centralized power. Such focused power, he wrote, is liable to abuse. That is why he concluded a distribution of power into separate departments is a first principle of free governments.

The Patriot Act honors Madison's "first principles" . . . giving each branch of government a role in ensuring both the lives and liberties of our citizens are protected. The Patriot Act grants the executive branch critical tools in the war on terrorism. It provides the legislative branch extensive oversight. It honors the judicial branch with court supervision over the Act's most important powers.

The Patriot Act Aids Law Enforcement

First, the executive branch.

At the Department of Justice, we are dedicated to detecting, disrupting, and dismantling the networks of terror before they can strike at our nation. In the past two years [since September 11, 2001], no major terrorist attack has been perpetrated on our soil.

Consider the bloodshed by terrorism elsewhere in that time:

• Women and children slaughtered in Jerusalem;

140

• Innocent, young lives snuffed out in Indonesia;
• Saudi citizens savaged in Riyadh;
• Churchgoers in Pakistan murdered by the hands of hate.

We are using the tough tools provided in the USA Patriot Act to defend American lives and liberty from those who have shed blood and decimated lives in other parts of the world.

The Patriot Act does three things:

First, it closes the gaping holes in law enforcement's ability to collect vital intelligence information on terrorist enterprises. It allows law enforcement to use proven tactics long used in the fight against organized crime and drug dealers.

Second, the Patriot Act updates our anti-terrorism laws to meet the challenges of new technology and new threats.

Third, with these critical new investigative tools provided by the Patriot Act, law enforcement can share information and cooperate better with each other. From prosecutors to intelligence agents, the Act allows law enforcement to "connect the dots" and uncover terrorist plots before they are launched.

> *"The Founders provided the mechanism to protect our liberties and preserve the safety and security of the Republic: the Constitution."*

Here is an example of how we use the Act. Some of you are familiar with the Iyman Faris case. He is a naturalized American citizen who worked as a truck driver out of Columbus, Ohio.

Using information sharing allowed under the Patriot Act, law enforcement pieced together Faris's activities:

• How Faris met senior Al Qaeda [terrorist] operatives in a training camp in Afghanistan.
• How he was asked to procure equipment that might cause train derailments and sever suspension systems of bridges.
• How he traveled to New York to scout a potential terrorist target.

Faris pleaded guilty on May 1, 2003, and on October 28, he was sentenced under the Patriot Act's tough sentences. He will serve 20 years in prison for providing material support to Al Qaeda and conspiracy for providing the terrorist organization with information about possible U.S. targets for attack.

The Faris case illustrates what the Patriot Act does. One thing the Patriot Act does not do is allow the investigation of individuals, quote, ". . . solely upon the basis of activities protected by the first amendment to the Constitution of the United States."

Even if the law did not prohibit it, the Justice Department has neither the time nor the inclination to delve into the reading habits or other First Amendment activities of our citizens.

Despite all the hoopla to the contrary, for example, the Patriot Act . . . which allows for court-approved requests for business records, including library records . . . has never been used to obtain records from a library. Not once.

Senator Dianne Feinstein recently said, quote, "I have never had a single abuse of the Patriot Act reported to me. My staff e-mailed the ACLU [American Civil Liberties Union] and asked them for instances of actual abuses. They e-mailed back and said they had none."

The Patriot Act has enabled us to make quiet, steady progress in the war on terror.

Since September 11, we have dismantled terrorist cells in Detroit, Seattle, Portland, Tampa, Northern Virginia, and Buffalo.

We have disrupted weapons procurement plots in Miami, San Diego, Newark, and Houston.

We have shut down terrorist-affiliated charities in Chicago, Dallas and Syracuse.

We have brought criminal charges against 286 individuals. We have secured convictions or guilty pleas from 155 people.

Terrorists who are incarcerated, deported or otherwise neutralized threaten fewer American lives. For two years, our citizens have been safe. There have been no major terrorist attacks on our soil. American freedom has been enhanced, not diminished. The Constitution has been honored, not degraded.

The Patriot Act and the Legislative Process

Second, the role Congress plays.

In six weeks of debate in September and October of 2001, both the House of Representatives and the Senate examined studiously and debated vigorously the merits of the Patriot Act. In the end, both houses supported overwhelmingly its passage.

Congress built into the Patriot Act strict and structured oversight of the Executive Branch. Every six months, the Justice Department provides Congress with reports of its activities under the Patriot Act.

> *"The Justice Department has neither the time nor the inclination to delve into the reading habits or other First Amendment activities of our citizens."*

Since September 24, 2001, Justice Department officials, myself included, have testified on the Patriot Act and other homeland security issues more than 115 times. We have responded to hundreds of written and oral questions and provided reams of written responses.

To date, no congressional committee has found any evidence that law enforcement has abused the powers provided by the Patriot Act.

Legislative oversight of the executive branch is critical to "ordered liberty." It ensures that laws and those who administer them respect the rights and liberties of the citizens.

There has not been a major terrorist attack within our borders in the two years. Time and again, Congress has found the Patriot Act to be effective against terrorist threats, and respectful and protective of citizens' liberties. The Constitution has been honored, not degraded.

The Patriot Act Encourages Judicial Oversight

Finally, the judiciary.

The Patriot Act provides for close judicial supervision of the executive branch's use of Patriot Act authorities.

The Act allows the government to utilize many long-standing, well-accepted law enforcement tools in the fight against terror. These tools include delayed notification, judicially-supervised searches, and so-called roving wiretaps, which have long been used in combating organized crime and in the war on drugs.

In using these tactics to fight terrorism, the Patriot Act includes an additional layer of protection for individual liberty. A federal judge supervises the use of each of these tactics.

Were we to seek an order to request business records, that order would need the approval of a federal judge. Grand jury subpoenas issued for similar requests by police in standard criminal investigations are issued without judicial oversight.

Throughout the Patriot Act, tools provided to fight terrorism require that the same predication be established before a federal judge as with similar tools provided to fight other crime.

In addition, the Patriot Act includes yet another layer of judicial scrutiny by providing a civil remedy in the event of abuse. Section 223 of the Patriot Act allows citizens to seek monetary damages for willful violations of the Patriot Act. This civil remedy serves as a further deterrent against infringement upon individual liberties.

Given our overly litigious society, you are probably wondering how many such civil cases have been filed to date. It is a figure as astronomical as the library searches. Zero.

There is a simple reason for this . . . the Patriot Act has not been used to infringe upon individual liberty.

The Patriot Act Has Not Been Used to Stifle Liberty

Many of you have heard the hue and cry from critics of the Patriot Act who allege that liberty has been eroded. But more telling is what you have not heard. You have not heard of one single case in which a judge has found an abuse of the Patriot Act because, again, there have been no abuses.

It is also important to consider what we have not seen . . . no major terrorist attacks on our soil over the past two years.

The Patriot Act's record demonstrates that we are protecting the American people while honoring the Constitution and preserving the liberties we hold dear. . . .

There is nothing more noble than fighting to preserve our God-given rights. Our proven tactics against the terrorist threat are helping to do just that.

For more than two years, we have protected the lives of our citizens here at home. Again and again, Congress has determined and the courts have determined that our citizens' rights have been respected.

Twenty-six months ago, terrorists attacked our nation thinking our liberties were our weakness. They were wrong. The American people have fulfilled the destiny shaped by our forefathers and founders, and revealed the power of freedom.

Time and again, the spirit of our nation has been renewed and our greatness as a people has been strengthened by our dedication to the cause of liberty, the rule of law and the primacy and dignity of the individual.

I know we will keep alive these noble aspirations that lie in the hearts of all our fellow citizens, and for which our young men and women are at this moment fighting and making the ultimate sacrifice.

What we are defending is what generations before us fought for and defended: a nation that is a standard, a beacon, to all who desire a land that promises to uphold the best hopes of all mankind. A land of justice. A land of liberty.

Thank you. God bless you. And God bless America.

Embedded Reporters During the Iraq War Improved War Coverage

by Jeffrey C. Bliss

About the author: *Jeffrey C. Bliss is an associate director at the Hoover Institution, which is devoted to advanced study of politics, economics, and political economy.*

When the Defense Department decided to place journalists alongside troops to cover events in real-time during the Iraq war, it ensured the fulfillment of two goals: the minimization of certain aspects of anti-American propaganda and the simultaneous provision of limited and focused information. What it also did was to bring reporters *into the tent.* As "embedded media," soldiers and scribes would travel and suffer together through battles, sandstorms, and less-than-five-star accommodations.

In short, it put them on the same team.

Although not every reporter went along with the program (some covered the war as independent, non-embedded "unilaterals" and some were outright hostile toward the U.S. military and the [George W.] Bush administration's policies before troops were even on the ground), the overwhelming response by Pentagon officials to the coverage has been positive: American forces were typically portrayed as professional, efficient, and humane, and "Operation Iraqi Freedom" was seen by most of the viewing public as a triumph. The experiment—the first new approach to military-media relations since the Vietnam War—was a success, and the levels of cynicism, general distrust, and enmity between the two sides were diminished, if not altogether swept aside, by embedding reporters with troops.

During World War II, war correspondents braved Nazi bombing raids, hunkered down in foxholes with combat infantrymen, and flew along on bombing runs over Germany. Reporters such as Ernie Pyle, Andy Rooney, and Edward R. Murrow made a name for themselves as they reported on Allied efforts—often glorifying the military's deeds and celebrating its victories. Their stories and those of their fellow correspondents kept the home front informed, bolstered morale, and built support for the war effort.

But just a little more than two decades later, journalists were covering the conflict in Vietnam, filing reports that many—especially the military—believed were not only biased against U.S. efforts but also playing a significant role in undermining support for the war against communism in Southeast Asia. Television coverage—which brought the horrors of war into the living rooms of America for the first time—was perceived as being particularly harmful to the war effort. Many in the military were left soured on the experience. Reporters had enjoyed nearly free range when it came to access during the war, and many in the Pentagon believed they had abused the privilege. Officials began operating on the premise that *the only good media were controlled media.*

During the 1980s and 1990s, Defense Department officials kept a safe distance from the press, but they realized the necessity of granting at least limited access during war. In 1983, U.S. forces invaded Grenada to rescue Americans, battle Cuban and other communist soldiers, and restore democracy to the Caribbean island-nation. Because journalists were forced to wait out the fighting on the island of Barbados, accurate—and favorable—coverage was scant. Likewise, in 1989, during military operations in Panama, Pentagon officials generally kept reporters from the front lines. Both the Pentagon and the media again deemed the coverage unsatisfactory.

At the onset of the Gulf War in 1991, journalists hoped there would be a change. To say the least, they were disappointed. The media pool was severely limited, the Saudi government withheld journalists' visas, and military briefings were conducted days after troops were deployed. Eventually, more than 1,500 journalists poured into Saudi Arabia, but they were held to tight restrictions. The media pool was small, only a few journalists were given access to battlefields, and their dispatches were frequently delayed. Only after coalition leaders realized that Iraq (of all places) was granting access did they acquiesce to some media requests.

"I was astounded by the failure of the system," Joseph L. Galloway, senior military correspondent for Knight Ridder Newspapers, said. "The United States fielded the finest combat force it had ever put in the field, and then

> *"We needed to have the maximum possible access of a free press operating on the battlefield."*

the commanders turned around and successfully hid that force from the American people."

A little more than a decade later, in the wake of the September 11, 2001, terror attacks on America, journalists were again off to a foreign war. This time the setting was Afghanistan, but the situation for many reporters was not much better. Although Defense Department officials made some efforts at improving media relations, most journalists were relegated to military facilities or guided tours. Some reporters did manage to work alongside troops or make their way independently into the hinterlands, but their numbers were small.

Then came Operation Iraqi Freedom.

While trying to garner support for a war that had more than its share of detractors at home and abroad, Pentagon planners saw the wisdom behind getting journalists in on the action. There was concern about a repeat of the visual unpleasantness of Vietnam, but officials believed the possible benefits far outweighed the negatives. So the Pentagon helped create and give credence to a new class of reporters: "embeds." Being knighted as an embedded journalist—one of the more than 600 assigned to the war—provided reporters and photographers with more than just a certain cachet, it provided them with the coin of the realm: access.

Press Access Benefits Both Citizens and Government

Although a host of people in and outside the military played a role in implementing the program—not to mention President George W. Bush and Secretary of Defense Donald Rumsfeld, who signed off on it—Joseph Galloway is credited with advancing the embedment idea (he also is called the father of the newly instituted media boot camp—an abbreviated introduction to military life and the dangers of combat for journalists, many of whom had never covered war). The noted coauthor of *We Were Soldiers Once . . . and Young* and *Triumph without Victory: The History the Persian Gulf War*, Galloway's experiences of reporting under fire date back to Vietnam. Understanding the importance of access and how all sides come up short when it is lacking, he appealed to top brass in favor of more "open and transparent" coverage. He told them, "Let the media through to your troops and they will fall in love with them just as you have done."

According to U.S. Air Force Lieutenant Colonel Larry Cox, who served as chief of the Defense Department's press desk during Operation Iraqi Freedom, recent experiences in the war on terror certainly gave the idea added impetus. "Embeds evolved from lessons learned, revelations, experiences out of the Afghanistan period," he told John Lawrence, writing for the *Columbia Journalism Review*. "We saw in Afghanistan that the Taliban, and to some extent Al Qaeda, made aggressive use of propaganda to get as much momentum behind their efforts as they could, to leverage the fact that we had relatively minimal on-the-ground independent press coverage. We needed to have the maximum possible access of a free press operating on the battlefield, not controlled by U.S. or the coalition, but in position to do third-person objective reporting that we knew would reflect and illuminate lies and exaggerations."

"It was President Bush and Defense Secretary Donald Rumsfeld who thought that embedding reporters with military units would help win the propaganda war at a time when the United States seemed to be losing it in the Arab world," George C. Wilson wrote in the *National Journal*. "If military leaders let reporters hear and see what they were doing, the resulting stories would do the administration more good than harm in the battle to win over Muslims to the American cause: This was a big part of the rationale behind the mandate to open it up."

In an interview with *Fox News Sunday*, General Tommy Franks went beyond the motives and hopes of his bosses, saying, "I'm a fan of media embeds, and it's for a very simple reason: I believe that the greatest truth that's available to the world about what's going on is found in the pictures that come from the front lines where the war is being fought. I believe that every step we remove ourselves from the fact of the picture, we become less precise in our description of what's happening. And so, if we believe in the First Amendment to our Constitution, and if we believe in the power of having our country know the truth, then the embeds have carried us a long ways in the direction of making that happen."

Coming from the head of the U.S. Central Command—a soldier who had served on the ground in Vietnam and risen through the ranks of a media-wary military—this was quite a statement. Franks was not only affirming the importance of press access but also in effect signaling that the press had an important role in the overall effort.

Embed Program Proved to Be Successful

"The war has been called the best-covered war in history, and certainly the visuals and reports from embedded reporters have been spectacular. They brought war into our living rooms like never before," says public relations analyst and former *San Jose Mercury News* reporter Katie Delahaye Paine. "The embedded reporter tactic was sheer genius. Taking reporters from behind the lines and putting them on the front lines with troops was an offer the media couldn't resist. This is a brilliant strategy and could well change the face of PR forever."

Paine, whose father and grandfather were war correspondents during World War II and the Cuban Revolution/Spanish-American War, respectively, had heard and read enough wartime accounts to know the importance of including journalists at the front. And as a public relations expert, she perceived the wisdom of embedding reporters as a solution to a problem that had dogged both sides for too long.

"The war has been called the best-covered war in history."

"The sagacity of the tactic is that it is based on the basic tenet of PR: It's all about relationships. The better the relationship with a journalist, the better the chance that journalist will pick up and report [a desired] message," she says. "So now journalists were making dozens—if not hundreds—of new friends among the armed forces. And, if the bosses of their newfound buddies wanted to get a key message or two across about how sensitive the U.S. is being to humanitarian needs or how humanely they are treating Iraqis, what better way than through these embedded journalists? As a result, most—if not all—of the stories being filed contained key messages the Department of Defense wanted to communicate."

An added benefit was that readers and viewers were also given a close-up look at the troops and the way they conducted themselves in the field. This was viewed as an opportunity to help eliminate some of the cynicism toward the U.S. military that has existed since Vietnam, according to General Richard Meyers, chairman of the Joint Chiefs of Staff. At a Pentagon "town hall meeting" reported on by Cybercast News Service, Meyers underlined the notion that U.S. military personnel had presented themselves better than anyone had ever hoped for.

"They've held up [microphones] to corporals and to lieutenants and to privates and you couldn't write a script for them better than their answers to all the questions," Meyers said. "And you wouldn't want to and it wouldn't be right to do that—but you didn't have to because they knew what they were fighting for, they knew how they were supposed to do their job."

Some Healthy Skepticism of Embedding

To be sure, though, not every journalist—embedded or otherwise—was entirely pleased with the Pentagon's program.

Writing for the *National Journal*, George C. Wilson was assigned to an artillery unit just behind advancing Marine units. He described the quick movements and tunnel vision that came with being attached to a single group "like being the second dog on a dogsled team. You see and hear a lot of the dog directly in front of you, and you see what is passing by on the left and right, but you cannot get out of the [harnesses] to explore intriguing sights you pass, without losing your spot on the moving team."

Addressing this issue, a recent report from the Project for Excellence in Journalism said, "One area of concern is whether embedded journalists, with a limited vantage point on the war and without complete control over where they go and when, are always capable of fully contextualizing the news they report. The most common criticism of the embedded reports was that they were only isolated pieces of a larger mosaic, and that relying too heavily on them would thus skew the picture viewers get. A review [of reports] suggested validity to this."

"Embedment has been beneficial in helping the military and the press each become more familiar with what the other does—under government-controlled circumstances," Wilson added. "Also, widespread embedment has generated thousands of stories about U.S. military action in Iraq, supporting the Bush administration's goal of winning popular approval for the war, at home and abroad. But these gains have been more than outweighed by the loss of the press' auditing function, which has been impeded, if not derailed altogether, by the severe constraints put on the embedded media. Embedment carries the danger of turning journalists into willing propagandists instead of auditors, into cheerleaders instead of reporters."

Sam Howe Verhovek, who reported on the war for the *Los Angeles Times* as a unilateral, said, "There's an inherent conflict built into embedding. From the military's point of view, when you embed somebody in your unit, they become family. For the reporter, that's very tricky. You want to keep objective distance from your source."

Writing for Slate.com, media critic Jack Shaffer noted, "One troubling side effect of the program was that it created a credentialing system among reporters: The embedded were considered official journalists, to whom the military would generally talk, and the unilaterals were often treated as pests with no right to the battlefield. In many instances, the military prevented unilaterals from covering the war, especially in the southern cities left in the invasion's wake: Basra, Umm Qasr, Nasiriyah, and Safwan.

"And while embedded TV journalists beamed back to the studio compelling footage of battlefield bang-bang, the networks failed to place the action in proper context," Shaffer noted. "Exchanges of small-arms fire were inflated into major shootouts by television, and minor (though deadly) skirmishes became full-bore battles. Also, the journalistic tendency to put a human face on every story hyperbolized coalition setbacks, such as the ambush of Private Jessica Lynch and her comrades."

Comprehensive Coverage Gives Context to Events

Larry Cox, the Pentagon's press desk chief, said if there were any biases he thought perspectives from embedded reporters and unilaterals served to even out one another. "Those close and direct experiences of embedded journalists are balanced by the slightly higher level of perspective that the non-embedded journalists have," Cox told the *Columbia Journalism Review.* "One of the beauties of being embedded is learning about the personality of the unit, about the color and the depth, the substance that you don't normally get if you're not associated with a unit in that way. That said, it is a type of coverage that's looking through a soda straw at a particular point in time on the battlefield. It would not have been sufficient if it had been the only opportunity for press coverage in this war. But it's not. It's one element. The others balance it and broaden it and lead to the overall goal for the military and the journalists, which is to provide an accurate picture of the war. A predictable and beneficial product of independent reporting is providing whatever information, good, bad or ugly, about the war that might exist. It is a goal unto itself to provide that in a free society. The goal of countering propaganda was a byproduct of a larger goal that derives from the operation of a free press in a free society."

Most reporters in the war zone appear to agree that embedment helped enhance coverage and few reported that they had experienced interference from military officials. Aside from instances when journalists were kept from reporting because of military, civilian, or personal security issues, indications are that they were generally allowed to write about or photograph whatever they desired.

Newsman Ray Quintanilla, who was embedded with the U.S. Army Third Infantry Division, disputed any claims that journalists candy-coated the news. "I didn't change anything because I was with a unit," Quintanilla told *Editor and Publisher* magazine. He also noted that, when military brass asked to review his reports, he turned them down cold. "The first day the captain asked if a major could read my stories and I laughed him off and said 'You gotta be kidding.' Nothing ever came of it."

> *"Most reporters in the war zone appear to agree that embedment helped enhance coverage."*

"In my view the recent media embed program for the Iraq operation was an unqualified success," Galloway said. "The media had relatively unfettered access to the front lines of a war for the first time since Vietnam—and in numbers that ensured a view of the operations across the spectrum. This is something the media had been demanding ever since Vietnam, at a time when military-media relations seemed to be in a death spiral. There was Grenada where the press was not allowed ashore until the war was over; Panama where the newly created ready reaction pool was flown south but locked up in a warehouse on an airbase until operations were over; the Gulf War where there were combat pools, under escort by military officers who had the power to censor their reports, and often frozen out of the action or unable to get their reports/film to the rear."

"Compared to the media freeze-outs of the Afghanistan campaign, the Panama invasion, and the taking of Grenada, the embed program is a huge improvement," Slate.com's Shaffer wrote. "Never in the history of war have more reporters been able to cover the conflict from the front as it happened. And just because the military ended up liking the embed program, it doesn't mean the program was bad."

Embedding Led to Excellent Coverage of the Iraq War

"The truth is, it's a win-win situation," Paine added. "We got more *and* better coverage of war than ever before, journalists had better access than ever before, and the coalition was able to get more of its messages across than ever before."

"The biggest winner was the military, which made the biggest leap of faith since they did not generally trust the media," agrees Galloway. "For the first time since Nam, the American public and the world got a clear view of American soldiers doing what they do so well in a tough combat environment."

According to the Project for Excellence in Journalism, "Americans seem far better served by having the embedding system than they were from more limited press pools during the Gulf War of 1991 or only halting access to events in Afghanistan."

"It will be interesting when the dust settles to see what the long-term effects are," said Torie Clarke, the Pentagon spokeswoman who was one of the chief supporters of the embedding program. She was quoted as saying she believes the embed program took the agenda-setting function for war coverage away from Iraq and other critics of U.S. policy and let the United States strut its stuff on a worldwide stage. "It was a good thing to do."

Gathering from the program's payoffs—more sympathetic and quicker coverage, as well as better relations between the military and the press—it wasn't just a good thing to do, it was the smart thing to do.

Chapter 4

How Should the Right to Free Speech Apply to Corporations?

Chapter Preface

In February 2003, just weeks before the invasion of Iraq, Stephen Downs, an Albany, New York–area lawyer, and his adult son went to a local mall wearing T-shirts that read "Peace On Earth," "Give Peace A Chance," and "No War With Iraq." By all appearances the father and son pair were seemingly exercising their constitutionally protected right to freedom of expression. As the two ate at the mall's food court, however, a security guard approached them and asked them to remove their shirts. The son complied, but the father refused on First Amendment grounds. The security guard contacted the police. The police asked the senior Downs to leave the mall and, when he refused, they arrested him and charged him with trespassing.

The point in question in this case was not whether Downs had the right to wear the shirt but whether he had the right to wear it on the mall's private property. Only a handful of states recognize the free speech rights of individuals on corporate-held private property, such as malls. New York state law protects the rights held by the owners of private property more than the rights of individuals who happen to be on that property. Notwithstanding the law's backing, when local activists protested Downs's arrest, the mall's management decided that it would be best to drop the charges against him. This case underscores a concern among civil libertarians: In an increasingly privatized, corporate environment, should the business interests of corporations trump a citizen's right to free expression?

An important legal precedent governs the relationship between corporations and free speech. In 1886, a headnote to a U.S. Supreme Court decision in the case *Santa Clara County v. Southern Pacific Railroad* contained the phrase, "Corporations are persons within the intent of the clause in section 1 of the Fourteenth Amendment to the Constitution . . . which forbids a State to deny to any person within its jurisdiction the equal protection of the laws." Ever since then, corporations have sought the same constitutional protections enjoyed by natural persons in the United States. At one time it was inconceivable that a corporation, an artificial construct, could be granted the same rights as a living human being. But as corporations have become more powerful, laws regarding them have evolved. Corporations now have come to enjoy some of the rights that individuals enjoy, even the right to free speech. Just as with any two individuals, however, occasionally a private citizen and a corporation find their free speech rights in conflict. The case of Stephen Downs and the New York mall provides an apt example.

The chapter that follows seeks to address the rights of corporations regarding free speech. Authors debate not only what free speech rights corporations should be granted but also what limitations corporations can place on the free speech rights of individuals on their property.

Corporations Should Be Granted the Same Free Speech Rights as Individuals

by Kathy Cripps

About the author: *Kathy Cripps is the president of the Council of Public Relations Firms. Part of her function as president of the Council is to advocate on behalf of member firms, their clients, and the overall profession.*

Just suppose that your bitter and vindictive next-door neighbor is quoted in a local newspaper article falsely charging you with mistreating the day-laborers helping you build a new garage. He accuses you of 'exploitation and cruelty,' even 'slavery.' He claims you withheld wages and refused to allow lunch or rest breaks.

You can't wait to set the record straight. But before you can, a local court issues an order saying you could be sued if you dared to publicly respond to those charges. An outrageous and inconceivable muzzling of your First Amendment guarantee of free speech, right?

Yet, incredible as it may seem, that is essentially what the California Supreme Court did to Nike, the Oregon-based maker of athletic shoes, in a recent decision that has chilling implications for corporations, consumers, and the US Constitution.

California's highest court, by a 4-3 vote, ruled recently that Nike's responses to critics who charge it with mistreating overseas workers should be classified as commercial speech that does not deserve full First Amendment protection. Despite the fact that the ruling threatens our freedom of speech, it has not received the attention and condemnation it so clearly warrants.

The Ruling and Its Implications

The ruling resulted from a 1998 lawsuit filed by Mark Kasky, a San Francisco environmental activist who accused Nike of unfair competition and fraud for stating that its overseas workers not only earned enough to live on, but were paid, on average, twice the local minimum wage. In ruling that the plaintiff can sue Nike for publicly defending itself against its critics, the California Supreme Court is seeking to silence public debate on one of the vital issues of the day.

> *"Free speech often is imprecise and flawed, but unless a free exchange of ideas is permitted, truth has little chance of being uncovered."*

In the clamor and heat of democratic debate, each side usually believes that they, and they alone, have truth on their side.

As long as all sides can make their case, the public has a chance to decide whose arguments have the most merit.

Free speech often is imprecise and flawed, but unless a free exchange of ideas is permitted, truth has little chance of being uncovered. As [the Enlightenment philosopher] Voltaire famously observed, 'In the exchanged of views, might truth emerge.'

The California Supreme Court ruling, however, adds a new and disturbing twist.

If it remains in place, lawyers will begin counseling businesses to withdraw from the public forum rather than risk a lawsuit over a viewpoint expressed in an advertisement or op-ed commentary. And the public, all of us, will suffer.

Restricting Speech Should Be a Last Resort

Nike has indicated it will appeal the decision all the way to the US Supreme Court,[1] which consistently has come down on the side of commercial free speech by striking down local and state bans on advertising. Of course, businesses are not allowed to fraudulently promote their goods and services.

And they must, quite reasonably, obey government safety and labeling requirements.

Writing for the US Supreme Court's majority in another case, an April 30th [2002] decision removing a ban that prevented pharmacies from advertising drugs mixed and created for a patient's specific needs, Justice Sandra Day O'Connor put it bluntly: 'If the First Amendment means anything, it means that regulating speech must be a last—not first—resort.'

My organization, the Council of Public Relations Firms, represents America's PR industry. We are taking a strong stance against the California Supreme Court decision as a matter of principle—and yes, self-interest as well.

Our 126 member firms are constantly advising corporations, trade associations, charitable organizations, educational institutions, and public interest groups on the most effective ways for them to respond to their critics.

The cardinal rule is to make your best case, but always tell the truth.

---

1. Nike's appeal was struck down.

If these agencies and their clients can be sued for simply seeking to broaden the scope of public debate, the public will be short-changed by hearing only one side of the debate.

We wholeheartedly agree with the opinion of Ann Brick of the American Civil Liberties Union's Northern California chapter, who argues that the California Supreme Court's decision 'shuts businesses out of the public debate on issues that directly affect them.' 'At bottom,' Brick added, 'it's up to the people, not the government, to decide who's right and wrong in a public debate on an issue like this. That's really what the First Amendment is all about.'

Our freedom as a country depends in large part on our freedom of expression.

Limiting our right to express our opinions and ideas erodes—and may destroy—that precious freedom. The four California Supreme Court justices who voted to restrict Nike's right to defend itself in the public arena should ponder the words of Thomas Jefferson: 'It is error alone which needs the support of government. Truth can stand by itself.'

'Difference of opinion,' he added, 'leads to enquiry, and enquiry to truth.'

And perhaps, at this turbulent time in our nation's history, another quotation is apropos: during the early, dark days of World War II, the legendary broadcast journalist Edward R. Murrow noted: 'We cannot defend freedom abroad by deserting it at home.'

Corporations Do Not Have the Right to Free Speech

by Carl J. Mayer and Brenda Wright

About the authors: *Carl J. Mayer is a former professor at Hofstra Law School. He has written widely on corporations and the Constitution. Brenda Wright is the managing attorney for the National Voting Rights Institute in Boston, Massachusetts.*

Editor's Note: The following brief was delivered before the U.S. Supreme Court in 2003 in Nike Inc. et al. v. Marc Kasky. *The court dismissed Nike's challenge.*

To preserve the integrity of the "marketplace of ideas," a business corporation's factual statements about its own operations must be subject to regulation for accuracy, regardless of whether they are categorized as commercial or noncommercial speech.

In this case,[1] Nike, a business corporation, seeks First Amendment protection for false factual statements about its own operations, by arguing that those statements do not constitute commercial speech under this Court's precedents. [This brief] submits that no purpose is served by parsing the distinction between commercial and non-commercial speech when a business corporation seeks to shield from regulation false factual statements about its own operations. Regardless of the pigeonhole into which they are placed, the factual assertions made by Nike may be regulated for their accuracy. "Untruthful speech, commercial or otherwise, has never been protected for its own sake." *Virginia State Bd. of Pharmacy v. Virginia Citizens Consumer Council, Inc.* . . .

> There is no constitutional value in false statements of fact. Neither the intentional lie nor the careless error materially advances society's interest in 'unin-

---

1. Marc Kasky had filed suit against Nike for making false claims regarding its business practices. Nike defended itself by claiming that its remarks were not commercial speech and protected by the First Amendment. Ultimately, the California Supreme Court decided in favor of Kasky.

Carl J. Mayer and Brenda Wright, Amicus Curiae Brief, *Nike Inc., et al. v. Marc Kasky*, U.S. Supreme Court, 2003.

hibited, robust, and wide-open' debate on public issues. . . . They belong to that category of utterances which are no essential part of any exposition of ideas, and are of such slight social value as a step to truth that any benefit that may be derived from them is clearly outweighed by the social interest in order and morality.

Gertz v. Robert Welch, Inc. . . .

Because nothing in this Court's precedents establishes a constitutional right for business corporations to make false statements of fact about their own operations, and regulation of the truthfulness of such statements imperils no First Amendment values, this Court should affirm the decision of the California Supreme Court regardless of how it determines the statements at issue should be categorized. . . . This conclusion is further enforced by the fact that, because of its corporate status, Nike's First Amendment rights stand on a different footing than those afforded to individuals, and certainly do not include First Amendment protection for the statements at issue here.

The Rights of the Listener

The speech of business corporations has been protected primarily for its presumed value to the listening public rather than because of a putative right of corporate self-expression. . . . In *First National Bank of Boston v. Bellotti* . . . when the Court held that corporations could not be banned from spending money to influence the outcome of a vote on a ballot initiative, the decision rested on the right of the public not to be deprived of different views within the "marketplace of ideas" rather than on any First Amendment right of business corporations to engage in such speech. . . . But neither *Bellotti* nor subsequent cases establish that a false factual statement by a corporation concerning its own business operations would obtain First Amendment protection under the rubric of its "capacity for informing the public.". . .

The "hearer-centered" basis for the protection of speech under the First Amendment is philosophically different from the traditional "speaker-centered" protection granted to individuals. . . . The "right to speak" protects the right of self-expression; the "right to hear," on the other hand, protects the interchange of ideas rather than protecting the dignity of the speaker. . . . As seen in the commercial speech context, . . . the "hearer-centered" protection of speech allows more expansive regulation of speech than "speaker-centered" protection. Similarly, the "hearer-centered" protection accorded to business corporations allows more expansive regulation of their speech than does the "speaker-centered" protection afforded to individual citizens. . . .

> *"Nike's First Amendment rights stand on a different footing than those afforded to individuals."*

When speech is protected on behalf of the listener, regulations that safeguard the ability of the listener to evaluate the information and thereby protect the integrity of the "marketplace of ideas" are permissible. For example, in *Austin v. Michigan Chamber of Commerce* . . . this Court upheld a regulation of corporate expenditures for political advocacy—protected for its value in the marketplace of ideas—which the Court had already determined unconstitutional as applied to a not-for-profit political advocacy organization. . . . In *Austin*, a business organization, organized as a corporation, challenged a statute prohibiting corporations from using corporate treasury funds for independent expenditures in support of or in opposition to candidates in elections for state office. The statute allowed corporations to make such expenditures from segregated funds used solely for political purposes. Although "expressive rights [were] implicated" by the prohibition of the use of corporate treasury funds, this Court nevertheless upheld the regulation. According to the Court, the regulation corrected for the advantages, gained by "the unique state-conferred corporate structure that facilitates the amassing of large treasuries," that corporations have over others in advancing their ideas by addressing the "distorting effects of immense aggregations of wealth . . . that have little or no correlation to the public's support for the corporation's political ideas," (*Austin*, 494 U.S. at 660). By contrast, the Court struck down the same requirement as applied to a not-for-profit political advocacy organization because the organization, which was formed for the dissemination of political ideas, did not pose the same problem of distorting the "marketplace of political ideas.". . .

> *"When speech is protected on behalf of the listener, regulations that safeguard the ability of the listener to evaluate the information . . . are permissible."*

Accurate Information Trumps Self-Expression

Like the commercial marketplace, the "marketplace of ideas" needs accurate information to function efficiently. Within the "marketplace of ideas," however, the countervailing First Amendment interest in individual self-expression generally prevents regulation of the content of speech. . . .

That countervailing First Amendment value has limited application to business corporations. Although the Court at times has assumed that corporations like Nike enjoy some limited "self-expressive" protection, the analyses in such cases clearly derive from the protection accorded to the listening public. . . . "Moreover, on the occasions when the Court has struck down regulations of the speech of business corporations, it has been to serve the integrity of the marketplace of ideas by preventing broad bans on speech concerning various public policy topics, . . . or has been akin to the protection of associational rights, such that a corporation cannot be compelled to "speak" contrary to its views. . . . There is no reason to grant First Amendment protection to false factual statements made by a business corporation about *its own operations*, however, because such statements *corrupt* the marketplace of ideas without serving any countervailing interest for speech protection.

In *Virginia State Bd. of Pharmacy v. Virginia Citizens Consumer Council, Inc.* . . . this Court recognized that the First Amendment provides some protection of commercial speech for similar reasons: because of the "consumer's interest in the free flow of commercial information.". . . Because the speech is protected for its informational value to the public, the Court recognized that regulations protecting against false or misleading information are permissible. . . . *Virginia State Bd. of Pharmacy* explained that regulations of the accuracy of speech are permissible when the speech has "greater objectivity and hardiness" than other types of speech. . . . For example, commercial speech satisfies the standard because it is "more easily verifiable by its disseminator than . . . news reporting or political commentary. . . . Also, commercial speech may be more durable than other kinds. Since advertising is the sine qua non of commercial profits, there is little likelihood of its being chilled by proper regulation and forgone entirely.". . .

This rationale for the permissibility of the regulation of truthfulness is just as applicable here—regardless of whether Nike's speech is categorized as commercial or non-commercial. Nike is in the best position to verify the accuracy of the particular speech at issue, and Nike's speech is unlikely to be chilled because it is motivated by Nike's own bottom line. The statements at issue, which concern Nike *itself* and how Nike conducts its own business, are within Nike's control and therefore Nike is in the best position to verify them. Thus, unlike in other First Amendment contexts in which the listening public may assess inaccuracies or inconsistencies by comparison with other contradictory speech, the public here cannot adequately assess Nike's speech because others have limited access to the facts.

This important fact—that the statements were about Nike itself—and the burden of proof under California's Unfair Competition Law, . . . distinguish the instant case from *New York Times v. Sullivan* . . . , and other defamation cases. In those cases, the facts at issue were not about the *speaker* but rather were about the plaintiff who brought the lawsuit. Moreover, the plaintiffs had only to prove the harm of the allegedly defamatory statements while the defendants, whose speech was at issue, had the burden to prove the truthfulness of the statements. This was an important factor for the Court's imposition of a heightened intent requirement in defamation cases regarding public officials. . . . Here, by contrast, the facts are about the speaker and it is the *plaintiff*—not the speaker-defendant—who has the burden of proving the falsity of the statements at issue. Thus, the procedural posture here is the mirror-image of the defamation and media cases that have come before the Court.

> *"There is no reason to grant First Amendment protection to false factual statements made by a business corporation about its own operations."*

Corporate Speech Is Designed to Enhance Profit

Moreover, Nike's communications—the communications of a business corporation—like commercial speech, are not likely to be chilled by regulation for truthfulness because of the presence of the profit motive. When a business corporation acts or "speaks," it is "with a view to enhancing corporate profit and shareholder gain." (1 *Principles of Corp. Governance*) . . . Even when a corporation engages in the activity related to the public welfare or for other reasons that are not directly business-related, there is generally a business-related motive for the conduct . . . Nike's conduct—and its factual assertions—were made with an eye toward maximizing shareholder value and therefore are unlikely to be chilled if regulated for truthfulness.

Indeed, Nike admits that its conduct was motivated by the desire to maximize shareholder value. . . . This view is also supported by various of Nike's [briefs], [which] state, "Because corporations are entities whose decision makers owe fiduciary duties to shareholders and owners, *no responsible corporate spokesman speaks on a company's behalf without being concerned about the effects, the statements may have on corporate sales and profits."* . . . But, contrary to the arguments of Nike and its [briefs], this does not make the profit-oriented motivation of the speech irrelevant in determining the constitutionality of regulating false statements about a corporation's own operations. To the contrary, it provides assurance that the kind of "chill" that sometimes prevents regulation of the accuracy of individuals' speech is unlikely to deter protected corporate speech.

> *"Even when a corporation engages in activity related to the public welfare . . . there is generally a business-related motive for the conduct."*

Regardless of the formal "category" of Nike's speech, Respondent's lawsuit is permissible because it serves the First Amendment interests of the listening public by protecting the integrity of the marketplace of ideas. Moreover, by establishing liability for specific asserted false factual statements, the challenged regulation is exactly tailored to ensure the accuracy of factual information asserted by a business corporation about itself in the marketplace of ideas. Accordingly, the Court should affirm the decision of the California Supreme Court.

Corporations Are Not Natural Persons

In the alternative, to the extent [the Supreme] Court's precedents establish First Amendment rights for corporations coextensive with those of individuals, the Court should use this case as an opportunity to overrule that constitutional interpretation.

Contrary to the arguments advanced [thus far] Nike has assumed that this Court's precedents grant the same level of First Amendment protection to non-commercial corporate speech as they do to speech of natural persons. In this section, [this brief] argues that, to the extent [the Supreme] Court has interpreted the First Amendment to grant protection to business corporations coextensive with that granted to individuals, [the] Court should use this case to overrule that constitutional interpretation.

Corporations, which are creations of state law, are not entitled to the same protections as individuals under the Bill of Rights. Corporations are artificial entities created by law for the purpose of furthering certain economic goals. A charter of incorporation is a *privilege*, not a right, conferred by state law that grants certain benefits to which a company would not otherwise be entitled. For example, the corporate form shields shareholders—the corporation's owners—from liability they would otherwise suffer for damages caused or debts incurred by their company. . . . Business corporations also enjoy perpetual existence and a host of other advantages to assist in their aggregation of wealth through commercial activity. . . . Given the benefits and advantages provided by the state, it is not unreasonable for the state to regulate business corporations to ensure that they do not use the economic benefits granted by the state for unfair advantage in other arenas of civic life. . . .

> *"Corporations, which are creations of state law, are not entitled to the same protections as individuals under the Bill of Rights."*

Specifically, it is reasonable for a state to regulate business corporations when they attempt to influence public policy and engage in public debate. Corporate speech, which by definition must be geared toward maximizing shareholder value over all else, does not express the views of citizens and therefore should not be given First Amendment protection coextensive with that provided to individual citizens. . . . Simply stated, corporations are not natural persons and should not benefit directly from the protections of the First Amendment. . . .

Corporations Were Never Meant to Have the Rights of Individuals

Neither the framers of the Constitution and the Bill of Rights nor the framers of the Civil War Amendments intended that corporations should be afforded the protections of constitutional provisions. First, although the Framers were clearly aware of corporations—state legislatures of the era chartered banks, canal companies, railroads, toll bridge companies, and trading companies as corporations—the Constitutional provisions do not specifically include corporations. . . . The exclusion of the term "corporation" from the express language of the Constitution is therefore significant.

Case law from early in this country's history also suggests that corporations were not intended to enjoy constitutional protections. The Court consistently relied on the "artificial entity" theory, viewing the corporation as nothing more than an artificial creature of the state, subject to government imposed limitations and restrictions. Under this view, corporations cannot assert constitutional rights against the state, their creator. . . . As Chief Justice Marshall observed:

> A corporation is an artificial being, invisible, intangible, and existing only in contemplation of law. *Being the mere creature of law, it possesses only those properties which the charter of creation confers upon it, either expressly, or as incidental to its very existence.* These are such as are supposed best calculated to effect the object for which it was created. . . .

Nineteenth century case law, both before and after the enactment of the Civil War Amendments to the Constitution, recognized that the Framers did not intend the Constitution to protect corporations as it protects natural persons. Thus, the Court ruled that corporations are not "persons" or "citizens" for purposes of Article III of the Constitution, *Bank of United States v. Deveaux,* and also that corporations are neither "citizens" nor persons for purposes of the Privileges and Immunities Clause of Article IV of the Constitution, *Bank of Augusta v. Earl.* . . . Subsequent to the passage of the Fourteenth Amendment, this Court determined that corporations are not citizens for purposes of the Fourteenth Amendment Privileges and Immunities Clause, . . . and that the liberty protected by the due process clause of the Fourteenth Amendment (through which the First Amendment is incorporated as against the states . . . "is the liberty of natural, not artificial persons," *Northwestern Nat'l Life Ins. Co. v. Riggs.* . . .

Even now, it is clear that business corporations do not enjoy the same level of constitutional rights or protections as natural persons. Corporations, for example, do not enjoy the privilege against self-incrimination.

> *"Case law from early in the country's history . . . suggests that corporations were not intended to enjoy constitutional protections."*

. . . They do not enjoy the protection of the privileges and immunities clause of the Fourteenth Amendment. . . . Nor do they have a right to privacy under the Fourth Amendment. . . . Indeed, this Court implicitly relied on the artificial entity theory to hold that corporations do not enjoy the same First Amendment protections as individuals. . . .

Corporations Are Not "Personified"

Although this Court on occasion has granted constitutional rights to corporations . . . , the Court has never provided a rationale for "personifying" corporations. Indeed, the initial grant of "personhood" under the Fourteenth Amendment to corporations was, to a certain extent, a judicial mistake. Corporate personhood is generally attributed to the Court's decision in *Santa Clara County v. Southern Pacific Railroad Co.,* . . . although the Court in that case specifically declined to address the issue. In *Santa Clara County,* Santa Clara County sued the Southern Pacific Railroad Company for failure to pay taxes, and the railroad presented the Court with six defenses, including the argument that corporations were persons under the Equal Protection Clause of the Fourteenth Amendment. Because one of the other five defenses was successful, the Court had no occasion to decide the question of corporate personhood and specifically declined to do so:

> If these [other] positions are tenable, there will be no occasion to consider the grave questions of constitutional law upon which the case was determined below; for, in that event, the judgment can be affirmed upon the ground that the assessment cannot properly be the basis of a judgment against the defendant.

> As the judgment can be sustained upon this [other] ground, it is not necessary to consider any other questions raised by the pleadings and the facts found by the court. . . .

Indeed, in a companion case, Justice Field in a concurring opinion lamented that the "tax cases from California" did not "decide the important constitutional questions involved." *County of San Bernardino v. Southern Pac. R. Co.* . . .

Nevertheless, it appears that the court reporter, J.C. Bancroft Davis, included a headnote stating, "The defendant Corporations are persons within the intent of the clause in section 1 of the Fourteenth Amendment to the Constitution of the United States, which forbids a State to deny to any person within its jurisdiction the equal protection of the laws.". . . Perhaps as a result, in dicta in three cases over the subsequent three years, this Court cited *Santa Clara County* without explanation for the proposition that corporations are persons within the meaning of the equal protection clause of the Fourteenth Amendment. . . . It is notable, however, that these cases nevertheless viewed legislative classifications based in part on corporate status as permissible. . . .

Notwithstanding the mistaken "personification" of corporations in *Santa Clara*, the Court's subsequent rulings reveal that this Court has not consistently applied the implications of the corporate personhood doctrine created by *Santa Clara*. Thus, shortly after *Santa Clara*, this Court ruled that corporations are "persons" for purposes of both due process and equal protection under the Fourteenth Amendment. . . .

Likewise, the Court utilized the artificial entity theory to deny corporations Fifth Amendment privileges against self-incrimination in *Hale v. Henkel*. . . . The Court held that the phrase "no person" in the privileges portion of the Fifth Amendment does

> *"It is clear that business corporations do not enjoy the same level of constitutional rights or protections as natural persons."*

not suggest that corporations should be included within the amendment's protections. The majority then rendered its most expansive rendition of the artificial entity theory, drawing a sharp distinction between the individual and the corporation:

> The individual may stand upon his constitutional rights as a citizen. . . . His rights are such as existed by the law of the land long antecedent to the organization of the state, and can only be taken from him by due process of law, and in accordance with the Constitution. . . .

Upon the other hand, the corporation is a creature of the state. . . . It receives certain special privileges and franchises, and holds them subject to the laws of the state and the limitations of its charter. Its powers are limited by law. It can make no contract not authorized by its charter. Its rights to act as a corporation are only preserved to it so long as it obeys the laws of its creation. There is a reserved right in the legislature to investigate its contracts and find out whether it has exceeded its powers. It would be a strange anomaly to hold that a state, having chartered a corporation to make use of certain franchises, could not, in the exercise of its sovereignty, inquire how these franchises had been employed, and whether they had been abused, and demand the production of the corporate books and papers for that purpose. . . .

Since the *Santa Clara* opinion, distinguished dissents have lamented corporate personhood. Justice Hugo Black famously remarked, "I do not believe the word 'person' in the Fourteenth Amendment includes corporations." . . . Justice Douglas observed, "There was no history, logic or reason given to support that view [that corporations are persons under the Equal Protection Clause]. Nor was the result so obvious that exposition was unnecessary." *Wheeling Steel Corp. v. Glander.* . . . And then-Justice Rehnquist argued that "[t]he State need not permit its own creation to consume it." *Bellotti, 435.* . . .

> *"Corporations are entitled only to those constitutional protections that are necessary to effectuate their purpose for existence."*

In sum, the Court should return to Chief Justice Marshall's standard for the regulation of business corporations: Corporations are entitled only to those constitutional protections that are necessary to effectuate their purpose for existence. As state creations, however, corporations should remain subject to state regulations that do not impinge on constitutional rights that are "incidental" (in the Justice Marshall sense, *i.e.* necessary) to their existence rather than become federalized by the grant of broad constitutional protections to artificial entities.

Corporate Speech Does Not Merit First Amendment Protection

The right to non-commercial speech is not "incidental" (in the Justice Marshall sense, *i.e.* necessary) to the existence of business corporations. As stated eloquently by then-Justice Rehnquist in his *Bellotti* dissent:

> It cannot be so readily concluded that the right of political expression is equally necessary to carry out the functions of a corporation organized for commercial purposes. A State grants to a business corporation the blessings of potentially perpetual life and limited liability to enhance its efficiency as an economic entity. It might reasonably be concluded that those properties, so beneficial in the economic sphere, pose special dangers in the political sphere. Furthermore, it might be argued that liberties of political expression are not at all necessary to effectuate the purposes for which States permit commercial corporations to exist. So long as the Judicial Branches of the State and Federal

Governments remain open to protect the corporation's interest in its property, it has no need, though it may have the desire, to petition the political branches for similar protection. Indeed, the States might reasonably fear that the corporation would use its economic power to obtain further benefits beyond those already bestowed. . . .

Finally, one critical function of the First Amendment is not served in any way by granting free speech rights to business corporations: the use of communication as a means of self-expression, self-realization, and self-fulfillment. . . . Communication by a business corporation does "not represent a manifestation of individual freedom or choice," nor does it necessarily represent the views of its shareholders, who do not share and have not invested their money for the advancement of "a common set of political or social views." *Bellotti.* . . . "To ascribe to such artificial entities an 'intellect' or 'mind' for freedom of conscience purposes is to confuse metaphor with reality.". . . When speech is not the product of individual choice and emanates from a speaker to whom "individual self-expression" is meaningless, the speech should not receive full First Amendment protection. . . .

Nike, a business corporation, is in the business of selling itself, its athletic apparel, and other products. Although it operates in the global marketplace, the factual assertions it made about itself and its business practices are simply not essential to its existence (except as a means to sell its products, in which case the statements at issue are commercial speech) nor were they necessary for self-expression, inasmuch as there is no "self" of a business corporation. Nike is an entity whose existence has been legislated into reality by the State and which should remain subordinate, not superior, to state government, which grants it the privilege of existence or of doing business within the state. Because the speech at issue was the speech of a business corporation, there is no reason to allow Nike to avoid defending itself against Marc Kasky's lawsuit.

Broadcast Media Conglomerates Promote Free Speech

by Anthony J. Dukes

About the author: *Anthony J. Dukes is an assistant professor at the School of Economics and Management at the University of Aarhus in Denmark. He has a Ph.D. in economics, and conducts research concerning the economics of advertising, marketing, and commercial media.*

A great deal of debate has arisen over the Federal Communications Commission's (FCC) proposed ownership guidelines, which were rejected by Congress last fall [2003]. Nevertheless, incentives for media companies to lobby for ownership reform still exist, and we are likely to see this debate again. Thus, a discussion of the issue is worthwhile.

The conflict begins with media companies such as Clear Channel Communications, CBS/Viacom, and others. They have appealed to the FCC to relax restrictions that prevent them from owning wider access to television viewers, radio listeners, newspaper readers, and generally anybody whom advertisers wish to reach. Current restrictions limit, for example, any single company from reaching more than 35 percent of the nation's television audience. The next FCC initiative probably will propose relaxing this to around 40 percent as well as relaxing other limitations on cross-ownership of media.

Members of the media industry desire looser ownership restrictions because they feel that there is much duplication in media production, which, when consolidated, would allow companies to provide media services, such as the production and delivery of your local news, more cheaply. For an example already in place, consider Baltimore-based Sinclair Broadcasting, which owns local-affiliate television stations in Michigan and in Alabama, among sixty other locations. Sinclair consolidates costs by using the same Baltimore employee to

Anthony J. Dukes, "The FCC and Media Regulation," *Phi Kappa Phi Forum*, vol. 84, Winter 2004.

broadcast weather reports for Flint, as well as for Birmingham. Generally such cost saving is an incentive for firms to merge. Regulatory authorities allow for these mergers if they feel that some of these savings are passed on to consumers via lower prices or innovative new products.

Many consumer groups and free-speech organizations see mergers in the media industry differently. Their opposition against looser ownership restrictions is rooted in the expectation that program diversity and journalistic plurality will be sacrificed. These groups argue that big media companies would grow even bigger, swallow up smaller media outlets, and consolidate the media industry into a few corporate giants. The giant media companies would then have even more control over what views, opinions, and programming the nation's citizenry would or would not see.

Economic Factors in the Consolidation Debate

An economic perspective can help sort out the elements of this debate. The media industry, which includes television, radio, newspapers and magazines, and the internet, to name a few, is unique when compared to most other industries such as, for instance, automobiles. For example, customers, or end users, pay for the cars that they wish to buy. However, the end user of a television program does not typically pay for that program. There is, of course the exception of pay-per-view shows, but that is not at issue in the current debate. And while we might pay a service fee for cable or satellite, we are not paying per use of the television programming.

Television and radio users pay for broadcasts indirectly by patronizing the advertisers who have sponsored the program. The bulk of media's revenues comes, in fact, from these advertisers rather than from service fees paid by your local cable or satellite provider. As a result of this unusual payment system, advertisers seek programming that reaches a lot of people. Commercial programming is thus chosen to appeal to popular tastes.

"Fewer media companies might actually provide more variety in programming and perspectives than a collection of many smaller media companies."

For instance, situation comedies about thirty-somethings and crime dramas are never in short supply, while educational or cultural programming is harder to find. We typically rely on public broadcasting, rather than commercial broadcasting, to provide the latter.

The surprising outcome of this payment system is that fewer media companies might actually provide more variety in programming and perspectives than a collection of many smaller media companies. To take a simple, illustrative example, suppose three-fourths of the population liked crime dramas, and only one-fourth liked educational shows. Two independent commercial-television stations seeking to maximize viewers would prefer to offer two different crime dramas rather than to offer educational programming because obtaining half of three-fourths is better than obtaining one-fourth. However, if only one company owned both commercial stations, then it would maximize its audience by offering one crime drama and one educational program because this strategy would capture the entire market. This theory suggests, therefore, that the proposed ownership policies of the FCC would broaden the variety of broadcast alternatives and avoid wasteful duplication of similar programming.

Media Companies Have Changed

So why do FCC critics, such as Americans for Radio Diversity and many others, not subscribe to this theory? Note that the theory assumes that the objective of media firms is to maximize its audience to attract advertising revenue. Suppose media owners, on the other hand, had political ambitions or sought to acquire power rather than profit. Then a consolidation of media ownership would lead to a loss in plurality of public discourse; power-seeking media owners, or those in the pocket of rich politicians, could take control of editorial content, deny the public alternative viewpoints, and propagate support for their own political agenda.

Such a situation is not without precedent. In the early twentieth century, media-mogul William Randolph Hurst used his newspaper empire to offer editorial support for his own senate bid and to give his lover's latest movies rave reviews.

But the media industry now is quite different from that of the early twentieth century. The key difference is that media companies are no longer made up of a singularly rich, Hurst-type magnate, nor are they owned by political institutions, such as the government. Rather, these media companies arc owned by investors who expect executives to run a profitable company, not to run for public office or shape policy. This more-modern form of corporate governance provides incentives for media companies to earn profits and puts the media industry in line with the audience-maximization assumption of the theory outlined above.

As an example, take NewsCorp's FOX Broadcasting, which is known to offer a center-right stance on public issues. Several years ago, FOX entered the television industry believing that many viewers felt conservative perspectives were lacking. It has been successful because it attracts viewers, which in turn attracts advertising revenue. This example illustrates how market incentives can fill the need for plurality in journalism.

Contrasting Viewpoints Prosper

That is not to say that the profit motive solves all of the media industry's potential problems. In particular, if existing media companies are permitted to use their market power to prevent entry by a new competing player, this power would have the undesirable consequence of denying the public an alternative perspective. Therefore, some degree of regulation in the media industry remains necessary. As such, it should be the FCC's role to ensure that competitive entry is possible.

It is also useful to point out that since June 2003, when the FCC proposal was announced, ReclaimTheMedia.org and hundreds of other groups have erected new media posts, on the internet for example, to organize an opposition voice. This outpouring of opposition precisely illustrates that it is easy to propagate contrasting viewpoints. Perhaps we forget how many more sources of opinion we have in today's world. Just look back a few years ago, before the internet and before Americans had more than a handful of television options (ABC, CBS, NBC, and a couple of UHF channels), and a limited number of local AM/FM radio stations.

Americans will always demand alternative perspectives, and profit-seeking media companies can supply them. With the Internet to keep them in check, there is little to fear from modest deregulation in the media industry.

Consolidation of Media Outlets Raises Concerns About Limits on Free Speech

by Gal Beckerman

About the author: *Gal Beckerman is a former editor at the* Columbia Journalism Review. *He is writing a history of the Soviet Jewry movement.*

The angels of the public interest, with large pink wings and glittering halos, descended on Michael Powell this fall [2003], five years after he had, somewhat sarcastically, first invoked them.

That was back in April 1998, when Powell was speaking to a Las Vegas gathering of lawyers. Only a few months had passed since his appointment to one of the five spots on the Federal Communications Commission, and the new commissioner had been invited to speak about a longstanding and contentious issue: Was it the FCC's responsibility to keep the media working toward the public good?

Powell made clear that he placed his faith in the invisible hand of the market: the business of the FCC, he said, was to resolve "matters that predominantly involve the competing interests of industry" and not some vague "public interest." The FCC had no role in deciding whether to give free airtime to presidential candidates, for example, or in forcing television channels to carry educational or children's programming. "Even if what is portrayed on television encourages or perpetuates some societal problem, we must be careful in invoking our regulatory powers," Powell insisted.

To highlight the point, Powell used biblical imagery. "The night after I was sworn in, I waited for a visit from the angel of the public interest," Powell said.

"I waited all night but she did not come. And, in fact, five months into this job, I still have had no divine awakening."

This September 4 [2003] the angels finally arrived.

Fifteen women dressed entirely in fluorescent pink and spreading frilly wings emblazoned with the words "Free Speech" stood on the sidewalk outside the large glass doors of the FCC. They banged on bongos and shouted chants, unfurling a large pink scroll containing their demands: full repeal of the new rules that Michael Powell had just shepherded into existence.

By this time, Powell had become FCC chairman and had overseen the biggest relaxation of media ownership rules in over thirty years. . . . But the day before, a federal appeals court in Philadelphia had granted an emergency stay barring the FCC from putting his new rules into effect. The court gave as one of its reasons "the magnitude of this matter and the public's interest in reaching the proper resolution." So the angels were celebrating, and they were not alone.

Strong Response to the Rule Changes

The massive public response to the rule changes, in fact, had been unprecedented. For months before and after the new rules were announced on June 2 [2003], opposition had been loud, passionate, and active. Hundreds of thousands of comments were sent to the FCC, almost all in opposition. It was the heaviest outpouring of public sentiment the commission had ever experienced.

Even more striking was the makeup of this opposition, what *The New York Times* called "an unusual alliance of liberal and conservative organizations." Together in the mix, along with Code Pink, the activists in angel wings, were the National Rifle Association, the National Organization for Women [NOW], the Parents Television Council (a conservative group focused on indecency in television), every major journalism association, labor groups like the Writers and Screen Actors Guilds, and a collection of liberal nonprofit organizations that had been focused on media issues for decades.

It is not every day that the ideological lines get redrawn over an issue, let alone an issue that had been destined to remain obscure and complex for all but telecommunications experts to debate. What's the glue that has held this unlikely coalition together?

Victoria Cunningham is the twenty-four-year-old national coordinator of Code Pink, a grass-roots women's organization that engages in wacky direct action. Code Pink has sung

"The massive public response to the rule changes, in fact, had been unprecedented."

Christmas carols outside [Secretary of Defense] Donald Rumsfeld's home and arrived at [New York Senator] Hillary Clinton's Senate office wearing underwear over their clothing to deliver her a "pink slip" of disapproval for her early support of the war in Iraq. I met with her a month after her group's boisterous visit to the FCC. Code Pink's office is little more than a broom closet on the fifth floor of a building a few blocks from the White House. Pink beads and rainbow flags cram the walls. Cunningham was wearing—what else?—a very pink shirt.

Why were her members, who number in the thousands, so interested in this issue? "Our people are informed enough that they understand what happens when there are only one or three or four companies that are controlling the information we get," Cunningham said. "A lot of our people would love to turn on the evening news and see a variety of opinions coming out."

Like everyone I talked to who was involved in the opposition to the FCC rules, Cunningham spoke of the intu-

> *"Further consolidation of the media . . . would only increase the lack of responsiveness to community needs."*

itive understanding most people had of an issue that seems complex on the surface. Over and over, as I attempted to understand what it was that was holding together this diverse coalition, I heard the same phrase: "People just get it." And I heard this from groups both left and right. The oddest invitation Cunningham said she had received in the last few months was to appear on Oliver North's conservative radio talk show to debate the FCC issue. "And when we talked about that," she said, "we just couldn't say anything bad to each other."

Rules May Not Respond to Local Community

Next, I made my way to a rather different scene, the headquarters of the United States Conference of Catholic Bishops, to talk with Monsignor Francis J. Maniscalco, its director of communications. No broom closet, the conference's home is in a giant modern Washington building behind a large sculpture of Jesus pointing to the sky.

Monsignor Maniscalco, a clerical collar under his soft, round face, spoke like a weathered telecommunications professional about his opposition to the FCC's new rules. The bishops are concerned about the loss of religious shows, like Catholic mass on television—but also the loss of a time when, he says, in order for broadcasters to keep their licenses they had to "prove they were being responsive to the local community." The further consolidation of the media that would be spurred by the new FCC rules, he said, would only increase the lack of responsiveness to community needs. "We see the media as being very formational of people, formational of a culture, formational of people's attitudes," he said, "and if certain strains of community life are not on television they are, by that very reason, considered less important, less vital to society."

Even though he and the conference had always opposed media consolidation, Maniscalco said, until recently they felt they were working in a vacuum. When the monsignor began talking about the current effort, though, he visibly brightened. His eyebrows, which are red, lifted, and he rolled forward in his chair. "The consumption of media is a passive consumption, it is a passive act in itself," he said. "And it is a passive audience that has said, 'We just have to take what they give us.' But interestingly enough, this seems to be something that has finally caught people's imagination, that they could make a difference in terms of turning back these rules and saying no, we don't see that as being very helpful to our situation."

Media industry insiders were taken by surprise at how fast these groups managed to come together and exercise political influence. In addition to the emergency stay issued by the Philadelphia federal appeals court on the day before Powell's six new rules were to go into effect, Congress has responded with zeal to their demands. Consider: on July 23 [2003], only a month after the rules were approved, the House of Representatives voted 400 to 21 to roll back the ownership cap to 35 percent. Then, on September 16, the coalition had an even greater success. The Senate used a parliamentary procedure, called a resolution of disapproval—used only once before in history—to pass a bill repealing all the new regulations. It passed 55 to 40, and was supported by twelve Republicans, and cosponsored, astonishingly, by none other than [Senator] Trent Lott. Such quick legislative action has generated excitement, but it is unlikely that the coalition will find such easy victory in the future. . . .

But these challenges don't take away from what has been achieved. Such ideologically disparate groups rarely find common cause. As Powell himself has pointed out, the reasons behind most of these groups' opposition are parochial and narrow. The unions are worried that more consolidation will lead to fewer jobs; the left-leaning groups are still shivering from what they saw as nationalistic coverage of the war; groups like the Parents Television Council want less *Buffy the Vampire Slayer* and more *Little House on the Prairie*. Yet there they were, at countless public hearings over the last half-year, the bishop sitting next to the gun lobbyist sitting next to a woman from NOW, all united around some common denominator.

Diverse Media Is Essential to a Strong First Amendment

To get a better idea of what that common denominator might be, I went to visit Andrew Schwartzman, the fifty-seven-year-old president of the Media Access Project, a small public-interest law firm that has been fighting big media and the FCC for more than three decades. Schwartzman was the lead lawyer in the case that led to the September 4 emergency stay.

A week after that triumph, he looked exhausted, his bloodshot eyes contrasting with his white hair and bushy moustache. He looked a little like Mark Twain—a very tired Mark Twain. He spoke slowly and deliberately. "Michael Powell has significantly misunderstood what this is about, to his detriment," Schwartzman said. "He repeatedly says, somewhat disdainfully, that all the disparate organizations are unhappy about what they see on the air. The right-wingers think the media is liberal and the left-wingers think the media is a corporate conspiracy, and they all can't be right. This is a way of dismissing and trivializing their position. For me, what these groups have in common is that they represent people who are within the relatively small group of Americans who choose to be active participants in the political process, the people who exercise their First Amendment rights aggressively. And even where their principal areas of interest may be the Second Amendment or other things, they understand the importance of the electronic mass media in the democratic process. And Michael Powell hasn't understood that."

> *"Radio was deregulated, leading to the growth of companies such as Clear Channel."*

What unites these groups, he told me, is that they all generally believe that the media are limited, and that this limitation comes from the fact that there is too much control in too few hands. This leads to a lack of diversity of voices, to programming that is out of touch with local concerns, to increasingly commercial and homogenized news and entertainment. And this is what has triggered people's passions. It is not the fear that their own voice won't echo loud enough, he said, but that further consolidation will produce media in which only the powerful few will be heard at all.

But why now? Neither Schwartzman nor anyone else I talked to could explain why, coming from so many different directions, all these groups landed in the same place at the same time. After all, this is not the first time that free-market enthusiasts have smashed up against the defenders of the public interest.

Media Consolidation and Abundant Backlash

The 1980s saw a major crack in the idea that the public interest was the top priority for the FCC. President [Ronald] Reagan's FCC chairman, Mark Fowler, presided over the death of the Fairness Doctrine, which required broadcast stations to provide airtime for opposing voices in controversial matters of public importance. Then in 1996 Congress passed, and President [Bill] Clinton signed, a major overhaul of U.S. telecommunications law, permitting greater media concentration. Radio was significantly deregulated, leading to the growth of companies such as Clear Channel, which now operates more than 1,200 stations in more than 300 markets. It was in that period that the national ownership cap for television stations went from 25 percent to 35 percent.

Such developments happened away from the public eye, in a place where only members of Congress and lobbyists roam. According to Celia Wexler, director and researcher for Common Cause, the nonpartisan citizens' lobby, those past fights were "very much inside the Beltway. It was very complicated, and there were no groups able to tell the story in a way that really made people understand what was at stake. There were media reformers who understood, who wanted a discussion of the public-interest obligations of broadcasters. But it didn't really catch fire."

At a morning session on media issues at a Common Cause conference, I saw how dramatically the situation had changed. Seats to the event were in hot demand. Next to me an elderly couple sat clutching newspaper clippings, one of which was headlined "new fee rules sap diversity in media owners."

Wexler, a small woman with the air of a librarian, was sitting on stage in a panel that included Gloria Tristani, a former FCC commissioner, who said of Michael Powell at one point: "I think he has lost touch with people or maybe never had touch with people in this country." The star of the morning, though, was John Nichols, a *Nation Washington* correspondent, who, together with Robert McChesney, another media reformer, started an organization called Free Press. Nichols has a professorial air, but he started his talk so dramatically that the couple next to me started nodding furiously.

He contended that, in the wake of [the September 11, 2001, terrorist attacks] and in the buildup to the war in Iraq [in 2003], Americans had come to realize how shallow and narrow were their media. "People said maybe I support this war, maybe I oppose it, but I would like to know a little more about who we're going to bomb," Nichols said. "And I would like to know more about what came before and how this works—not just cheerleading. And all of that churned, combined, to have a profound impact."

This was an explanation I had heard from other liberal groups involved in the media movement. But it still didn't explain why conservatives had chosen this particular moment to join this coalition. As with the liberals, there have always been conservative groups that have opposed media deregulation, most notably the Catholic Church, but the message never resonated widely.

That, too, has changed. Take, for example, the Parents Television Council, an organization with 800,000 members that monitors indecency. The group regularly sends letters to the FCC when a show contains what they call "foul language" or racy subject matter. In August, L. Brent Bozell, the council's president, joined Gene Kimmelman of Consumers Union, a longtime advocate of media reform, in an editorial that was published in the *New York Daily News*, writing that in spite of their ideological differences they "agree that by opening the door to more media and newspaper consolidation, the FCC has endangered something that reaches far beyond traditional politics: It has undermined the community-oriented communications critical to our democracy."

"The smaller and more local the media are . . . the more attuned to community standards of decency."

Conservatives see a link between the growth of big media and the amount of blood and skin they see on television. The smaller and more local that media are, the argument goes, the more attuned to community standards of decency. If local stations could preempt what was being fed from New York and Los Angeles, then programming could be more reflective of family values. Here again, the sense is that media have become too large and all-encompassing and lost touch with their audience.

Melissa Caldwell, director of research at the council, points out that the new ownership rules were a way for big media companies to buy up even more local stations. This is worrisome, she explained, because locally owned broadcast affiliates tend to be more responsive to community standards of decency. The council's surveys, Caldwell says, show that network-owned stations almost never preempt network shows, "whereas locally owned and operated stations were more likely to do so. We don't want to see the networks become even less responsive to community concerns than they already are."

Opposing the FCC on Media Consolidation

By the end of September, with his rules in deep freeze, Powell, speaking to *The New York Times*, expressed exasperation with the effectiveness of the opposition. "Basically, people ran an outside political campaign against the commission," Powell was quoted as saying. "I've never seen that in six years."

At the core of this "campaign" were four groups—Consumers Union, led by Kimmelman, and the Consumer's Federation of America, represented by Mark Cooper, as well as Andrew Schwartzman's Media Access Project and the Center for Digital Democracy, run by Jeffrey Chester. The four men (who often referred to themselves as the "four Jewish horsemen of the apocalypse") played the central role in translating the growing anger and frustration of the Left and the Right into a cohesive movement.

Early on, these groups realized that to fight the FCC they would need more political power than their dependable but small progressive base could offer. One of their first steps, in addition to beginning a conversation with conservative groups like Parents Television Council, was to call on labor organizations like the Writers Guild and AFTRA [the American Federation of Television and Radio Artists], which could provide the resources and the manpower to get the message out.

By the beginning of 2003, a loose coalition was in place. And at that point, Powell's personality, of all things, began to play a galvanizing role. In pronouncement after pronouncement, he trumpeted the importance of these new rules—highlighted by his decision to vote on all of them in one shot. He insisted that their rewriting would be based purely on a scientific examination of the current broadcasting world.

It was true, as Powell claimed, that reexamining the rules was not his idea. The District of Columbia Court of Appeals, interpreting the 1996 Telecommunications Act, had ordered him to conduct a biennial assessment. But Powell had many chances to include the public in this review, and he did not. No public hearings were necessary, he said; the facts would do the talking, and would point to the rightness of his free-market convictions. "Michael Powell deserves a public-interest medal because he practically single-handedly created this enormous opposition," said Jeffrey Chester.

In December, Powell announced a single public hearing, to be held in what one opponent jokingly referred to as "the media capital" of Richmond, Virginia. Soon, groups who had been only peripherally involved in the loose coalition became increasingly angered by Powell's intransigence. One story often invoked to illustrate the unifying power of Powell's stubbornness involves a meeting that took place between members of the Hollywood creative community and labor groups, including producers and writers, and Kenneth Ferree, the chief of the media bureau at the FCC. According to several people present at the gathering, when a request for public hearings was made, Ferree was dismissive and rude, saying he was only interested in "facts," not "footstomping." "The sense of helplessness and anger that he generated by that meeting was enormous," said Mona Mangan, executive director of Writers Guild East.

> *"Media had become a political issue, as deeply felt as the economy, health care, or education."*

If Powell's refusal to hold public hearings galvanized the opposition in one direction, the desire of another commissioner, Michael J. Copps, to engage with the public on this issue also played a key role. Copps, one of the two Democrats on the FCC, was unhappy with Powell's insistence on keeping the issue within the Beltway. When Powell finally announced that the number of public hearings would be limited to one, Copps issued a statement that read like the complaints of the growing grass-roots opposition. "At stake in this proceeding are our core values of localism, diversity, competition, and maintaining the multiplicity of voices and choices that undergird our marketplace of ideas and that sustain American democracy," he said.

"The idea that you are changing the basic framework for media ownership and you don't really want to make this a public debate was a reflection of Powell's own sort of arrogant, narrow mind-set," said Chester. "He didn't understand that this is about journalism, this is about media. No matter what the outcome, you have to go the extra mile to encourage a serious national debate."

Through the winter and early spring, Copps organized unofficial hearings around the country in collaboration with groups like the Writers Guild, earning the nickname Paul Revere in some quarters. As media reform groups searched for a wide range of witnesses to speak at these hearings, the coalition grew to include groups like the National Rifle Association and the National Organization for Women. Out of the meetings came the first sense that this issue could resonate.

Public Outcry Over Media Consolidations

In the spring, after Powell refused to delay the June vote for further discussion, the FCC was flooded with calls and letters. Petitions were signed with hundreds of thousands of names and comments. Something was happening. Despite the scant press coverage, citizens were responding. The Internet helped to make this response immediate and numerous, mostly through an Internet-based public interest group called MoveOn.org, which had been an organizing force against the Iraq war, capable of turning out thousands upon thousands of signatures and donations in a matter of days. Now it turned its attention to media reform, and the result surprised even its organizers.

"We thought it was just kind of a weird issue because it's this wonky regulatory thing, it's not a typical MoveOn issue like stopping the drilling in the Arctic," said Eli Pariser, MoveOn's young national campaigns director. "After we heard from a critical mass of people we decided to pursue it and see what happened. And when we went out with our petition we got this amazing response."

A few days before the September 16 Senate vote on the resolution of disapproval, I accompanied lobbyists from Consumers Union and Free Press as they delivered a huge MoveOn petition. Lining one of the halls in the Hart Senate Office Building were stacks upon stacks of paler, 340,000 names in all. It was the quickest and largest turnover MoveOn had ever experienced, including its antiwar effort.

As the activists, young and in rumpled, ill-fitting suits, delivered these petitions to Senate aides, everyone was struck by the fact that they were more than just names printed on paper, more than a rubber-stamp petition drive. Many of the statements seemed heartfelt. Sometimes they were only a line, "I want more diversity and freedom of speech," and sometimes long letters, taking up whole pages. People expressed their personal dissatisfaction with what they saw when they turned on the TV. But mostly, they expressed passion. It popped off the page. People in Batesville, Arkansas, and Tekamah, Nebraska, were angry. Media had become a political issue, as deeply felt as the economy, health care, or education. Senate Republicans and Democrats alike understood this. A few days later, they voted to repeal all the new regulations.

A Consensus

When I asked the coalition partners how long their alliance could last beyond the battle over the ownership rules, their answers were uniform: not long. If the Parents Television Council and the Writers Guild ever sat down and tried to figure out rules for TV, the decency monitors would demand stricter limits on sex and violence, and the screenwriters who make up the guild would recoil in horror, shouting about the First Amendment.

But on the question of what these groups' larger and long-term objectives were for the media, I did get some kind of consensus. At the most fundamental level, there is a demand for a forum, for a place where diverse ideas can be heard and contrasted. The ideal seemed to be media that better reflect America, with its diversity, its ideological contentiousness, its multitude of values and standards.

When I asked Monsignor Maniscalco how he would want broadcasters to act in an ideal world, I assumed he would posit some narrow vision of an all-

Catholic twenty-four-hour news channel, but he didn't.

"We would like them to take a chance on things that are noncommercial, that are simply not on television," the monsignor said. "Not for the sake of how much money they can make, but because they represent significant aspects of the community. We would really like to see the concept of broadcasting in the public interest be recognized by these people as a legitimate aspect of their work."

When I posed the problem of whether he could eventually agree to share airtime with all the groups in this, coalition, groups like NOW with which he had fundamental and deep disagreements, Monsignor Maniscalco had a simple answer: "You could say that the goal is for the media to give us access so we can finally have a space to argue amongst ourselves."

Telemarketers Should Be Able to Contact Potential Customers

by Solveig Singleton

About the author: *Solveig Singleton is a lawyer and senior analyst with the Washington, D.C.–based Competitive Enterprise Institute.*

Freedom means joy; we can marry and form a family with whomever we please, although not so long ago so-called "mixed" marriages were illegal. Freedom means risk; you can mortgage your house to start a small business selling ceramics or cleaning services and succeed or fail by your own efforts. Freedom means toleration; Buddhists and Baptists may live or work under the same roof. Most Americans cheerfully take the good with the bad and accept that law is too clumsy an instrument—and lawyers too imperfect as artisans—to regulate the world into perfection. Yet the annoyance of being called by telemarketers, it seems, we cannot endure. A wise camel looks askance at such legislative straws.

The Federal Trade Commission [FTC] has proposed the creation of a federal "do-not-call" list.[1] Telemarketers would face stiff penalties for calling a consumer who placed his name on the list. The idea of a do-not-call list is wildly popular across the board; it first was championed by George W. Bush-appointed FTC chairman Tim Muris and lauded by the irrepressible [Representative] Ed Markey [D-Mass.], his keen ear ever-attuned to the heartbeat of the nation. "You have a box-office, smash, runaway hit on your hand!" he said. Markey even staged a telemarketing call to his cell phone in the middle of his little speech to illustrate the issue, in case anyone in his audience did not know what telemarketing was, or needed a demonstration that it can be annoying to be interrupted.

---

1. The federal do-not-call list went into effect in late 2003.

But lawmaking is not a movie or a dance. The muse of the moment, the pulse of the populist, these are things our country and Constitution must endure. When Congress is attuned to the trivial, where does our freedom go? If we insist that the federal government step in to protect us from phone calls during dinner, when will we not ask them to intervene? Let's get our priorities straight.

Defining What Constitutes a Nuisance

But wait a second. Does freedom really need to mean that other people have the right to call us at dinner? Isn't that a kind of intrusion? Freedom doesn't mean that your neighbor has the right to pump smoke into your house or blast music through the walls. Even an old-fashioned view of property rights says that the freedom of others stops when they create a nuisance. Point taken, but is telemarketing really that much of a nuisance? It only takes a second to pick up the phone and put it down and, particularly in these days of the cordless handset, one need not even get up. It doesn't entail any disturbance that one might not reasonably foresee when one buys a phone. And regulation of telemarketing affects ordinary behavior [making a phone call] well outside the bounds of the household. Maybe it's ultimately a matter of degree, but telemarketing ranks low on the list of seriously intrusive nuisances.

> *"That annoyance and inconvenience do not make good grounds for federal regulation can be a hard point for people to accept."*

That annoyance and inconvenience do not make good grounds for federal regulation can be a hard point for people to accept. I was on a radio talk show once talking about this issue when someone called in to disagree. Telemarketing is more than just an annoyance, the caller insisted, and declared that telemarketing calls had driven her "literally crazy." But it became clear as she talked that in fact they had not. She was still perfectly rational, neither institutionalized, nor on Halcyon, nor even in need of counseling; by "literally crazy" she really meant "annoyed and occasionally inconvenienced." Which is my point exactly.

Controlling Calls Without Government Regulation

This does not mean that folks in a free country simply are stuck with annoyances. They are, of course, free to invent their way around the problem—and many have. Entrepreneurs have stepped in to offer a wide array of services and products that help block telemarketing calls. Caller ID works reasonably well for that purpose. As telemarketers usually show up as "unknown caller," one usually can assume that such calls come from telemarketers. Some phone companies offer services that block such calls. And there are devices such as the TeleZapper and the Phone Butler.

These devices don't work perfectly, but they are bound to get better all the time. Here is why: They all compete with each other. Competition gives the consumer a choice of products—the consumer can look over the options to see which methods work best, which can be tailored to their preferences and which are the most cost-effective. By contrast, the FTC's do-not-call list is a one-size-fits-all solution. The FTC has no profit motive to make it work better, to build in innovative technologies, to tailor it to individual customers, to bring the costs of operating it down over time. It will be hard for private businesses to compete with the FTC. Who will

> *"The do-not-call proposal . . . raises free-speech questions."*

force telemarketers to pay for access to the all-important no-call list. So what will happen to the market for all the innovative services and devices that block telemarketing? Unless the FTC's list is a flop, that market and the investment money available to innovators will shrink substantially. And consumers will lose another range of choices.

But there's another objection to my line of argument. Won't consumers be better off with the federal solution to the problem than with the private-sector solutions? After all, the federal solution is "free," but you have to pay extra for the various gizmos that block telemarketers in the private sector. That is a short-sighted view, though. Can it really cost us all less to solve a problem by getting lawyers involved? That is unlikely.

What it will do is create another regulatory tax. The FTC has asked Congress to authorize them to charge telemarketers to pay for the list. The charges ultimately would be reflected in higher costs for businesses and higher prices for consumers.

More importantly, the private-sector gizmos are only costly in the short run. In the long run, those prices would come down because of competition. And consumers who rarely are at home to be annoyed by unwanted callers need pay nothing at all. Finally, some private-sector offerings to telemarketing-sensitive consumers already are free. One credit-card company, for example, prominently advertises "no telemarketing," but charges nothing extra. But all these choices —what product to buy, how much to pay, whether to buy at all—are foreclosed by a federal solution.

Regulation Is Uneven

Competition in other areas might be affected by the do-not-call list as well. The FTC has little authority to regulate calls from telephone companies, for example. The Federal Communications Commission [FCC], however, does have the legal authority to regulate telemarkating by phone companies. Now it makes little sense to regulate most businesses one way and the phone companies another way. So the FTC hopes that the FCC also will create do-not-call rules for phone companies. So far, so good. The problem is that telemarketing has played a big role in introducing competition between phone companies. Way back when AT&T was broken up in the 1980s, it took customers a long time to realize that they had a choice of phone companies. A lot of them learned about MCI and Sprint and switched when offered the option by telemarketing. The battle for more phone competition is not over yet, and limits on telemarketing might mean that consumers are slower to realize they have choices.

The do-not-call proposal also raises free-speech questions. Even business callers have free-speech rights, though the courts say that advertising and soliciting may be more closely regulated than other speech. [The courts may be wrong about this, as a matter of constitutional history. There is no evidence that the Constitution originally was intended to give businesses less constitutional protection than other human endeavors.]

And the ruling affects more than business callers. Some of the biggest users of telemarketing are charities such as the Red Cross. Political candidates also call to round up potential voters. Finally there are research companies and pollsters who may work with charities, political candidates or businesses, but who do not sell anything.

Of these groups, the FTC has no authority over charities and politicians. But the FTC can regulate the telemarketing firms that charities and political groups use. It still is not clear to what extent telemarketing firms would be exempted from do-not-call rules when they are calling on behalf of charities such as the Red Cross. So far it looks as though they would not be exempted. This does raise troubling free-speech questions. Regulation of the hours that telemarketers can call is one thing, but a flat ban on calling someone on the do-not-call list is another. It probably would not occur to many people that placing their names on the list also would result in their never hearing about a group that needs their support to which they might be quite sympathetic, whether it is a new animal shelter or a political cause.

Regulation Stifles Freedom

All of this goes to a more fundamental point, it is easy to take freedom for granted. When we hear a message from a telemarketer, we do not think of the role that message plays in a larger landscape of competition and commerce, of civil society and political debate. A lot of our freedoms may at first glance appear tiny, insignificant, even annoying. The display of a million different kinds of toothbrushes momentarily may irritate a confused shopper just trying to pick one. But it is all part of a larger whole.

Americans are uneasy about the looming size of government. Tax bills are a part of that; this April, add together the amount you pay in taxes to the federal, state and local governments. Most people will be startled to find that even if their federal rate is below 30 percent, their total liability may amount to almost 50 percent. Another part of it is the difficulty of doing business without paying for a million lawyer-hours and bankrolling extensive liability insurance. In the face of this growth of government, the proposal to establish a federal do-not-call list for telemarketers seems insignificant. And so it is a reasonably practicable if not perfect solution to an unbelievably minor problem. But if we cannot resist inviting federal agencies in to regulate this issue, when will we not invite them in?

Telemarketing Is Not Protected Free Speech

by Bill Lockyear et al.

About the authors: *Bill Lockyear is the attorney general of California.*

Editor's Note: This is an amici curiae brief submitted in October 2003 to the 10th Circuit Court of Appeals in the case Mainstream Marketing Services, Inc. et al. v. Federal Trade Commission. *The court ruled in favor of the FTC, upholding the constitutionality of the do-not-call regisrty.*

America is frustrated with telemarketing. To help individuals reclaim a measure of peace and privacy in their homes, the States and, later, the federal agencies had to step in. . . .

When America demanded protection from these all too common and bothersome calls, the States' regulatory response was restrained and thoughtfully crafted. The States' DNC [do-not-call] laws do not impose a blanket, government-imposed restriction on commercial solicitations. Rather, these laws depend on individual choice to activate their protection. In addition, States have found that DNC laws can be tailored to ensure that only those calls that are the most prevalent and unwelcome are eligible to be blocked. The States' experiences demonstrate that applying the law to unsolicited commercial calls will directly and materially advance residential privacy and do so in the most effective, yet least restrictive manner. The States' experiences show that exempting some noncommercial calls can be consistent with maintaining residential privacy.

When the federal agencies enacted their DNC rules there was a body of State experiences supporting distinctions between commercial and noncommercial speech. With their individual DNC laws, the States have served as a proving ground for the development of innovative ways to protect residential privacy. These laws have been tested at the State level, and their provisions have proven to be principled and effective. . . .

Bill Lockyear et al., Amicus Curiae Brief, *Mainstream Marketing Services, Inc., et al. v. Federal Trade Commission*, U.S. Court of Appeals for the Tenth District, October 2003.

Telemarketers Have No Right to Call Unwilling Listeners

The Colorado District Court held that because the FTC's [Federal Trade Commission's] DNC rules targeted commercial speech, they must be analyzed under the commercial speech test set forth in *Central Hudson Gas & Electric v. Pub. Serv. Comm'n* (1980). In reaching this conclusion, however, the Colorado District Court did not consider the substantial right of unwilling listeners to exclude unwanted speech from their homes. This substantial right must be measured against the total absence of any right of a commercial telemarketer to deliver an unwanted message into the home. Because there is no First Amendment right to force unwanted commercial calls into the home, an analysis under *Central Hudson* is unnecessary.

In *Hill v. Colorado*, the Supreme Court recognized that the right of an unwilling listener to avoid unwanted speech is one of our most established and inviolate rights: "It is an aspect of the broader 'right to be let alone' that one of our wisest Justices [L. Brandeis] characterized as 'the most comprehensive of rights and the right most valued by civilized men.'" At issue in *Hill* was a Colorado statute that prohibited sidewalk counselors from breaching an 8-foot buffer around individuals entering health clinics. This law pitted the right of an unwilling listener "to be let alone" against the right of another to communicate. After carefully balancing these interests, the Court upheld the right of the unwilling listener. In reaching this conclusion the Court relied heavily on *Rowan v. U.S. Post Office* and *Frisby v. Schultz*, in which the Court held that the "right to avoid unwelcome speech has special force in the privacy of the home and its immediate surroundings."

In *Rowan*, the Court entertained a challenge to a federal statute that allowed residents to block future mailings to their home if they notified the Postmaster that they received advertisements for "matter which the addressee in his sole discretion believes to be erotically arousing or sexually provocative." The Court explained that "Congress has erected a wall—or more accurately permits a citizen to erect a wall—that no advertiser may penetrate without his acquiescence."

The *Rowan* Court gave great weight to the recipients' right to decide what speech to allow into their homes. Allowing the resident to make this choice struck an eminently reasonable balance, the Court stressed, because it did not operate to substitute the government's judgment for that of the resident.

> *"There is no First Amendment right to force unwanted calls into the home."*

The Court observed that "the right of every person 'to be let alone' must be placed on the scales with the right of others to communicate. . . ." After weighing these rights the Court concluded that "a mailer's right to communicate must stop at the mailbox of an unreceptive addressee."

The possibility that valuable communication might be restricted prompted no equivocation by the Court in *Rowan:*

We therefore categorically reject the argument that a vendor has a right under the Constitution or otherwise to send unwanted material into the home of another. If this prohibition operates to impede the flow of even valid ideas, the answer is that no one has a right to press even 'good' ideas on an unwilling recipient.

In *Frisby*, the Court again emphasized that "there simply is no right to force speech into the home of an unwilling listener."

Thus, *Rowan* and *Frisby* recognize a strong right of an unwilling listener to exclude unwanted speech from his or her home. *Hill* took this right a step further and upheld speech restrictions where core speech was directed to an unwilling listener in a public setting.

Taken together the *Rowan-Frisby-Hill* holdings create a balancing test whenever the right of an unwilling listener to exclude unwanted speech is pitted against the rights of a speaker. In this balancing test, the right of the unwilling listener is given special weight when the message is directed into the unwilling listener's home. This right is stronger yet when the resident—not the government—makes the decision that the communication may not enter the home, as is the case here.

As in *Rowan*, the federal DNC rules allow individuals—not the government—to decide whether commercial solicitations may cross their homes' thresholds. Moreover, the DNC rules apply to individuals in the privacy of their homes. Here, the unwilling listener is more accurately described as an objecting listener. Mainstream [Marketing, the chief plaintiff] seeks

> *"The right of the unwilling listener is given special weight when the message is directed into the unwilling listener's home."*

to override the established rights of an objecting listener by interjecting a commercial solicitation into the privacy and serenity of his or her home. As in *Rowan*, the right of the objecting listener to stop this solicitation must prevail.

The Colorado District Court discounted the individual choice provided for under the federal DNC rules because it felt that the noncommercial speech exemptions unduly influenced the individual's choice. This conclusion is contrary to the evidence and the Supreme Court's recent decision in *Watchtower Bible & Tract Society v. Village of Stratton.*

In *Watchtower*, the Supreme Court indicated that it is permissible to draw a distinction between commercial and noncommercial speech when regulating solicitations directed into the privacy of the home. Though the Court held that the challenged ordinance swept too broadly because it regulated religious speech, the Court noted . . . that had the ordinance applied only to commercial solicitations, it may have been narrowly tailored to advance residential privacy.

Also, because noncommercial calls are not as prevalent or bothersome to individuals as unsolicited commercial calls, there is a valid basis for distinguishing between commercial and noncommercial speech. When a valid basis exists to distinguish between commercial and noncommercial speech, (such as when seeking to protect residential privacy) the regulatory system must be upheld.

The federal DNC rules give meaning to the strong right of objecting listeners to exclude unwanted commercial solicitations from their homes. When balanced against the right of the commercial solicitor to call into the home, the right of the objecting listener must prevail. Thus, under *Rowan-Frisby-Hill*, the federal DNC rules need not be analyzed under *Central Hudson*.

The Federal DNC Rules Are Valid Under *Central Hudson*

Even if the Court determines that *Central Hudson* provides the appropriate analytical framework for deciding the constitutionality of the federal DNC rules, the rules pass constitutional muster, and the decision below must be reversed.

Under *Central Hudson*, the government may regulate truthful, non-deceptive commercial speech if "(1) [the government] has a substantial state interest in regulating the speech, (2) the regulation directly and materially advances that interest, and (3) the regulation is no more extensive than necessary to serve the interest."

In its October 7, 2003, order granting the FTC's motion for a stay pending appeal, this Court has already undertaken a thorough analysis of why the federal DNC rules pass the *Central Hudson* test. . . .

As discussed above, it is well established that the government has a substantial interest in protecting residential privacy.

The governmental interest here, an interest in allowing people to make their own choices about whether they wish to accept unsolicited commercial telemarketing calls, is focused and specific to the individuals who seek to invoke their well-established right as objecting listeners to exclude unwanted solicitations from the home. The DNC regulations protect only those people affirmatively seeking protection; the regulations burden only that speech which is directed at *unwilling* listeners. There can be no question that this governmental interest is substantial.

The already ample record concerning the government's substantial interest in this regard is bolstered by the experiences of the States in adopting their own DNC laws. Many of the States' DNC laws refer to this interest. The FTC was made aware of this public interest early in its rulemaking process, at a forum organized to discuss the possibility of a national DNC list. An FTC representative asked why more and more States were enacting DNC laws. A representative from the Kentucky Attorney General's Office explained that:

> *"The DNC regulations protect only those people affirmatively seeking protection."*

> I cannot tell you how intense, how strong an issue this is to the people. We get calls by the hundreds, the legislators report to us it is far and above the biggest

issue which they get any calls on, that people are saying that they absolutely want some means of controlling the calls that come into their home.

Also, as a representative from the National Association of Attorneys General explained, States that enacted DNC laws found the public response to be immediate and overwhelming; more than one state agency had its own telephone system overwhelmed by calls from individuals eager to sign up. This public outcry for protection from unwanted telemarketing calls was the basis for Congressional and State legislative action.

Finally, although Mainstream has consistently relied on *US West, Inc. v. FCC*, to argue that there is not a substantial interest in protecting residential privacy, *US West* does not apply here.

In *US West*, this Court agreed that privacy "may rise to the level of a substantial state interest." At issue in that case was an FCC [Federal Communications Commission] regulation that sought to protect consumer calling records from being divulged by the telephone company. Here, the federal DNC rules are trying to protect the choice of an objecting listener to exclude unwanted solicitations from intruding upon the serenity of the home—a clearly established right.

The *US West* Court distinguished the privacy interest before it from those cases that have recognized a state's interest in protecting against unwanted intrusions caused by solicitations. The *US West* Court specifically noted that it was not dealing with the privacy interest that protects against a telemarketing intrusion. Rather, it indicated that the privacy interest in consumer calling records was a new interest. The Court specifically distinguished this emerging privacy interest from the privacy interest that protects against the unwanted intrusion into an individual's home caused by solicitations. Because *US West* was dealing with a different interest it is inapplicable.

> *"The right to residential privacy . . . is at least a substantial interest . . . under well established First Amendment precedent."*

The right to residential privacy, free from unwanted solicitations, is at least a substantial interest, if not a compelling interest under well established First Amendment precedent. Accordingly, the rules meet the first part of the *Central Hudson* test.

Mainstream argues, essentially, that the rules fail to materially advance the government's stated interest, because they would not block all (or nearly all) forms of telephone solicitation. This argument is not only contrary to the evidence, but assumes a legal standard that is far more stringent than *Central Hudson* and its progeny.

The Regulatory System Is Likely to Reduce Unwanted Calls

Mainstream argues that the federal DNC rules cannot be constitutional unless all telephone solicitation calls are blocked. *Central Hudson* does not require this all-or-nothing approach. So long as the DNC rules achieve a reasonable fit between "the legislature's ends and the means chosen to accomplish those ends," the Court will "leave it to the governmental decisionmakers to judge what manner of regulation may best be employed."

As this Court recognized in its October 7 [2003] order, these two sets of regulations, and their likely effect, should not be considered in isolation. This case demonstrates the wisdom of the Supreme Court's observation "that the Government [need not] make progress on every front before it can make progress on any front." Here,

> "Commercial and charitable solicitations need not be subject to identical regulations."

the District Court's focus on the FTC front ignored the fact that this battle has been waged on many fronts. The problem of intrusive, unwanted telemarketing calls is ubiquitous, and the States and the federal government have addressed it in a variety of ways. Each step along the way has improved individuals' ability to protect themselves from unwanted telemarketing calls. As would be expected (indeed, encouraged) in our federal system, the States have tried different approaches, serving as laboratories for the development of governmental solutions to a problem that is of widespread concern. While none of these varied approaches has fully and permanently solved the problem—no law ever does—they have each materially advanced the government's interest in addressing it. Under the District Court's reasoning, none of these laws would have been allowed to take effect, because each would have been struck down as less than a complete solution.

The likely effect of the FTC and FCC regulations must be examined in a context that includes the efforts of both agencies as well as those of the States. With regard to the federal agencies, each has the authority to enforce its own rules; each agency will bring its own particular strengths to those efforts, so federal enforcement will benefit from the FTC's experience in consumer protection and the FCC's expertise in the use of communications technologies. In addition, the States have statutory authority to prosecute violations of both agencies' regulations. State prosecutors are well positioned to recognize and respond to patterns of violations that affect particular regions of the country and their own States' citizens. State and federal authorities will also be able to join resources when that is appropriate, and to coordinate their work in order to maximize the overall effectiveness of the regulations.

In particular, the effectiveness of the FTC's regulations cannot be evaluated without considering the effect of the FCC's regulations, because the FCC regulations reach businesses (such as common carriers and banks) and intrastate calls that are not within the FTC's jurisdiction. Viewed in that light, the District Court's assumption that the FTC's regulations would block 40% to 60% of all unwanted telephone solicitations suggests that the combined regulations would reach a substantial majority of all telephone solicitation calls, and an even higher percentage of the commercial telemarketing calls found by Congress to be most intrusive.

Furthermore, the experiences of the States with DNC lists suggest that Mainstream underestimates the extent to which telemarketing calls will be reduced. For example, Indiana has enacted a DNC law that exempts certain categories of charitable and commercial solicitation calls. Despite these exclusions, independent research showed that individuals who signed up on the Indiana DNC list saw the number of solicitation calls (including exempt calls) decline by more than 80%.

Thus, by covering a substantial number of the calls that are placed to the home, the rules materially and directly protect residential privacy. This same logic persuaded the Eighth Circuit to uphold the TCPA's [Telephone Consumer Protection Act's] ban on fax advertising, which applied only to commercial entities but exempted noncommercial faxes. The federal DNC rules take a similar approach. They give the individual an option to eliminate those telemarketing calls that account for a substantial number of the calls that disrupt the serenity and privacy of the home.

Recognizing Differences Between Commercial and Charitable Solicitations

This Court has recognized and analyzed the reasons why the FTC properly concluded that commercial and charitable solicitations need not be subject to identical regulations. The record shows that individuals consider commercial calls to be more intrusive than charitable solicitations. In a regulatory system intended to allow individuals to make their own choices about which calls to receive, it would be counterproductive to ignore that distinction; it is a distinction that is directly related to the purpose of the regulations.

There is empirical evidence showing that people find charitable solicitations to be less intrusive than sales calls. During Congressional hearings on the TCPA, the House Committee on Energy and Commerce studied the nature of the telemarketing intrusion. It found that individuals generally have two objections to telemarketing. The first pertains to the volume of unwanted calls and the second relates to whether the call is expected. Based on the evidence that it received, the House Committee found that individuals are more accepting of noncommercial calls because they are more expected. This evidence that individuals expect these calls supports the decision by the FTC and FCC to exempt noncommercial calls. *American Blast Fax* again supports the distinction drawn between commercial and noncommercial solicitations on this basis.

> *"The [do-not-call] regulations are tailored to exclude only those calls that individuals want excluded."*

These considerations show why the DNC regulations are unlike the ordinance invalidated in *Cincinnati v. Discovery Networks*. That ordinance distinguished between commercial and noncommercial speech solely because of the view that commercial speech had less value under the Constitution, rather than for any reason related to the aesthetic interests behind the ordinance. Individuals' receptiveness to these exempt calls serves to distinguish this case from the regulation at issue in *Discovery Networks*. Here, there is ample evidence that excluding noncommercial speech is consistent with the goal of protecting residential privacy.

Also, the Cincinnati ordinance directly prohibited the dissemination of speech (the commercial or noncommercial nature of which was in question) via newsracks that were owned by the speakers (the two companies) and located on public property (the city sidewalks). In contrast, the government enforces the registry provisions at issue here only if a telephone subscriber first chooses to invoke them; the registry provisions apply to speech that is clearly commercial in nature, in that the prohibition on calls to people who have signed on to the registry applies only to solicitations that seek to persuade consumers to buy or invest in something; and the instrumentality for dissemination of the telemarketer's commercial speech—the consumer's telephone—does *not* belong to the speaker and generally is located on private property.

The Government Must Balance Competing Interests

Any measure of the effectiveness of the regulations must be based on more than just the percentage of telemarketing calls that will be blocked. If the agencies' sole interest had been to block all telemarketing calls, they could have achieved that goal with a straightforward, all-encompassing ban on telemarketing. It is evident from the regulatory record and rationale that both agencies sought to achieve a *balance* of competing legitimate interests.

In *United States v. Edge Broadcasting*, the Supreme Court made it clear that the effectiveness of an effort at balancing cannot be measured against absolutist goals. In *Edge*, the Court considered the constitutionality of a federal statute that generally prohibited the broadcast of lottery advertisements. An exception allowed broadcasting of information concerning state-sponsored lotteries, but only by broadcasters located within States that sponsored lotteries.

The statute was challenged by a broadcaster who operated in North Carolina (a non-lottery State), but primarily broadcasted to listeners across the State line in Virginia (a lottery State). Measured against a goal of preventing lottery promotions from reaching listeners in non-lottery States, the statute was clearly overinclusive, because it also blocked some lottery promotions from listeners in neighboring lottery States. It was also underinclusive, because listeners in non-lottery States would hear promotions broadcast from lottery States. Finding the statute constitutional, the Court recognized that the purpose of the legislation was not to eliminate all lottery promotions, but to balance the competing interests of lottery states and non-lottery States.

Here, it is evident that the FTC and FCC sought to do something other than eliminate all telemarketing calls. Rather, their obvious goal was to achieve a balance, reducing telephone solicitation calls to those who prefer not to receive them, preserving a means by which individuals could choose something other than all-or-nothing exclusion of such calls, allowing commercial solicitors to generate income by calling those who do not object, and allowing charitable solicitors to seek donations and advocate issues while respecting individuals' wishes. The rulemaking records and the federal legislative record show that there was an ample basis for the agencies to conclude that their chosen approach would have a substantial impact on unwanted telemarketing calls without undue effect on the other interests at stake.

> *"The mere fact that a statute regulates commercial speech does not mean that the statute is a content-based restriction."*

By giving individuals the right to block the most prevalent and unwanted calls, the federal DNC rules directly and materially advance residential privacy. Thus, the federal DNC rules satisfy the second part of the *Central Hudson* test.

The Federal DNC Rules Are Not More Extensive than Necessary

The federal agencies do not have to prove that the rules are the least restrictive alternative, or that there are no conceivable alternatives to the DNC rules. The law instead requires that the "regulation not burden more speech than is necessary to further the government's legitimate interest."

Courts have held that individual-initiated restrictions on commercial speech satisfy the tailoring requirement of the *Central Hudson* test.

The DNC regulations are tailored to exclude only those calls that individuals want excluded. Individuals who want to block calls from all or most telemarketers can do so through the national registry. Individuals who register may continue to receive calls from businesses with whom they have an established business relationship, but individuals can block those calls as well by asking those businesses to cease calling. To the extent individuals are willing to accept calls from some but not all telemarketers, they may choose to register their telephone numbers, then provide authorization to those companies whose calls they are willing to accept. Alternatively, individuals can bypass the registry, and choose to rely on company-specific lists. Because of this flexibility, there is no reason why a telemarketer will be blocked from calling a willing listener.

In the Colorado District Court, *Mainstream* alleged that the federal DNC rules go too far because the federal agencies did not consider call blocking options available through call blocking services, electronic gimmicks and industry self-regulation as less restrictive alternatives. These alternatives are either costly or ineffective. In addition, the FTC and FCC had an ample basis, given their prior experience, for concluding that regulations based only on a company-specific list were "seriously inadequate" in protecting residential privacy.

Moreover, the regulations include a "safe harbor," so that telemarketers who are doing what is necessary to comply with the law will not be held strictly liable for an inadvertent call to a telephone number on the registry.

Also, Mainstream's suggested alternatives are not viable to protect residential privacy. A less restrictive alternative must be at least as effective as the rules in advancing this important interest. Here the federal DNC rules are tailored to just those individuals who seek its protection. They cost individuals nothing and are effective in preventing the bulk of the unwanted calls from ringing into the home in the first instance. The alternatives are costly and many times do not prevent the ringing of the phone in the first instance.

Finally, all of Mainstream's suggested alternatives assume that the States and federal agencies should not play a role in regulating practices that disturb residential privacy. Protecting the well-being and tranquility of the home, however, are matters squarely within the States' and federal agencies' police powers. The DNC rules and state laws are a valid exercise of this power, notwithstanding the existence of self-help devices, all of which are not as effective as the DNC rules and State laws.

Not Subject to Strict Scrutiny

In the Colorado District Court, Mainstream claimed that the federal DNC rules amount to a content-based restriction because they target commercial solicitations while exempting noncommercial solicitations. The mere fact that a statute regulates commercial speech does not mean that the statute is a content-based restriction. This theory would subject all commercial speech regulations to heightened scrutiny, which has been consistently rejected. . . . This Court has previously held that even if a regulation can be viewed as content-based, if it concerns commercial speech it is still subject to analysis under the *Central Hudson* standard. Therefore, strict scrutiny does not apply here.

The First Amendment Does Not Protect Unwanted Commercial Speech

The States have had considerable experience in crafting and enforcing their DNC laws. This experience supports the fact that the right of an objecting listener to exclude unwanted solicitations from intruding upon his or her residential privacy is an established and inviolate right. Thus, a commercial telemarketer must stop its message at the threshold of the home of an unwilling listener.

The States' experiences also support the federal agencies' conclusion that their regulations will protect residential privacy, and are no more restrictive than necessary. The federal DNC rules are consistent with residential privacy and the First Amendment.

Corporations Threaten Freedom of Speech

by Lawrence Soley

About the author: *Lawrence Soley is a professor at Marquette University in Milwaukee. He is also the author of* Censorship, Inc.

During the 1990–1991 Persian Gulf War, Margaret Gilleo of Ladue, Missouri, put up signs in her front yard reading, "Say 'No' to War in the Persian Gulf, Call Congress." When the signs were stolen and vandalized, she complained to the police, who informed her that she—not the thief—was violating the law. The police told Gilleo that Ladue had an ordinance against posting yard signs, and she had broken it. "I was very angry at this," says Gilleo. "I said 'this is the United States of America and we have free speech.'"

Gilleo petitioned the Ladue City Council for a variance permitted under the ordinance. It refused. So she put a small sign inside her window reading, "For Peace in the Gulf."

The council responded by adopting another, stiffer ordinance prohibiting all but ten kinds of signs. "For sale," "residential identification," and commercial signs would be permitted under the new ordinance; most others (including window signs) were prohibited because they "create ugliness, visual blight and clutter, and tarnish the natural beauty of the landscape," according to the City Council.

In response, Gilleo filed suit against the city in the U.S. District Court, which quickly struck down the ordinance as an unconstitutional restriction on political speech. The city appealed this decision, but in 1994 the Supreme Court upheld the lower court, concluding that "a special respect for individual liberty in the home has long been part of our culture and our law; that principle has special resonance when the government seeks to constrain a person's ability to speak there."

Regulating Speech in the Private Sector

Although courts have consistently struck down government bans that restrict speech such as the Ladue ordinance, they have consistently upheld similar bans

Lawrence Soley, "The Invisible Gag," *Dollars & Sense*, May/June 2003. Copyright © 2003 by Economic Affairs Bureau. Reproduced by permission of *Dollars & Sense*, a progressive economics magazine, www.dollarsandsense.org.

imposed by private entities. For example, "Homeowners' associations—private corporations that govern planned developments and condominiums—are free to adopt restrictions on the speech and behavior of residents that, if adopted by government, would be unconstitutional.

Homeowners are not the only ones facing censorship in the private sector. Because the Supreme Court has taken the position that the First Amendment protects citizens against speech restrictions imposed by governments, not the private sector, corporations can impose an almost endless array of restrictions on speech. Corporations can restrict the release and distribution of internal documents, claiming that they are copyrighted or private property; restrict speech on corporate-owned property; terminate employees who speak out about corporate practices; pressure the mass media to kill or alter stories with threats of lawsuits or by withdrawing advertising dollars; or file lawsuits against critics and activists, claiming injury to their businesses as a result of speech.

Corporations' power to censor has increased at the very time that courts have struck down government-imposed limitations on speech, such as flag desecration laws. The increased power of corporations to censor arises from three closely-related factors: an increasingly conservative Supreme Court's deference to private sector property rights; the gigantism and power of modern corporations, brought about by the merger frenzy of the 1980s and 1990s; and the shrinking of the public sector, the arena where citizens can exercise constitutionally-protected speech rights. In fact, when government has withdrawn from a particular sector, private interests have entered the vacuum and exercised private property rights, reducing the public's freedom of speech. For example, the city of Milwaukee, like most cities, closed a public street to allow the construction of a shopping mall, the Grand Avenue Mall. The mall is considered private property, even though located on former government property, and even though government offices, including those of the University of Wisconsin, are located there. Free speech is not permitted in the mall.

Ironically, about the only limits on corporate censorship are those imposed by government, such as the National Labor Relations Act, which prohibits companies from restricting

> *"Homeowners' associations ... are free to adopt restrictions on the speech and behavior of residents that, if adopted by government, would be unconstitutional."*

employees' speech about unions, and affirmative disclosure laws, such as those adopted by the Securities and Exchange Commission and the Environmental Protection Agency, which require corporations to disclose specific types of information such as executive stock sales. Because corporations have so many methods available to them for restricting speech, corporations represent a greater threat to free speech today than government.

Free Speech in Planned Developments

In *Murphy v. Timber Trace Association* (1989) and *Linn Valley Lakes Property Owners v. Brockway* (1992), bans on signs imposed by homeowners associations were declared legal by courts. In *Linn Valley Lakes*, the court observed that "there is nothing constitutionally impermissible per se in a private agreement restricting signs in a residential neighborhood, and enforcement thereof does not constitute improper state action."

The rationale for allowing these bans is that the contracts and covenants governing planned developments and condominiums are considered by courts to be private agreements, rather than government or "state action." These contracts and covenants have been upheld by courts even though most residents are unaware of the content and binding nature of the restrictions when they move in, and even though many housing associations function like governments, collecting garbage, plowing streets, operating "community" pools, and assessing taxes in the form of maintenance fees.

As of 1999, 42 million Americans—about one in seven—were living in planned developments governed by associations. In Maryland, nearly one-third of residences are in planned developments. In some areas, including the Washington, D.C. area, Florida, Arizona and California, the majority of housing units built [between 1998 and 2003] have been in planned developments.

Because the rules and restrictions on behavior in planned communities are viewed by courts as voluntary, contractual agreements, corporations

"Corporations represent a greater threat to free speech today than government."

such as Disney, Mobil Oil and the American Nevada Corp. that build these communities can write covenants imposing a multitude of restrictions on residents' behavior. These restrictions often limit the colors of exterior paint residents can use on their dwellings, the types of grass they can plant, and the colors of drapes they can hang. In some cases clotheslines, birdbaths, and basketball hoops are prohibited; some covenants prohibit parking pickups and campers within the developments. Most regulate the posting of yard signs.

The Estrella housing development in Phoenix, built by convicted savings and loan embezzler Charles Keating, Jr., banned pornographic videos and magazines from the community—even from residents' bedrooms. The massive, city-like Columbia development in Maryland, built by the Rouse Co. with financing from Connecticut General Life Insurance Co., prohibited Green Party members from collecting signatures to place Ralph Nader on the presidential ballot at a waterfront arts festival held on Columbia property.

So many housing associations in Maryland banned the display of yard and window signs—including yard signs for candidates running for public office—that the state legislature finally passed a law allowing residents to post them. The law prohibited associations from banning signs supporting candidates and ballot measures for thirty days before, and seven days after, an election.

Although a self-serving act on the part of politicians because they were the primary beneficiaries of the law, the Maryland law nevertheless represents an example of how legislation can protect speech—and democracy—from being undermined by the private sector.

The Rise of Corporate Power

The power of corporations to censor speech has grown enormously during the past quarter century. Prior to the 1970s, it was the government that gagged speakers—albeit often at the urging of the private sector. For example, nearly all of the criminal anarchy laws passed by states during the World War I era, which prohibited the advocacy of political syndicalism, were adopted at the urging of those businesses and industries being organized by the Industrial Workers of the

"The power of corporations to censor speech has grown enormously during the past quarter century."

World (I.W.W.). Similarly, the speech bans adopted by cities targeting I.W.W. speakers during the 1920s were adopted at the urging of retailers, who feared that street corner orating interfered with their sales. And many book bans imposed by school and library boards, such as those targeting John Steinbeck's *The Grapes of Wrath*, were implemented at the urging of the affected industries.

During the 1960s and 1970s, when courts started overturning government-imposed restrictions on speech, the private sector sought ways to regulate speech without state action. To achieve this goal, corporations asserted that free speech interfered with their property rights, an argument that the Supreme Court had rejected in 1945 when it declared: "when we balance the Constitutional rights of property against those of the people to enjoy freedom of press and religion . . . the latter occupy a preferred position." In that decision, *Marsh v. Alabama*, the Supreme Court declared company-owned towns to be the functional equivalent of public places, observing that the "more an owner, for his own advantage, opens up his property for use by the public in general, the more do his rights become circumscribed by the statutory and constitutional rights of those who use it."

The *Marsh* decision was applied to shopping centers by the Supreme Court in 1967, when it ruled that union organizers have a right to picket on shopping center property during a labor dispute, noting that the "similarities between the business block in Marsh and the shopping center . . . are striking." The Court found no reason why access to a business district in a company-owned town was constitutionally protected, but access to mall property functioning as a business district was not.

In 1972, the Supreme Court, now dominated by conservative justices appointed by President [Richard] Nixon who were more inclined to protect property than speech rights, began reversing these earlier decisions. In *Lloyd Corp. v. Tanner* (1972) and *Hudgen v. National Labor Relations Board* (1976), the Court majority concluded that mall and shopping center owners had a right to ban speech on their property because "the First and Fourteenth Amendments safeguard the rights of free speech and assembly by limitations on state action, not on action by the owner of private property.". . . As a result of these decisions, shopping centers, malls and most other corporate-owned properties in all but three states are now closed to free speech. In California, Colorado and New Jersey, the state supreme courts ruled that their state constitutions protect speech in malls. Consequently, shoppers in the remaining 47 states, probably without even realizing it, leave their free speech rights at the curb when they enter a shopping center or mall parking lot.

The restrictions on speech in malls are often arbitrary, as recent events at Crossgates Mall near Albany, New York demonstrate. On March 3, 2003, 61-year-old Stephen Downs was arrested and taken away in handcuffs because he refused to obey mall security guards, who ordered him to remove a T-shirt he was wearing, which he had made at a mall store, or else leave the mall. The T-shirt read, "Peace on Earth" and "Give Peace a Chance." (The mall later dropped the charges after a public outcry.)

Not only are corporate property owners able to restrict public speaking and displays, they are free to limit the distribution of newspapers and other literature on their properties. For example, Northwest Airlines Corp. banned *City Pages*, an alternative newspaper in the Twin Cities, from its properties after the newspaper ran articles opposing state funding for the airline.

Censorship on the Internet

In the past, property was defined as physical or intellectual property. Several recent court decisions, however, have extended property rights to cyberspace, allowing Internet service providers (ISPs) to control information entering and leaving their servers. These court decisions undermine the tremendous potential of the Internet to extend speech and access to information.

> *"Shopping centers, malls and most other corporate-owned properties in all but three states are now closed to free speech."*

In 1997, America Online (AOL) blocked incoming e-mail messages sent to subscribers, and was sued by the sender, Cyber Promotions. AOL, the largest ISP with over 35 million subscribers, argued that it was the electronic equivalent of a mall, not a company town or a common carrier, and the federal court agreed. "AOL's e-mail servers are privately owned and are available only to the subscribers who pay a fee for their usage," the judge concluded. As a result, AOL can bar e-mail messages sent by "non-AOL subscribers."

This court decision allows AOL-Time Warner and other ISPs to limit incoming messages and to pick and choose the material entering their systems. Among other messages that AOL–Time Warner has censored were e-mails sent by Harvard University to applicants, informing them of their acceptance to the school. AOL claims that it mistakenly identified the Harvard e-mails as spam. Even so, the mistake shows that AOL is vigorously censoring e-mails, even those that subscribers want.

The ISP also makes it difficult to access competitors' web pages, and uses filters to block access to certain websites, particularly those with adult-oriented content.

Suppressing Public Scrutiny

Just as corporations can close their property to public discourse, they can also keep documents from the public, even when the documents affect public discourse, claiming it to be private, they can also keep documents from the public, even when the documents affect public health and welfare. The Freedom of Information Act and state open records laws, which require government agencies to be somewhat open, do not apply to the private sector.

For example, lead pigment manufacturers were knowledgeable about the hazards of lead, and suppressed the information, just as asbestos manufacturers did. Pharmaceutical companies also kept a lid on information about the dangers associated with drugs such as Fen-phen, Duract, Rezulin, and Propulsid, all of which have since been withdrawn.

> *"Just as corporations can close their property to public discourse, . . . they can also keep documents from the public, even when the documents affect public health and welfare."*

The tobacco companies offer the perfect illustration of the ways that corporations can effectively curb discussions about their products. The tobacco companies have used a whole host of tactics to curtail discussion about their practices, including secrecy clauses in employment contracts, speech-restrictive lawsuits, gag orders, and pressures on the mass media. Most of these tactics are now widely employed by corporations in other industries to curb public debate about issues affecting their industries.

Tobacco companies Philip Morris (now renamed Altria, Inc.) and Brown & Williamson used secrecy clauses embedded in employment contracts to silence in-house scientists, including Victor DeNoble and Jeffrey Wigand. When hired, DeNoble and Wigand signed secrecy agreements prohibiting them from talking about their employers, even after their employment ended. Both men were aware of company research showing nicotine to be highly addictive. DeNoble conducted research showing that nicotine altered brain chemistry and tried to publish his results in the journal *Psycho-pharmacology*, but Philip Morris withdrew the article. Both DeNoble and Wigand were eventually discharged and warned that if they disclosed what they knew about tobacco research, they would be sued.

Many other corporations require new employees to sign secrecy agreements as a condition of hire or threaten to fire employees to limit the disclosure of damning evidence about industry practices. To curtail the use of these tactics in the nuclear power and financial securities industries that are regulated by the federal government, Congress passed "whistleblower protection" laws to keep corporations in these industries from gagging their employees. But in most industries, in the absence of whistleblower laws, companies can easily silence employees.

> *"Lawsuits . . . filed against those who participate in debates about public issues are known as strategic lawsuits against public participation."*

Even with whistleblower laws in place, companies still attempt to gag employees. For example, Commonwealth Edison punished employees who complained about safety problems at its Zion nuclear power plant in Illinois. The company demoted six employees who complained and transferred them to menial jobs. The company lowered its evaluation of another employee, and discharged yet another who reported 60 problems with the plant. The latter employee could not find another job after being dismissed.

Threatening Litigation to Control Expression

Beyond silencing employees, corporations have lots of tricks up their sleeves to prevent the public from finding out about corporate practices. One of the most common is to file a lawsuit, or to threaten to file a lawsuit, against critics, charging that some imaginary harm has been done to the company by their speech. The most common harms asserted in lawsuits are defamation, business interference, copyright violation, patent infringement, and civil rights violations.

For example, toy manufacturer Mattel, Inc., maker of the Barbie doll, filed a trademark infringement suit in 1999 against Seal Press, publisher of *Adios, Barbie*, a book of essays criticizing Barbie's "tall, thin and white" body image. Mattel asserted that the book's use of the Barbie image on the front cover caused trademark confusion. Lacking the financial resources to defend itself in court, the Seal Press settled the suit, agreeing to retitle the book and redesign the cover of subsequent editions.

Similarly, when former Brown & Williamson executive Jeffrey Wigand revealed what he knew to CBS' "60 Minutes," the tobacco company threatened to sue the CBS television network for "tortious liability" if it aired the interview. Fearing that a lawsuit would impede the sale of the network, CBS executives ordered "60 Minutes" to cancel the broadcast.

In an apparent effort to undermine its competitor, ABC network owner Disney Corp. released a feature film, *The Insider*, in 1999 about CBS' decision to kill the Wigand interview. Brown & Williamson then threatened to sue Disney for distributing the film. Lawsuits such as this one, filed against those who participate in debates about public issues, are known as strategic lawsuits against public participation or SLAPPs.

The term "SLAPP" was coined by University of Denver professors George W. Pring and Penelope Canan to describe lawsuits brought against private citizens and groups because they petitioned some branch of government, but the term is now widely used to describe lawsuits filed to punish or inhibit speech. SLAPPs or threats of SLAPPs have been used to curb debates about pollution and global warming by oil and coal firms, about land use by developers and builders, and by a host of other industries.

Some of the most widely publicized SLAPPs include suits filed against North Kingstown, Rhode Island resident Nancy Hsu Fleming by Hometown Properties, Inc., the operator of a nearby landfill that Hsu contended was producing groundwater contamination; a suit filed by the head of the Florida Petroleum Marketers Association against an environmental magazine for declaring the association and its leader to be "Public Enemy Number One"; and a suit filed against the *National Catholic Reporter* by Briggs & Stratton Corp. alleging that an article critical of the company's decision to move jobs to the South and Mexico was libelous. Although there are few statistics available on SLAPPs, a study by Florida's Attorney General concluded that at least 21 SLAPPs had been filed in that state between 1985 and 1993.

Realizing that SLAPPs are designed to punish speakers rather than rectify wrongdoing, a number of states, including Rhode Island, California, Minnesota and Nebraska, have passed laws making it easy to dismiss SLAPPs. The Rhode Island legislation was motivated by the publicity surrounding the Hometown Properties, Inc. suit against Fleming, one that dragged on for years.

Methods Used to Limit Public Discourse

Although Disney disclosed how CBS buckled under to tobacco company pressures in *The Insider*, it did not disclose that the ABC network had done so as well. A segment of the ABC program "Day One," broadcast in 1995, alleged that the tobacco companies "spiked" the nicotine in cigarettes. Philip Morris and R.J. Reynolds SLAPPed ABC, alleging the program was libelous.

On the eve of the sale of the ABC network to Disney, the tobacco company lawsuits were quickly settled. ABC agreed to publicly apologize for airing the segment and agreed to pay the tobacco companies' legal expenses. The settlement included a non-disclosure agreement prohibiting ABC and tobacco company executives from publicly commenting on the case.

Despite the non-disclosure agreement, *USA Today* obtained a copy of the settlement and other documents, which showed the evidence to be "at odds with both the tobacco company's public statements and the network's apology." The newspaper concluded that ABC actually had documents showing that the tobacco companies "spiked" cigarettes.

Non-disclosure agreements such as these are commonly used today by corporations and other institutions to limit the release of publicly-damning information. They were used by Ford and Firestone to hide the dangers posed by the ATX tire on Ford Explorers, and by the Catholic Church to hide the sexual abuse of children by priests.

In addition to secrecy agreements, SLAPP suits and gag orders, the tobacco companies also successfully pressured the mass media into killing articles about the hazards of smoking with threats to withdraw, or by actually withdrawing, advertising. That pressure was applied for decades. In the early 1950s, the tobacco companies prohibited the showing of "no smoking" signs and all references to cancer on the television shows they

> *"Non-disclosure agreements . . . are commonly used today by corporations . . . to limit the release of publicly-damning information."*

sponsored. During the 1960s and 1970s, they withdrew advertising from such magazines as *Reader's Digest* and *Mother Jones* that carried stories about the hazards of smoking. By the 1980s and 1990s, most magazines carrying tobacco advertisements stopped carrying stories about the dangers of smoking. Statistical studies published in such journals as the *New England Journal of Medicine*, *Women's Health*, and *Journalism Quarterly* showed that the more tobacco advertising found in a magazine, the less likely it was to provide coverage about the hazards of smoking.

The effectiveness of this advertiser pressure was not lost on other corporations, which have similarly pressured the news media to stop carrying negative stories about their industries. Studies published in *American Journalism Review and Journal of Advertising* found that the real estate, automotive, airline, and retailing industries routinely influence news coverage.

Fighting Corporate Censorship

Although there is little that ordinary citizens can do to stop advertising censorship, except perhaps to boycott advertising- and corporate-dominated media, there are many things that can be done to limit other types of corporate censorship. Legislation can be passed making it difficult to file SLAPPs. In several states, including California, a coalition of media, unions and activist groups effectively lobbied for anti-SLAPP statutes. California and Minnesota have very broad anti-SLAPP statutes that make it difficult for frivolous suits to pass judicial scrutiny. In states such as Pennsylvania, however, where corporations rather than coalitions of free speech advocates were the primary lobbyists, anti-SLAPP legislation was eviscerated.

Victims of SLAPPs can also file counter lawsuits, called SLAPPback suits. In cases where this has been done, SLAPP victims have sometimes been awarded large verdicts by juries. Shell Oil was hit with a $5.1 million jury verdict for suing a consumer advocate who complained to a state health agency about a Shell home plumbing product. In July 1998, a New Jersey jury awarded Jo Ann Baglini and her husband $1.5 million for being maliciously prosecuted by a developer whose zoning changes the Baglinis had opposed.

Citizens can also push for laws opening malls up to free speech. In New York, where Stephen Downs was arrested for trespassing because he refused to remove his anti-war T-shirt, representative Steve Englebright (D-Suffolk) introduced an assembly bill (A.B. 4163) amending the state civil rights law to require malls of at least twenty stores to permit some form of public expression in common areas. Similar bills can be introduced in other states.

Activists and legislators can also demand that any corporation receiving indirect or direct public subsidies open its property to free speech. Currently, many malls, manufacturers and even professional sports teams are heavily subsidized by taxes, but nevertheless claim that the property on which they operate is private. For example, the Milwaukee Brewers baseball corporation plays in a stadium built by taxpayers, yet claims that the stadium is private property—and has had activists arrested for protesting the team's sales of merchandise made in Central American sweatshops on stadium property. Activists can challenge these private property claims by passing out leaflets, unfurling banners, holding up placards, and engaging in other forms of speech.

Residents of planned developments and condominiums can organize for change within their developments, demanding that residents be allowed to post signs and distribute leaflets door-to-door. In addition, residents can demand that legislators adopt laws such as the Illinois Condominium Property Act, which prohibits housing associations from adopting rules that "impair any rights guaranteed by the First Amendment to the Constitution."

Organizations to Contact

The editors have compiled the following list of organizations concerned with the issues presented in this book. The descriptions are derived from materials provided by the organizations. All have publications or information available for interested readers. The list was compiled on the date of publication of the present volume; the information provided here may change. Be aware that many organizations take several weeks or longer to respond to inquiries, so allow as much time as possible.

The American Civil Liberties Union (ACLU)
125 Broad St., 18th Fl., New York, NY 10004-2400
(212) 549-2500
e-mail: aclu@aclu.org • Web site: www.aclu.org

The mission of the ACLU is to preserve the protections and guarantees outlined in the Constitution and the Bill of Rights. The ACLU maintains the position that civil liberties must be respected, even in times of national emergency. It publishes several fact sheets and position papers, including "Overview of Post-9/11 Court Cases" and "Civil Liberties After 9/11: The ACLU Defends Freedom."

The American Library Association (ALA)
50 E. Huron St., Chicago, IL 60611
(800) 545-2433
Web site: www.ala.org

The American Library Association is the oldest and largest library association in the world, with members in academic, public, school, government, and special libraries. The mission of the ALA is to provide leadership for the development, promotion, and improvement of library and information services and the profession of librarianship in order to enhance learning and ensure access to information for all. The ALA produces *Booklist* and *American Library* magazines.

The Cato Institute
1000 Massachusetts Ave. NW, Washington, DC 20001-5403
(202) 842-0200
Web site: www.cato.org

The Cato Institute is a nonprofit public-policy research foundation headquartered in Washington, D.C. It seeks to broaden the parameters of public-policy debate to allow consideration of the traditional American principles of limited government, individual liberty, free markets, and peace. The institute produces numerous papers and publications, including various policy studies and *Regulation* magazine.

Concerned Women for America (CWA)
1015 Fifteenth St. NW, Suite 1100, Washington, DC 20005
(202) 488-7000
Web site: www.cwfa.org

The mission of CWA is to protect and promote Biblical values among all citizens—first through prayer, then education, and finally by influencing society—thereby reversing what it sees as the decline in moral values.

Electronic Frontier Foundation (EFF)
454 Shotwell St., San Francisco, CA 94110
(415) 436-9333
e-mail: information@eff.org • Web site: www.eff.org

EFF is a donor-supported membership organization working to educate the press, policy makers, and the general public about civil liberties issues related to technology and to act as a defender of those liberties. EFF initiates and defends court cases preserving individuals' rights, launches global public campaigns, introduces leading-edge proposals and papers, hosts frequent educational events, engages the press regularly, and publishes a comprehensive archive of digital civil liberties information.

First Amendment Center
1207 Eighteenth Ave. South, Nashville, TN 37212
(615) 727-1600
e-mail: info@fac.org • Web site: www.firstamendmentcenter.org

The First Amendment Center works to preserve and protect First Amendment freedoms through information and education. The center serves as a forum for the study and exploration of free-expression issues, including freedom of speech, of the press, and of religion; the right to assemble; and the right to petition the government.

Freedom Forum
1101 Wilson Blvd., Arlington, VA 22209
(703) 528-0800
e-mail: news@freedomforum.org • Web site: www.freedomforum.org

The Freedom Forum is a nonpartisan foundation dedicated to free press, free speech, and free spirit for all people. The Freedom Forum funds the operations of the Newseum, an interactive museum of news under construction in Washington, D.C.; the First Amendment Center; and the Diversity Institute.

Free Press
100 Main St., PO Box 28, Northampton, MA 01061
(413) 585-1533
Web site: www.freepress.net

Free Press is a national, nonpartisan organization working to increase informed public participation in crucial media-policy debates, and to generate policies that will produce a more competitive and public interest–oriented media system with a strong nonprofit and noncommercial sector.

Free Speech Coalition
PO Box 10480, Canoga Park, CA 91309
(866) 372-9373
Web site: www.freespeechcoalition.org

The Free Speech Coalition is the trade association of the adult entertainment industry. The coalition promotes the acceptance of the industry in America's business community and supports greater public tolerance for freedom of sexual speech. The coalition produces the *Free Speech X-Press* newsletter and the *Free Speaker FSC* magazine.

The Heritage Foundation
214 Massachusetts Ave. NE, Washington, DC 20002-4999
(202) 546-4400
e-mail: info@heritage.org • Web site: www.heritage.org

The Heritage Foundation is a research and educational institute—a think tank—whose mission is to formulate and promote conservative public policies based on the principles of free enterprise, limited government, individual freedom, traditional American values, and a strong national defense. The foundation produces many books and position papers, including "Leadership for America" and "Defending the Homeland."

Morality in Media, Inc.
475 Riverside Dr., Suite 239, New York, NY 10115
(212) 870-3222
e-mail: mim@moralityinmedia.org • Web site: www.moralityinmedia.org

Morality in Media, Inc. is a national, not-for-profit, interfaith organization established to uphold decency standards in the media. It conducts public information programs to educate and involve concerned citizens, and maintains the National Obscenity Law Center, a clearinghouse of legal materials on obscenity law. Morality in Media publishes two monthly online news columns, "Especially for Parents," and "A View from Riverside Drive."

National Coalition Against Censorship (NCAC)
275 Seventh Ave., New York, NY 10001
(212) 807-6222
e-mail: ncac@ncac.org • Web site: www.ncac.org

The National Coalition Against Censorship is an alliance of fifty national nonprofit organizations, including literary, artistic, religious, educational, professional, labor, and civil liberties groups. United by a conviction that freedom of thought, inquiry, and expression must be defended, the NCAC works to educate the public about the dangers of censorship. The coalition publishes a quarterly newsletter, *Censorship News*.

National Coalition for the Protection of Children and Families
800 Compton Rd., Suite 9224, Cincinnati, OH 45231
(513) 521-6227
e-mail: ncpcf@nationalcoalition.org • Web site: www.nationalcoalition.org

The National Coalition for the Protection of Children and Families (formerly the National Coalition Against Pornography) is a nonprofit organization dedicated to eliminating pornography and advancing Christian values in the area of sexuality. It seeks to effectuate debate and change in public policy related to sexual ethics. Its publications include *Sex & Young America: The Real Deal.*

People for the American Way
2000 M St. NW, Suite 400, Washington, DC 20036
(800) 326-7329
e-mail: pfaw@pfaw.org • Web site: www.pfaw.org

People for the American Way seeks to advance pluralism; individuality; freedom of thought, expression, and religion; a sense of community; and tolerance and compassion for others, as well as to protect the principles set forth in the Constitution. It produces several online educational materials and pamphlets.

World Press Freedom Committee
11690-C Sunrise Valley Dr., Reston, VA 20191
(703) 715-9811
e-mail: freepress@wpfc.org • Web site: www.wpfc.org

The World Press Freedom Committee is an international umbrella organization that includes forty-four journalistic groups—print and broadcast, labor and management, journalists, editors, publishers, and owners on six continents—united for the defense and promotion of the freedom of the press.

Bibliography

Books

Kristina Borjesson, ed.   *Into the Buzzsaw: Leading Journalists Expose the Myth of a Free Press.* New York: Prometheus Books, 2002.

James Bovard   *Terrorism and Tyranny: Trampling Freedom, Justice, and Peace to Rid the World of Evil.* New York: Palgrave Macmillan, 2003.

Paul S. Boyer   *Purity in Print.* Madison: University of Wisconsin Press, 2002.

Michael Brenson   *Visionaries and Outcasts: The NEA, Congress, and the Place of the Visual Artist in America.* New York: New Press, 2001.

Ronald Collins and David Skover   *The Trials of Lenny Bruce: The Fall and Rise of an American Icon.* Naperville, IL: Sourcebooks MediaFusion, 2002.

Michael Kent Curtis   *Free Speech, "The People's Darling Privilege": Struggles for Freedom of Expression in American History.* Durham, NC: Duke University Press, 2000.

Michaelangelo Delfino and Mary E. Day   *Be Careful Who You Slap.* Los Altos, CA: MoBeta, 2002.

Fiona Donson   *Legal Intimidation.* London: Free Association Books, 2000.

Herbert N. Foerstel   *From Watergate to Monicagate: Ten Controversies in Modern Journalism and Media.* Westport, CT: Greenwood Press, 2001.

Robert Justin Goldstein, ed.   *The War for the Public Mind: Political Censorship in Nineteenth-Century Europe.* Westport, CT: Praeger, 2000.

Robert Hargreaves   *The First Freedom.* Stroud, UK: Sutton, 2002.

Philip D. Harvey   *The Government vs. Erotica: The Siege of Adam and Eve.* Amherst, NY: Prometheus Books, 2001.

Marjorie Heins   *Not in Front of the Children: 'Indecency,' Censorship, and the Innocence of Youth,* New York: Hill and Wang, 2001.

Nat Hentoff   *The War on the Bill of Rights and the Gathering Resistance.* New York: Seven Stories Press, 2003.

Richard T. Kaplar, ed.	*The First Amendment and the Media, 2001.* Washington, DC: Media Institute, 2001.
Richard Leone and Greg Anrig, eds.	*The War on Our Freedoms: Civil Liberties in an Age of Terrorism.* New York: Century Foundation, 2003.
David Lowenthal	*Present Dangers: Rediscovering the First Amendment.* Dallas, TX: Spence, 2002.
Robert W. McChesney and John Nichols	*Our Media, Not Theirs: The Democratic Struggle Against Corporate Media.* New York: Seven Stories Press, 2004.
Linda R. Monk	*The Words We Live By: Your Annotated Guide to the Constitution.* New York: Hyperion, 2003.
Aryeh Neier	*Taking Liberties: Four Decades in the Struggle for Rights.* New York: Public Affairs, 2003.
Robert S. Peck	*Libraries, the First Amendment, and Cyberspace.* Chicago: American Library Association, 2002.
William H. Rehnquist	*All the Laws but One: Civil Liberties in Wartime.* New York: Vintage Books, 2000.
Lawrence Soley	*Censorship, Inc.: The Corporate Threat to Free Speech in the United States.* New York: Monthly Review Press, 2002.
Thomas L. Tedford and Dale A. Herbeck	*Freedom of Speech in the United States.* 4th Ed. State College, PA: Strata, 2001.
Tinsley E. Yarbrough	*The Rehnquist Court and the Constitution.* Oxford, UK: Oxford University Press, 2000.

Periodicals

Dell Champlin and Janet Knoedler	"Operating in the Public Interest or in the Pursuit of Private Profits? News in the Age of Media Consolidation," *Journal of Economic Issues*, June 2002.
Robert Corn-Revere	"Indecency, Television, and the First Amendment," *Consumers Research*, February 2004.
Sean R. Gallagher and Marianne N. Hallinan	"Privacy Versus Freedom of Speech: Telemarketing and Government's Ability to Limit It," *Colorado Lawyer*, October 2004.
William Norman Grigg	"Censoring America: An Attempt to Squelch Ads for a Controversial New Film Illustrates How 'Campaign Finance Reform Has Created a New Corps of Federal Speech Police," *New American*, July 26, 2004.
Nat Hentoff	"Getting It Right," *Editor & Publisher*, November 5, 2001.
Pamela Taylor Jackson and James Ronald Stanfield	"The Role of the Press in a Democracy: Heterodox Economics and the Propaganda Model," *Journal of Economic Issues*, June 2004.
Russell Jacoby	"The New PC: Crybaby Conservatives," *Nation*, April 4, 2005.

Bibliography

Charles Levendosky	"President Bush: Make Those Protesters Disappear," *Humanist*, January/February 2004.
Alexandra Marks	"Kids on Internet: Controls or No Controls? A Philadelphia Court Case Weighs Whether Mandatory Computer Filters Curb Free Speech," *Christian Science Monitor*, March 29, 2002.
Ian Marquand	"All Free Speech Cases Affect Journalism," *Quill*, April 2003.
Jay Mathews	"The Perils of Campus Candor," *Washington Post*, November 10, 2002.
Robert W. McChesney and John Nichols	"Holding the Line at the FCC," *Progressive*, April 2003.
Roger Parloff	"Can We Talk?" *Fortune*, September 2, 2002.
Elisabeth Sifton	"The Battle over the Pledge," *Nation*, April 5, 2004.
Eugene Volokh	"First Myths," *National Review Online*, January 5, 2004. www.nationalreview.com.
Lorraine Woellert	"Will the Right to Pester Hold Up? The First Amendment Protects Marketers, but Spam May Shift the Equation," *Business Week*, November 10, 2003.

Index

ABC network, 204
Abu Ghraib, prison abuse scandal at, 92
advertising, American public does not
   want, 72
Alien Registration Act (1940), 114
Altria, Inc., 202
American Booksellers Foundation for
   Free Expression (ABFFE), 134
American Civil Liberties Union
   (ACLU), 15, 59, 109
American Federation of Television and
   Radio Artists (AFTRA), 178
American flag
   burning of, is a legitimate expression of
      dissent, 42–43
   constitutional amendment protecting,
      19–21
      threatens First Amendment rights,
         44–45
      unfounded arguments by proponents
         of, 43–44
   government's legitimate interest in
      protecting, 18–19
   is a cherished symbol, 21–22
   must be protected, 21–22
American Library Association (ALA),
   15, 134
America Online (AOL), 201
American Protective League, 121
Americans for Radio Diversity, 170
Ansolabohere, Stephen, 85–86
antiterrorism policies, 125–26
   must respect First Amendment values,
      127–28
   recommendations for, 131–33
   violate or threaten First Amendment
      guarantees, 126–31
Arnett, Peter, 123
art/entertainment
   artistic freedom for, 61–62
   government should not censor, 59–60
   individual decisions on viewing, 63

rating system for, 101, 102
regulating indecency in, 63–64
self-censorship in, during wartime,
   119–20
sexual speech in, 60
see also media violence
Ashcroft, John, 139
   antiterrorism policies and, 125, 126
   on Freedom of Information Act, 130
Ashcroft v. ACLU (2004), 52, 55
Associated Press, the, 93
Austin v. Michigan Chamber of
   Commerce, 160

Bache, Benjamin, 112
Bader, Eleanor J., 133
Baker, Marge, 42
Barber, Bretton, 119
Baseball Hall of Fame, 136, 137
Beckerman, Gal, 172
Beethoven, Ludwig van, 113
Bickford, Geoffrey, 118
bin Laden, Osama, 127
Bipartisan Campaign Reform Act
   (BCRA) (2002), 66–67
Blanton, Tom, 92
Bliss, Jeffrey C., 145
Bond, Julian, 114
bookstores, 134
Bowers v. Hardwick, 57
Bozell, L. Brent, 177
Bradlee, Ben, 88–89, 93
Breyer, Stephen, 55
Brick, Ann, 157
Brockett v. Spokane Arcade Inc. (1985),
   54–55
Brown & Williamson, 202, 203–204
Bryant, Daniel J., 134
Buckley v. Valeo (1976), 82–83, 84, 97,
   98
Burger, Warren, 54
Burk, John Daly, 112

Bursey, Brett, 121
Bush, George H.W., 90
Bush, George W., 14, 66–67, 90

California Supreme Court, 155–56, 157
campaign finance reform
  arguments by opponents of, 97–98
  debate on, 66–67
  hurts citizens, 86–87
  is a recent development, 82–83
  is rooted in prior laws, 96
  limits speech, by banning political ads, 86
  soft money and, 83–86, 96–97
  support for, 98–99
  see also Shays-Meehan bill
campaign spending
  on issue ads, 96
  from soft money, political party differences in, 95–96
Campus Watch, 122
Canan, Penelope, 204
censorship
  corporate, 197–98, 200–201
    fighting, 205–206
  Internet self-regulation and, 101
  media violence motivates, 60–61
  opposing, 59–60
  by private pressure groups, 64
  during wartime, 119–20
Center for Digital Democracy, 178
Center for Public Integrity, 93
Central Hudson Gas & Electric v. Pub. Serv. Comm'n (1980), 188, 190, 191–92
Chang, Nancy, 133, 135
charitable solicitations, 185, 193–94
Chemerinsky, Erwin, 111, 115
Cheney, Dick, 90–91, 93
Chester, Jeffrey, 178
Child Online Protection Act (COPA), 52, 53–54
child pornography, 57–58
Children's Internet Protection Act (CIPA) (2000), 77
Cincinnati v. Discovery Networks, 194
Citizens Flag Alliance (CFA), 18, 43
Civil War era, 112
CleanPlay (video company), 17
Clear Channel Communications, 70, 121, 137, 138, 168
Cline, Victor B., 34, 36
Clinton, Bill, 97, 176

Coalition of Journalists for Open Government, 93
Code Pink (activist organization), 173–74
Cole, David, 110
Cole, Jeffrey, 100
colleges, speech at
  categorizing types of, 28
  codes for, harm classroom discussion, 47–49
  defining nature of speaker and, 27–28
  "forum" for, 28–29
  restrictions on, timing and effects of, 29–30
Colorado District Court, 188, 195
Colson, Charles, 89
Columbia University, 122
Commission on Children at Risk, 33
Common Cause conference, 176–77
Communications Decency Act (CDA) (1996), 25, 53, 59, 100–101
Communist Party, 114
Comstock, Barbara, 109
Comstock Law (1873), 59
Constitution, amendment process for, 19–20
  see also First Amendment; Fifth Amendment
Constitution Project's Liberty and Security Initiative, 126–27
Consumer's Federation of America, 178
Cooper, Mark, 178
Copps, Michael J., 179
corporations
  critics of, threatening litigation, 203–204
  documents kept from the public by, 202–203
  fighting censorship by, 205–206
  free speech rights of
    accurate information vs. self-expression and, 160–62
    are designed to enhance profits, 162
    denial of, California Supreme Court ruling on, 155–56
    do not merit First Amendment protection, 166–67
    lack of constitutional right for, 158–59
    personification and, 164–65
    rights of the listener and, 159–60
  Internet censorship by, 201–202
  public discourse limited by, methods of, 204–205

restrictions on signs in planned
  developments by, 199–200
restrictions on speech by, 197–98
rights of, 154
rise of power by, to censor speech,
  200–201
Council of Public Relations Firms, 156
Cox, Larry, 147, 150
Craven, S. Michael, 31
Cripps, Kathy, 155
Cunningham, Victoria, 173
Cyber Promotions, 201

Dahl, Elizabeth, 125
Dartmouth Medical School, 33
Debs, Eugene, 113
De Genova, Nicholas, 122–23
Democratic National Convention (1968),
  114
Democratic Party, 95
Dennis v. United States (1951), 114
DeNoble, Victor, 202
Department of Justice, 15, 130
Diller, Barry, 69
Disney Corp., 203–204
dissent. *See* political dissent
Dixie Chicks, 15, 123, 138
Domestic Enhancement Security Act
  (2003), 93
Donahue, Phil, 117, 123
Downs, Stephen, 154, 206
Doyle, Sarah, 119
Dukes, Anthony J., 168
DVD content, legislation on altering, 17

Eberle, Bobby, 136
Ellsberg, Daniel, 89
Englebright, Steve, 206
Espionage Act (1917), 118
Estrella housing development, 188, 199

Fairness Doctrine, 176
Family Entertainment and Copyright Act
  (2005), 17
Faris, Iyman, 141
Federal Bureau of Investigation (FBI),
  130–31, 132
Federal Communications Commission
  (FCC)
  media ownership rules and, 74, 168, 172
  opposition to, 178–79
  telemarketing regulation and, 184, 192,
    195–96

*Federal Communications Commission v.
  Pacifica* (1978), 63–64
Federal Elected Commission (FEC), 96
Federal Election Campaign Act (FECA)
  (1974), 82
Federalist Society, 139
Federal Trade Commission (FTC), 182,
  184, 192, 195–96
Feinstein, Dianne, 142
Ferree, Kenneth, 179
Fifth Amendment, 165
films, rating system for, 101, 102
Finan, Chris, 134, 135
First Amendment
  antiterrorism measures violate, 126–31
  Ashcroft on, 139
  assault on, during WWI, 112–13
  campaign finance reform and, 97
  corporate free speech and, 159, 162–65,
    166–67
  diverse media is essential under,
    175–76
  does not protect unwanted commercial
    speech, 196
  flag amendment threatens rights under,
    44–45
  flag desecration and, 20
  forms of speech not protected under, 14
  individual decisions and, 63
  media ownership controls and, 106
  pornography and, 37–38
  public opinion on, 15, 116
  speech at colleges and, 27–28
  violation of, during wartime, 111–15
First Amendment survey, 15, 116
First National Bank of Boston v. Bellotti,
  159
527 groups, 66
flag. *See* American flag
Fleischer, Ari, 14
Fleming, Nancy Hsu, 204
Foner, Henry, 117, 120
founding fathers
  on debate, 139
  did not permit flag desecration, 19
  on freedom of the press, 71
Fowler, Mark, 176
FOX Broadcasting, 170
Franks, Tommy, 148
Freedman, Samuel G., 50
Freedom Forum, 15, 116
Freedom of Information Act (FOIA),
  126, 130, 132, 134

freedom of the press
  assault on, 111–12
  founding fathers on, 71
  government control on
    public opinion and, 92–93
    before/after September 11, 90–92
  is key to upholding democracy, 93
  Pentagon Papers case and, 88–89,
    93–94, 114–15
  public's right to know about
    government activities and, 89–90
  stifling of, during war on terror, 91–92,
    126–27
Free Press (organization), 177
Frisby v. Schultz, 188, 189

Galloway, Joseph L., 146
Gephardt, Richard, 86
Gilleo, Margaret, 197
Gilmore, Glenda, 118, 122
Glassner, Barry, 120
Gutmann, David, 34

Halliburton (company), 93
hard-core pornography, 54, 56
Harvard Law School, 46
hate crimes, 23
hate speech
  has a slow-acting effect, 23–24
  limiting, threatens legitimate debate,
    50–51
  line between legitimate free speech and,
    49–50
  may influence actions, 25
Hersh, Seymour, 92
Hill v. Colorado, 188
Hollywood celebrities, 117, 136–38
Homeland Security Act, 92
homeowners' associations, 198, 199–200
Hometown Properties, Inc., 204
Hoover, J. Edgar, 114
Horne, Gerald, 123
*Hudgen v. National Labor Relations
  Board* (1976), 201
Hudson, David, 110
Hunt, E. Howard, 89
Hurst, William Randolph, 170

immigrant detainees
  First Amendment issues and, 128–29
  recommendations for, 131–32
immigration proceedings, secrecy of,
  129–30

Industrial Workers of the World (IWW),
  200
Internet
  health information found on, by youth,
    77
  labeling, does not censor content, 101
  may require special regulation, 24–25
  media content and, 73
  self-regulation on, 100–101
Internet Filter Review, 56
Internet filters
  blocking of health sites with, 78–80, 81
  finding pornography while using, 80
  home use of, 78
  legislation on, 77
  parents must educate themselves on,
    101–103
  study determining effectiveness of,
    76–77
Internet pornography
  children's access to, 38
  finding, with Internet filters, 80
  incidental exposure to, during health
    information searches, 79, 80
  prevalence of, 56
  regulation of, has been flawed, 53–54
  restricting youth access to, 52–53
Internet service providers (ISPs),
  201–202

Japanese American concentration camps,
  113
Japanese TV/film, 61
Johnson, Nicholas, 68
Justice Department, 91

Kaiser Family Foundation, 76
Kansas Republican State Committee, 96
Kasky, Mark, 155–56
Keating, Charles, Jr., 199
Kerry, John, 95
Kessler, Gladys, 129
Kimmelman, Gene, 177, 178
Korean War era, 113–14
Kutchinsky, Berl, 40

Lanares, Guillermo, 50
Langhauser, Derek P., 27
Lantos, Tom, 120
Lawrence, John, 147
Lawrence v. Texas (2003), 57
Leahy, Patrick, 92
Leets, Laura, 23

legislation
   on communications technology, 17
   on Internet blocking, 77
   on Internet pornography, 52–54
   on media consolidation, 176
Levi, Edward, 126
Lewis, Charles, 88
libraries, 133, 141–42
Linfield, Michael, 14, 111
Linn Valley Lakes Property Owners v.
   Brockway (1992), 199
Lloyd Corp. v. Tanner (1972), 201
Lockyear, Bill, 187
Lo, Katherine, 119
Long, Alexander, 112
lottery advertisements, 194
Lyon, Matthew, 112

Madigan, Charles, 92
Maher, Bill, 14
Mangan, Mona, 179
Maniscalco, Francis J., 174–75, 180–81
Mapplethorpe, Robert, 55, 60
Markey, Ed, 182
Matoush, Joseph, 119
Mattel, Inc., 203
Mayer, Carl J., 158
McCain, John, 70, 86
McCarthy era, 117
McChesney, Robert W., 68, 177
McGruder, Aaron, 123
Media Access Project, 175–76
media industry
   choices in, 106–107
   complexity of supply and demand in,
      72–73
   consolidation in
      abundant backlash to, 176–78
      contrasting viewpoints on, 170–71
      economic factors in, 169–70
      opposition to, 169, 171, 179–81
   corporate monopoly of
      debunking myths on, 105
      public concern over, 74–75
      in radio, 70
   diversity in, 104–105
   is essential to a strong First
      Amendment, 175–76
   First Amendment does not justify
      ownership control of, 106
   increased democracy with, 105
   Internet's impact on, 73
   localism is not disappearing in, 105

   ownership rules for, relaxation of
      changes in media companies and, 170
      debate on, 168–69
      opposition to, 173–75, 178–79
   policy making in, 68–69
      changing, 73
      corporate interests and, 69
      movements opposing, 73–74
      public participation in, 69–70
   pressure to generate profit in, 71–72
   regulation of, is not needed, 106
   see also art/entertainment; freedom of
      the press; news; television
media violence, 60–63
Mehlman, Ira H., 49
Meyers, Richard, 149
Miller v. California (1973), 37, 54, 63
Milwaukee Brewers, 206
Mitchell, John, 114
Motion Picture Association of America
   (MPAA), 102
MoveOn, 66, 180
movie piracy, 17
Muris, Tim, 182
Murphy v. Timber Trace Association
   (1989), 199
Myers, Richard, 92

National Center for Missing and
   Exploited Children, 38
National Endowment for the Arts (NEA),
   120
National Freedom of Information
   Coalition, 93
National Labor Relations Act, 198
National Organization for Women, 179
National Rifle Association, 179
Neas, Ralph G., 42
Nelsen, Craig, 50
Nevins, Bill, 119
Newhall, Amy, 122
news
   embedded reporters during Iraq war for,
      145
      benefit citizens and government,
         147–48
      excellent and comprehensive coverage
         with, 150–52
      healthy skepticism of, 149–50
      success of, 148–49
   pressure to generate profit in, 71–72
   war coverage by, 145–47
   see also freedom of the press

New York Times (newspaper), 88, 106,
    114
Nichols, John, 177
Nike, 155, 158–59, 161, 162–63
Norr, Henry, 123
Nussbaum, Martha, 54

obscenity
    defining, 37–38, 63
    difficulties in, 54–55
    indecency vs., 63–64
    national standard does not exist for,
        55–56
O'Connor, Andrew, 118
O'Connor, Sandra Day, 55, 156
Onek, Joseph, 125
Opotow, Susan, 24
O'Reilly, Bill, 122–23

Paine, Katie Delahaye, 148, 151
Parents Television Council, 177, 178
Pariser, Eli, 180
pedophilia, 39–40
Persian Gulf War (1991), 146
Philip Morris, 202
Phone Butler, 183–84
Pipes, Daniel, 122
planned developments, 199–200
political dissent
    democracy and, 123–24
    flag burning as an expression of, 42–43,
        44
    right to, controversy over, 15
    stifling
        during war on terror, 116–17, 119–20,
            121–23, 126
        con, 137–38
        during wartime, 117–18
    using private property for, 154
political speech
    banning political ads limits, 86
    link between political spending and, 83
    unconstitutional restriction on, 197
Pope, Darrell, 40
pornography, 64
    adverse behavioral effects of, 34–35
    adverse societal effects of, 36–37,
        39–40
    children have unprecedented access to,
        38–39
    defining obscenity and, 54–55
    demonstrating direct cause and effect
        and, 40–41

disintegrated view of sexuality and,
    32–33
government should not allow
    prosecution for, 56–57
harms public morality, 31–32
lack of connectedness with others and,
    33–34
lax regulation encourages, 37–38
legislation on, is useless, 57–58
national standard for obscenity and,
    55–56
sexual stimulation with, 35–36
see also Internet pornography
Posner, Richard A., 14
Powell, Michael, 172–73, 175, 176, 177
presidential election
    2000, 95
    2004, 66
Pring, George W., 204
public opinion
    on advertising, 72
    on First Amendment rights, 15, 116
see also political dissent

Quintanilla, Ray, 151

radio, corporate monopoly of, 70
Rehnquist, William H., 55, 166–67
Reno v. ACLU (1997), 53
Republican Party, 95
Revolutionary War era, 111–12
Rich, Frank, 55–56
R.J. Reynolds, 204
Robbins, Tim, 117, 119, 136–37
Rosen, Jeffrey, 52
Rowan v. U.S. Post Office, 188
Rumsfeld, Donald, 90, 124
Russell, Mark, 120

Salazar, Ken, 187
Samples, John, 82
*Santa Clara County v. Southern Pacific
    Railroad* (1886), 154, 164–66
Sarandon, Susan, 117, 137
Scalia, Antonin, 55, 57, 116
Scarborough, Joe, 123
Schrecker, Ellen, 123–24
Schwartzman, Andrew, 175–76, 178
Scott, David, 40
Seal Press, 203
Sedition Act (1798), 111–12
Sedition Act (1918), 113, 118
September 11 terrorist attacks, 89–90, 120

information control prior to, 90–91
see also war on terror
sexual speech, censorship of, 60
Shaffer, Jack, 150
Sharkey, Jacqueline, 90
Shaw, Clay, 86
Shays-Meehan bill, 86–87, 96, 98
Shell Oil, 205–206
Siems, Larry, 135
Sinclair Broadcasting, 168–69
Singleton, Solveig, 182
"SLAPP," 203–204, 205–206
Smith, Howard W., 114
Smith, Toni, 118, 119
Snyder, James, Jr., 85–86
Soley, Lawrence, 197
Solomon, Alisa, 116
Solomon, John, 91
Starr, Paul, 71
Stevens, John Paul, 57
Sullivan, Kathleen, 54
Swift Boat Veterans for Truth, 66

Telecommunications Bill (1996), 25
telemarketers
  charitable, 193–94
  "do not call" rules for, 182–83, 187
    are likely to reduce unwanted calls,
      191–93
    are not more extensive than necessary,
      195–96
    are valid, 190–91
  First Amendment and, 196
  have no right to call unwilling listeners,
    188–90
  nuisance from, is not grounds for
    regulation, 183
  regulation of
    balance of competing interests and,
      194–95
    for charities and political groups, 185
    controlling calls without, 183–84
    cost issues with, 184
    does not apply to phone companies,
      184–85
    stifles freedom, 185–86
  right to privacy and, 191
Telephone Consumer Protection Act
  (TCPA), 193
television
  increased diversity in, 105
  labeling/rating system for, 102
  violence on, 61, 62

TeleZapper, 183–84
Texas v. Johnson (1989), 44
Theaters Against War, 120
Thierer, Adam, 104
Thomas, Clarence, 55
tobacco companies, 202, 204, 205
2 Live Crew (rap group), 59

United States Institute for Peace, 122
United States v. Edge Broadcasting, 194
University of Illinois, 133
USA PATRIOT Act (2001), 91
  aids law enforcement, 140–42
  controversy over, 15, 109
  creation of, 140
  encourages judicial oversight, 143
  government powers under, 110, 133–34
  has not been used to stifle liberty,
    143–44
  legislative process and, 142–43
  opposition to, 134–35
U.S. Post Office, 71
U.S. Supreme Court
  on artistic freedom, 61–62
  on campaign finance, 66, 82, 97, 98
  on commercial speech, 161
  on corporate speech, 156, 159–60,
    162–63, 164–66
  flag rulings by, 19, 21, 44–45
  on Internet pornography, 52
  on Internet regulation, 25
  on obscenity, 37–38, 54–55, 57–58, 63
  on prosecution for sexually explicit
    speech, 56–57
  on protecting property vs. speech rights,
    200–201
  on rights for corporations, 154
  on telemarketing, 188–89
US West, Inc. v. FCC, 191

Vallandingham, Clement L., 112
V-chip, 102
Verhovek, Sam Howe, 150
Vietnam War, 114, 146
Volokh, Eugene, 46

Warner, James, 43
war on terror
  fears of First Amendment violations
    during, 115
  free speech during, 14–15
  information control by government
    during, 91–92

McCarthy era compared with, 117–18
opposition to, by liberal celebrities,
 136–37
patriotism during, violence and, 118–19
protesting, democracy and, 123–24
public fear and, 92–93, 120–21
stifling public opposition to, 116–17,
 119–20, 121–23, 126
 con, 137–38
using private property to state
 opposition to, 154
see also antiterrorism policies; USA
 PATRIOT Act
wartime
 government hiding facts from public
 during, 89–90
 news coverage during, 145–47
 stifling dissent during, 117–18
 violation of civil liberties during,
 111–15
Washington Post (newspaper), 88, 114
*Watchtower Bible and Tract Society v.
 Village of Stratton,* 189
Watergate scandal, 89
Weich, Ronald, 111
Weissberg, Shelli, 119
Weitzel, Pete, 92

Wexler, Celia, 176, 177
Wheaton College, 118
whistleblower protection laws, 203
White, John, 113
Wigand, Jeffrey, 202, 203
Wilson, George C., 148, 149–50
Wilson, Woodrow, 121
Windfalls of War (report), 93
World Church of the Creator (WCOTC),
 24
World War I era, 112–13, 117, 118, 200
World War II era, 113–14, 145–46
Wright, Brenda, 158
Writers Guild, 178, 179

youth
 access to pornography by, 38–39
 dissent distrusted by, 123
 Internet health searches by, 77
 restricting Internet pornography from,
 52–53
 see also Internet filters

Zayid, Maysoon, 119
Zillman, Dolf, 40
Zinn, Howard, 117, 123